Paula Vogel

MICHIGAN MODERN DRAMATISTS
Enoch Brater, Series Editor

Michigan Modern Dramatists offers the theatergoer concise, accessible, and indispensable guides to the works of individual playwrights, as interpreted by today's leading drama critics. Forthcoming books in the series will consider the works of Sam Shepard, Samuel Beckett, and Wendy Wasserstein.

Paula Vogel

Joanna Mansbridge

THE UNIVERSITY OF MICHIGAN PRESS
ANN ARBOR

Published in the United States of America by
The University of Michigan Press
Printed and bound by CPI Group (UK) Ltd, Croydon, CR0 4YY

2017   2016   2015   2014   4   3   2   1

A CIP catalog record for this book is available from the British Library.

ISBN 978-0-472-07239-2 (hardcover : alk. paper)
ISBN 978-0-472-05239-4 (pbk. : alk. paper)
ISBN 978-0-472-12069-7 (e-book)

For my greatest teachers,
Mary Ellen Hengen and
Christopher Mansbridge

Acknowledgments

A book does not get made without many people contributing their knowledge, time, and skill. My thanks go to the proficient staff at the New York Public Library for the Performing Arts, for providing access to recorded productions and other archival materials, and to Kathryn Rickman at Arena Stage Theater, for providing production photos. Thanks to the superb photographers, Chris Dzombak, T. Charles Erikson, Gerry Goodstein, Joan Marcus, Carol Rosegg, and Marie Schulte, who contributed the photographs reprinted here. Thank you to the efficient editorial staff at the University of Michigan Press for all of their work on this book. Thanks especially to Alexa Ducsay for patiently answering my many questions and for being so helpful, to Carol Sickman-Garner for her excellent copy editing, and to Marcia LaBrenz for her skilled editorial work and communication throughout the production process. Thanks to Enoch Brater, series editor, for his support and feedback. Very special thanks to LeAnn Fields, whose expert guidance on this project has been of immeasurable worth. Thank you to my anonymous readers, who reviewed earlier drafts of the manuscript; their astute, attentive comments made this book better and demonstrate one of the best things about the profession: peer review. Parts of chapters 3 and 6 were published in *Modern Drama* and *Comparative Drama*, and I thank both journals for allowing portions of those articles to be reprinted here.

A book is also the end product of a long process. This book had an earlier life as my doctoral dissertation at the Graduate Center, City University of New York. All my thanks go to my committee members, David Savran, Steven Kruger, and Mario DiGangi. Their incisive feedback on my early work was invaluable, their graciousness an added bonus. Thanks especially to David, whose influence is everywhere present in these pages. I am very grateful to the Social Sciences and Humanities Research Council of Canada for the fellowship that supported my doctoral research and for the small institutions grant that I received while at St. Francis Xavier University, which allowed me to do the research necessary to transform the dissertation into the book you hold in your hands. Thank you to Anne Humphreys for the Upper West Side apartment I had the privilege of staying in while doing this later research. Finally, my sincerest thanks to Paula Vogel, who responded to all of my questions and, along the way, taught me so much about what theater can do. My profound thanks for her generosity, her keen insights, and her plays.

I give warmest thanks to friends and family. First, my enduring gratitude goes to Peter Dickinson, scholar, mentor, and friend extraordinaire. It has been my best fortune to learn from and work with Peter, whose intelligence, grace, and generosity are matchless. For the many amazing dinners and great conversations, I thank you and Richard Cavell. Thank you to Shannon Hengen and Francis Mansbridge, in whose steps I follow, for their loving guidance and support. Thanks to my fellow Fellows, Ornaith O'Dowd and Kristen Van Hooreweghe, for the law school fun and the ongoing camaraderie. Thank you to Paul Shoebridge, Nicole Harrison, Noah, and Theo for the home downstairs, where I wrote most of this, and for the life, love, and laughter upstairs. Thank you to my three sisters, Krista Mansbridge, Kayleen Mansbridge, and Megan Mansbridge, whom I love and admire so much and who were often my imagined audience as I wrote. Thanks to my nieces and nephews—Alexandria, Zachary, Rose, Fynn, William, Margaret May, and Theo—for reminding me of everything good in the world. Heartfelt thanks to James Gibson for his cherished presence and support. Finally, I give a lifetime of thanks to my parents, Mary Ellen Hengen and Christopher Mansbridge, whose integrity, wisdom, and love have taught me countless lessons and been my most cherished guides.

Contents

Introduction: A Dramaturgy of Defamiliarization

To see a Paula Vogel play is to participate in a three-way dialogue with the dramatic canon, social history, and contemporary American culture. Her plays respond to and rewrite works by William Shakespeare, Thornton Wilder, Edward Albee, Sam Shepard, and David Mamet, rearranging their plots, revising their conflicts, and recasting their dramatis personae. As they speak back to the canon, Vogel's plays also initiate a conversation with contemporary culture, staging vexed issues like domestic violence, pornography, and AIDS in ways that promote, rather than stifle, dialogue. She does not write "about" AIDS, pornography, and domestic violence, however; instead, she examines how they have come to be framed as "issues"—as sensationalized topics—and focuses on the histories and discourses that have gone into defining them, as well as on the bodies that bear their meanings. Vogel crafts collage-like playworlds that are comprised of fragments of history and culture and that feel, at once, inclusive and alienating, familiar and strange, funny and disturbing. At the center of these worlds are female characters negotiating with the images and discourses that circumscribe their lives and bodies. Although frequently at odds with the social worlds they populate, these characters also forge a sense of belonging, often through the creative forces of fantasy, memory, storytelling, and other unauthorized acts.

Gender, sexuality, authority, family, fantasy, memory, history— these are the topoi of Vogel's drama, the questions her plays pose, and the ideas they investigate. While grounded in these ideas, the nonlinear structure of her plays works to loosen, reframe, and defamiliarize the identities and issues that have been shaped by them and fixed as "just the way things are." Vogel's unique dramaturgy—the aesthetic architecture of her plays—is characterized by sharp juxtapositions, formal innovation, and campy humor, and this non-naturalistic technique defamiliarizes subjects like pornography and AIDS by presenting them as products of history, public discourse, and collective political fantasy. Her plays suggest the way each generation unconsciously recites the same scripted responses to these subjects, while also pointing toward ways of building a more expansive vocabulary. The recursive, juxtapositional structure of Vogel's playworlds undermines habituated responses, insisting instead on a mode of spectatorship that tolerates, and even takes pleasure in, contradictions and that consciously participates in an ongoing cultural dialogue. Revising—literally "to see again"—the dramatic canon and social history, Vogel also revises our perception of the present.

A Biographical Sketch

Born on November 16, 1951, in Washington, DC, to a Jewish father and a Catholic mother, Vogel is the youngest and only daughter of three children. Her father, Donald Stephen Vogel, was an advertising executive from New York City, and her mother, Phyllis Rita Bremerman, was from New Orleans and worked as a secretary for the US Postal Service Training and Development Center. At five years old, Vogel "fell in love" with Mary Martin's performance of Peter Pan, which initiated her interest in theater and, in particular, the musical. When she was eleven, her father left home, and she and her brother Carl remained with their mother, while her elder brother, Mark, lived with their father. After this formative family event, Carl became Vogel's protector.[1] In high school, she took a drama class, discovering in theater "a spectrum of possibilities in terms of gender" and "a home that could include [her] sexuality."[2] It was also in high school that Vogel recognized her love for women, coming out as a lesbian at seventeen years old. After graduating high school, she attended prestigious Bryn Mawr College, where she wrote her first play, a musical version of The Hunchback of Notre Dame.[3] After two years at Bryn Mawr, Vogel transferred to Catholic University of America, where she finished her BA in drama in 1974. Wanting to pursue graduate studies, Vogel applied to and was rejected by the Yale School of Drama (the same year that Wendy Wasserstein and Christopher Durang were accepted). She instead attended Cornell University, where she studied under Bert States and Marvin Carlson and completed all of the requirements for her doctorate in theater arts, except the dissertation. She taught intermittently in the Theatre Arts and Women's Studies departments at Cornell from 1977 to 1982. In 1985, Vogel began teaching playwriting at Brown University, where she remained for twenty-three years, training some of the most exciting new playwrights in the country, including Nilo Cruz, Gina Gionfriddo, Lynn Nottage, Adam Bock, and Sarah Ruhl. On September 26, 2004, in Truro, Massachusetts, Vogel married her long-time partner Anne Fausto-Sterling, a professor of biology and women's studies at Brown University.[4] In July 2008, in what must have been a satisfying turn of life events, Vogel accepted a position as the Eugene O'Neill Chair of the Playwriting Department at the Yale School of Drama. At the end of the 2011–12 academic year, Vogel stepped down as chair to focus on new projects, such as *One Hundred Years of Vengeance*, a co-commission from Yale Repertory Theater and Oregon Shakespeare Festival, workshopped in 2012 with director Rebecca Taichman. She continues teaching at Yale as a lecturer in playwriting.

Vogel's working-class beginnings inform her playwriting practice. She recalls the day she told her mother that she wanted to work in theater, a declaration that caused her mother to react "as if a death in my family had been announced, instead of my future." Vogel explains, "I was the first generation in the family that had graduated high school and the first generation to go to college. . . . Theatre in my neighborhood was aligned with dinner theatre, or mystery theatre trains, or cruises you might take on an anniversary."[5] As a playwright with working-class beginnings and an Ivy League education, an insatiable intellect, a capacious imagination, and a taste for both high and low culture, Vogel writes with a language that is both erudite and irreverent and creates playworlds that are both material and abstract. Her characters are not the bourgeoisie of traditional realist drama, but rather working-class wives, husbands, mothers, daughters, and prostitutes. (For Vogel prostitution is working class labor.) The divisions among her female characters often revolve around economic disparities as much as gender, sexual, or political differences.

Vogel is a materialist, concerned with bodies, with history, and with the history of bodies. Even so, she also traffics in the theoretical and ephemeral. These above autobiographical details are important for the background they provide to Vogel's body of work. And indeed her plays often do contain autobiographical elements, most obviously in *The Baltimore Waltz* (1992) and more subtly in her other plays. However, I offer no autobiographical readings in the study that follows, as this seems a limited interpretive approach and not one that gets at the broad cultural and historical scope of her plays.

Vogel has written over twenty plays, eleven of which have been produced and ten published. She has also written for television, including screenplays for *How I Learned to Drive* and *The Oldest Profession*. Vogel's early unpublished work, such as *The Swan Song of Sir Henry* (1975) and *The Last Pat Epstein Show before the Reruns* (1979), reflects a persistent concern for history, popular culture, and representations of gender in both. Vogel won her first award for playwriting as a graduate student in 1976 for *Meg* at the Ninth Annual American College Theatre Festival in Washington, DC, a prize that earned her some recognition and, more important, an agent at William Morris. In 2002, the American College Theatre Festival designated this prize as the Paula Vogel Playwriting Award, which is given out annually to "the outstanding student-written play that celebrates diversity and encourages tolerance while exploring issues of disempowered voices not traditionally considered mainstream." Vogel achieved national recognition, along with an Obie Award and Pulitzer nomination, for her 1992 play, *The Baltimore Waltz*, which she wrote in commemoration of her brother Carl Vogel, who died from AIDS in 1987. She won a Guggenheim Fellowship in 1995, and her reputation as one of America's most important playwrights was firmly established in 1997 with *How I Learned to Drive*, which won the Pulitzer Prize for Drama, as well as New York Drama Critics, Obie, Drama Desk, Outer Critics, Lortel, Pell, and Hull-Warriner awards. She was also awarded the Susan Blackburn Award in 1998 and the Pen/Laura Pels Award for Playwriting in 1999. In 2005, Vogel received the Academy of Arts and Letters Award for Literature and, in 2006, was inducted into the Academy of Arts and Sciences. In 2010, Vogel was the recipient of the Inge Festival Distinguished Achievement in the American Theater award. On March 19, 2014, Vogel's most recent play, *Don Juan Comes Home From Iraq* premiered at Philadelphia's Wilma Theater. A revision of *Don Juan Returns From the War* (1936) by Bertolt Brecht's younger contemporary Ödön von Horváth, this newest addition to the Vogel oeuvre is in keeping with the playwright's penchant for responding to the canon and asking pressing questions about the present. The play focuses on veterans of the wars in Iraq and Afghanistan as they return home to a country largely divorced from the impacts of war. Displacing time and space and depicting a dream-like landscape, this latest play also demonstrates Vogel's ongoing interest in form, her search for new ways to tell familiar stories.

Early Influences

Vogel's artistic perspectives are eclectically informed by Russian formalism; Kenneth Burke; canonical playwrights like Brecht, Artaud, and Strindberg; and "all the songs of Judy Garland; every Broadway musical; and a gay brother, who, when I was seventeen, took me to see John Waters."[6] Revealing something of her unique strategy as a playwright who identifies as both a feminist and a lesbian, Vogel considers Strindberg "an extremely powerful ally for me as a woman dramatist because in him there is a fear and a power of women not approached by any other dramatist."[7] As theater scholar David Savran argues, Vogel's playwriting performs a masquerade in the way it "represents a revision and repossession of a highly masculinized textual practice."[8] Identifying topics that make her uncomfortable—sexism, homophobia, violence—Vogel writes not as a way to blame, but as a method through which to investigate the historical discourses and cultural narratives that have gone into shaping a sexist, homophobic, and hostile late-capitalist social system. And while she praises playwrights such as Caryl Churchill and María Irene Fornés for their ground-breaking work, Vogel reveals, "When people ask who [my] prototype is . . . as a feminist playwright, I say Chekhov, Williams, and Guare." Vogel appreciates these playwrights for giving their female characters a "complicated desire" and a "psychological complexity equal to the male characters." Vogel singles out John Guare as "the greatest living American playwright," finding inspiration in his lush language, his relentless reinvention, and his irrepressible "love of women."[9] That she revises the texts of a predominately white, male canon of playwrights suggests Vogel's crafty use of the very institutions that have marginalized her as a woman, feminist, and lesbian. As French sociologist Pierre Bourdieu asserts, "the strategy *par excellence* is the 'return to sources,' which is the basis of all heretical subversion and all aesthetic revolution, because it enables the insurgents to turn against the establishment the arms which they use to justify their domination."[10]

Vogel's engagement with the canon is an engagement with history as it is passed down through a selectively chosen body of texts and traditions. With its origins in Christian theology, canonization carries with it notions of timelessness and sacredness. However, as Savran points out, "canonization is not a mystical but a historical process. It represents an itinerary of cultural legitimization that privileges and excludes certain kinds of texts as well as their makers and consumers; it constructs hierarchies; it tries to sublimate and etherealize the commercial character of art; and it establishes aesthetic, ideological, and moral values and standards that masquerade as disinterested and universal."[11] Both inspired by the tradition she has inherited and outraged by her exclusion from it, Vogel read the canon, critically and voraciously, with a keen feminist eye that looked for tools, devices, and techniques that could be productively employed to pose her own questions. Theater critic Alisa Solomon articulates a feminist approach to a masculinist dramatic canon that coincides with Vogel's approach to playwriting. Solomon writes, "though as a feminist, I certainly recognize the misogyny within the Western dramatic tradition and resent women's frequent exclusion from that tradition, I am not ready to join some of my colleagues in ditching canonical plays as irrelevant or hostile to feminist concerns. I'd rather widen the openings that theatre's denaturalizing effects provide to expose and exploit Western drama's revelation of gender's artificiality."[12] Vogel puts Solomon's method into practice, "expos[ing] and exploit[ing]" western drama's revelation of gender's artificiality, its historicity, and thus its changeability.

Believing that "form *is* content," Vogel is a self-described formalist. She explains her theoretical approach to playwriting in an interview with critic Ann Linden:

> I think that one gets to the postmodern by deconstructing the modern. And that's what formalism does. If you follow someone like Ken-

neth Burke or if you follow the Russian formalists all the way to the letter, they're very much active in deconstruction. I sort of see a play traveling through time as unraveling its own devices. I mean, when I think about Bertolt Brecht and the separation of elements, I literally see the elements separating in terms of the textual elements. The plot and the character aren't doing the same thing.[13]

Vogel mobilizes a variety of dramatic forms, like circular and repetitive structures, to reconfigure Aristotelian elements, reorient audience expectations, and subvert habitual ways of seeing, thinking, and feeling. Vogel uses juxtaposition to jar her audiences into seeing familiar scenes in unusual ways. In this way, her plays develop an awareness of the relationship between aesthetic and social conventionality—that is, between the genre conventions that shape our expectations in the theater and the social conventions that shape our understandings of things like gender, sexuality, and family in everyday life. Like Bertolt Brecht, Vogel uses the structure of her plays to disrupt habituated patterns of identification. Unlike Brecht, Vogel cultivates affective engagement and empathy. Specifically, she cultivates negative empathy, which works against conditioned moral responses by structuring an emotional connection to characters that, under normal circumstances, would be reductively categorized and dismissed.

"Defamiliarization," for Vogel, "is the purpose of drama."[14] Taking up Russian formalist Victor Shklovsky's notion of defamiliarization, a term adapted by Brecht and renamed *Verfrumsdungeffekt*, Vogel foregrounds the forgotten, the habitual, and the ubiquitous, recontextualizing and re-presenting them in unexpected ways. Shklovsky's theory emphasizes sensual experience as opposed to rational knowing. As Shklovsky puts it, the "purpose of art is to impart the sensation of things as they are perceived and not as they are known," to make "the stone *stony*," a technique achieved by complicating dramatic conventions and making "forms difficult." Shklovsky insists that *"art is a way of experiencing the artfulness of an object; the object is not important,"*[15] an aesthetic theory that underpins all of Vogel's work. She invites audiences *to see differently*, to look at people and subjects from an oblique angle. Juxtaposing broad comedy and serious drama, high and low culture, sex and gender, language and sensation, Vogel asks her audience—and her students—to look from the edge of things, rather than from the center.

Vogel is a gifted mentor and beloved teacher, and as suggested by the many references to lessons and learning in her plays, her work as a teacher and her work as a playwright inform one another. The reciprocal relationship between her dramaturgy and her pedagogy emerges from her belief that we are not, as Lady Gaga would have it, "born this way," but rather, to borrow the words of Rodgers and Hammerstein, "we have to be carefully taught." Vogel sees her role in the classroom as that of facilitator. "I don't actually teach," she insists. For her, playwriting is a collaborative task, beginning with peer-directed workshops and propelled by "a brain trust at the table." In the classroom, she seeks to stretch the aesthetic muscles of her students, frequently encouraging them "to change the engines of their plays," writing a language-driven play, for example, rather than a plot-driven one, or a spectacle-driven work, rather than a character-centered one. Perhaps surprisingly, Vogel dissuades students from putting their politics into their plays and stays away from talking about theme- or thought-driven plays. Instead, she asks her students to focus on the structure of their plays and to "concentrate on the theatrical devices that deliver the theme," rather than the theme itself. The politics, she assures her students, will be there. She assigns writing exercises that, like her plays, are formal experiments aimed at developing a flexible adaptation of traditional Aristotelian elements.

Vogel asks her students to write plays that must be plays, pressing them to consider why their story has to be told on the stage, and not in a film or novel. One of the first assignments she gives to an incoming class is to have them write a play that is impossible to stage (such as a play with a dog as the protagonist), a task that demands a highly theatrical imagination and challenges the perceived limitations of the stage and live performance. Vogel adapted this assignment from Austrian playwright and enfant terrible Wolfgang Bauer, who developed the notion of unplayable plays or *mikrodramen* (microdramas), which set out to stage condensed ideas in seemingly impossible ways. Vogel also challenges her students to "bake-offs," an exercise that has them write a play in twenty-four hours using the conventions of a particular genre, such as Restoration comedy. For lessons in character development, she gets her students to draw from a real-life profile on the FBI's "Most Wanted" list and then write a scene that defies the profile.[16] This is a formalist's lesson in how to structure negative empathy, and one that promotes inclusive and complex understandings of justice in theater and in the social world beyond it.

Vogel's dramaturgy of defamiliarization is informed by the concept of *plasticity*. *Plasticity* is the term she uses to describe the theatrical spectacle as a living, malleable entity that changes according to its context and collaborators. According to Vogel, there are four levels of plasticity, or spectacle: the plasticity of the playworld (how the world feels); the plasticity of the stage (how the world is presented visually); the plasticity of the page (stage directions, pauses, tempo); and the plasticity of the playwright (how the artist is present in the play). As a conceptual and practical tool, plasticity produces playworlds grounded in an organic principle of changeability. Vogel's plays adapt to the conditions of each production; her playworlds are not determined in advance but are altered by the collaborative process; her characters are shaped by history, but they are also shaping history with each performance. Vogel's dramaturgy is informed by these four interlocking levels of spectacle, which together imbue her plays with a distinctive visual and affective texture.

An Embodied Aesthetic

For Vogel, "every new play is a theory,"[17] a theory that she is positing about the culture in which she lives. As a writer for the stage, Vogel develops play-theories that require fleshing out, literally and figuratively, with the actors, audiences, and crew all working to realize Vogel's embodied aesthetic. For her, "playwriting is really not about writing. It's about structuring, about gaps between language that are really filled in by the collaborators and the process."[18] Perhaps it is more apt to say that Vogel constructs plays, rather than writes them, and she does so in ways that reorient conventional habits of theatrical spectatorship, which, traditionally, encourage identification with a universalized male protagonist. With female characters at the center of the play action, Vogel's plays implicitly grapple with this question: "How can I seduce the men in the audience to identify directly, to empathize directly with the female subject, and [how can I] retrain women in the audience to identify directly with the female subject?"[19]

As well as being a self-described formalist, Vogel is a self-described feminist. Her feminism is best described not as an identity, but rather as a practice, a way of asking questions, and a process of reflecting on the psychosocial processes of internalization that perpetuate sexist and homophobic beliefs in both women and men. She contends:

> For me being a feminist does not mean showing a positive image of women. For me being a feminist means looking at the things that disturb me, looking at things that hurt me as a woman. We live in a misogynist world and I want to see why. And I want to look and see why not just men are the enemy but how I as a woman participate in the system.[20]

For Vogel, we are all complicit. Gender and sexuality are not fixed identities, but learned dispositions in Vogel's playworlds, and her characters often challenge the social, historical, and theatrical conventions through which normative gender and sexuality establish their authority, even as they are also bound by them. The presentation of gender in Vogel's plays highlights the performativity of gender, which feminist philosopher Judith Butler has influentially theorized as the citation of authorized acts that, over time and through repetition, become recognized as "properly" feminine and masculine. Butler explains:

> Gender is in no way a stable identity or locus of agency from which various acts proceed; rather, it is an identity tenuously constituted in time—an identity instituted through a *stylized repetition of acts.* Further, gender is instituted through the stylization of the body and, hence, must be understood as the mundane way in which bodily gestures, movements, and enactments of various kinds constitute the illusion of an adding identity.[21]

Gender acts gain their authority through the citation of already legitimized acts. There is, therefore, no ontology of gender, no original gender act; rather, as Butler explains, the "reality" of gender is produced as "an effect" of the repeated acts, "which congeal over time to produce the appearance of substance."[22] Citing normative gestures of gender works in much the same way as citing canonical texts; both quote established authority to legitimize an act or text. Citations may, however, "misquote" authority if, for example, a man performs gestures coded as feminine or a woman behaves in a conventionally masculine way—or if a feminist playwright rewrites a male-authored dramatic canon. In her revisions of canonical texts, Vogel deliberately misquotes, saying what has not yet been said and rephrasing what has been said over and over. Her plays point to the way certain bodies are ignored or reproduced as stereotypes in order to secure the boundaries of the normative. Highlighting how gender is learned and enacted at all levels of American culture, Vogel's female characters impersonate femininity in ways that make visible the performance of gender as a product of history and authority.

These characters, however, are not presented as victims of patriarchy, nor are they valorized simply because they are women. Rather, they are presented as participants in the discourses that produce inequality, both the subject and objects of history. Uninterested in developing a feminist or lesbian aesthetic, creating an alternative female canon, or idealizing women on stage, Vogel found herself excluded by feminist theater and theory in the early stages of her career. In the 1980s, when she was writing the first drafts of *Hot 'n' Throbbing* and *And Baby Makes Seven*, Vogel struggled to find theaters that would produce her work. If her plays were staged, they were not always warmly received, by either critics or audiences. Theater scholar C. W. E. Bigsby succinctly summarizes the complicated reception of Vogel's plays in the early stage of her career: "Her plays were not offered as an antidote, still less as a palliative, but they were offered as an irritant. She aimed to disturb and for much of the 1980s she found herself operating in a theatre where that was not a priority."[23] *Baby*'s first production, in 1984, was vehemently criticized by lesbian audience members who were outraged by the representation of a lesbian couple who created imaginary boy children to animate their private life. When it comes to "representing" as a lesbian playwright, Vogel insists: "I don't speak for all lesbians and I don't want to."[24] As Split Britches was staging campy butch-femme performances in downtown New York City to wide acclaim, Vogel was writing "straight" plays for a theatrical institution not open to irreverent representations of lesbian relationships. She herself admits, "I guess I've sort of fallen between the different models of what feminist theatre is . . . or queer theatre."[25] Rather than developing an aesthetic based on her sexual orientation or gender, Vogel tried to show how these crystallize as social identities over time and, also, how revised iterations of these identities can dissolve this crystallization, if only slightly.

The 1980s was an important decade for women, gay, and lesbian playwrights, with Wendy Wasserstein, Beth Henley, and Marsha Norman all being produced on Broadway and winning major awards, including Henley's Pulitzer Prize in 1981 for *Crimes of the Heart* and Norman's in 1983 for *'night Mother*. Moreover, Jane Chamber's *Last Summer at Bluefish Cove* (1980) and Larry Kramer's *Normal Heart* (1985) were landmark plays that used the conventions of realism to stage lesbian and gay experiences respectively. Along with these playwrights, David Mamet, John Patrick Shanley, August Wilson, and Sam Shepard were writing celebrated plays that registered a competitive American culture increasingly divided politically between right and left, as well as culturally along lines of class, sexuality, gender, and racial difference. The 1980s saw the emergence of the "culture wars," a series of social debates between the political left and right, characterized by a backlash against feminism and civil rights, a reassertion of family values and traditional gender roles, and an emerging hegemony grounded in individualism and other economically driven values of Reaganomics. Consequently, the radical theatrical experiments of the 1960s and 1970s and the formation of groups like the Open Theater and Living Theatre gave way, in the 1980s, to a decade of aesthetic, as well as economic and social, conservatism.

Significantly, all of the successful plays cited above were written in the still-dominant genre of American theater—realism. As anyone familiar with feminist theater criticism in the 1980s will know, realism was the target of a wholesale critique during this period, identified as a deeply conservative genre that reaffirms dominant (i.e., white, heteronormative, masculine) values by reproducing a seemingly stable and unchangeable playworld. In her seminal work of feminist theater criticism, *The Feminist Spectator as Critic* (1988), Jill Dolan points out that realist plays like Norman's and Henley's were accepted into the canon because they adhere to established aesthetic conventions and cater to a generic white, male spectator. Dolan writes, "a profitable success on Broadway [meant] meeting the canon's requirements for institutional and economic recognition" and conforming "to the rule of universality by transcending the historical moment and speaking to a generic spectator." [26] The aesthetic conventions of universality and timelessness obscure the white, male subject authorizing (and often authoring) these conventions, while excluding all who fall outside the realm of the universal—women, people of color, and homosexuals. Embracing realism as the established form of commercial theater, the American stage in the 1980s was more concerned with maintaining convention, rather than challenging or disturbing it.[27] Vogel's plays, with their experimental dramaturgy and difficult subject matter, did not fit these criteria. Instead, they encouraged unconventional habits of identification and challenged audiences to consider the ways they participate in producing the values and beliefs presented in the spectacle before them.

It was in the 1990s—amid an intellectual climate defined by poststructuralist theories of gender, sexuality, and embodiment and a popular climate rife with identity politics—that Vogel's plays found receptive audiences. Vogel's breakout play, *The Baltimore Waltz*, was staged at New York City's Circle Repertory Theater in February 1992 and was praised by critics and audiences for its imaginative, irreverent, and yet sensitive representation of AIDS. Coming on the heels of Tony Kushner's groundbreaking *Angels in America* (1991–92), *Waltz* contributed to a new era of plays that dealt with AIDS not as a marginal issue but as central cultural question. *Waltz* also marked Vogel as a courageous, witty, and innovative playwright. After this success, her earlier works, such as *Desdemona* and *And Baby Makes Seven*, were produced at off-Broadway theaters like Circle Repertory and Lucille Lortel. With the resounding success of *How I Learned to Drive* at the end of the decade, Vogel was recognized as an important voice in American theater. New York City's Signature Theater devoted its 2004–5 season to Vogel's work, staging *The Baltimore Waltz*, as well as revised versions of *Hot 'n' Throbbing* and *The Oldest Profession*, which further secured her place in the American dramatic canon.

Vogel's dramaturgy is grounded in an understanding of history as an embodied participation in the cultural narratives that inevitably, albeit differently, shape bodies and consciousnesses. Her plays use history to question the present, with the past punctuating the present and interrupting linear movement. Her plays often move recursively, displacing teleological plot and its promise of final resolutions with a past that continually folds back onto the present, usually in the form of memory. The past is not invoked as a way to legitimize the present or to reclaim a time nostalgically remembered as less complicated than today, nor is it a story set "long, long ago." History is, for Vogel, an affective encounter with a past that continues to permeate the present and that, if recognized, can complicate how we live in the contemporary moment. As she explains:

> The connection I have with time is something that causes enormous emotional repercussions for me. . . . I don't think that there's a neat demarcation, politically, ethically, between history and the present moment. . . . History is simply a way . . . to analyze shifting interconnections among politics, social history, economics, culture, gender. History is simply the name we give a discrete moment when we analyze those connections.[28]

For Vogel, history is a method, a way of seeing and examining how the past continues to shape the present. And theater—literally "a place to see"—is an ideal place to witness history unfolding. History emerges in Vogel's plays in the language and bodies of her characters, in the choices they make, in the relationships they form, and in the memories they recall and revise.

Along with this multitemporality, Vogel's plays also mobilize multiple psychic registers at once. Just as past and present overlap in her plays, fantasy operates in dialectical relation to reality. Reality and fantasy are interpenetrating states of mind and interlocking social practices that are, at once, individual and collective, private and public; her plays give a material historicity to fantasy, showing the social stereotypes and conventions that structure our imaginations. Her plays deliberately confuse distinctions between reality and fantasy, as well as between history and memory, while implicitly questioning the authority that goes into making these distinctions in the first place.

Fusing the interruptive dramaturgy of Brechtian epic theater with fragments of American popular culture, Vogel's plays oscillate between gestic distance and affective engagement. In *Unmaking Mimesis*, theater scholar Elin Diamond develops a gestic feminist criticism that productively brings together the Brechtian aesthetic of distance and historicization with Derridian *différance* and feminist theory's focus on gender, sexuality, spectatorship, and the body.[29] Diamond explains why Brechtian theory is useful for feminists seeking to show gender and sexuality not as natural, but as socially constructed over time: "Brechtian historicization insists that [the] body is not a fixed essence but a site of struggle and change," and his theories give "us a way to put that history in view."[30] The body, from this perspective, is not understood as the property of an individual person, but rather as a social situation. In her canonical revisions, Vogel revises the Brechtian "not . . . but"—an acting technique that foregrounds the choices available within every social act—into something closer to "yes, and!"—a writing technique (and the first rule of improvisation) that acknowledges the choices available *and* adds other possible choices. Vogel's "yes, and!" is a supertextual defamiliarization strategy that takes up and talks back to the plays written by her predecessors, along with the histories they convey, and gives them other words, bodies, and contexts. Her playworlds and the characters in them are part of an ongoing dialogue, a "yes, and!" contribution to a canonical and cultural history always in process.

Diamond's description of the "polymorphous thinking body" of the performer is an especially useful way of understanding Vogel's female characters. Although Diamond uses this term to differentiate performance from traditional theater, it is applicable to Vogel's presentational style and non-naturalistic construction of character, which displaces notions of interiority and psychological realism with characters that assume a knowing distance from the lives and bodies they inhabit. Diamond theorizes performance as a mode that "dismantles textual authority, illusionism, and the canonical actor's body, in favor of the 'polymorphous thinking body' of the performer, a sexual, permeable, tactile body."[31] The notion of a polymorphous thinking body is helpful for the way it disrupts traditional divisions of body (typically associated with the feminine) and mind (typically associated with the masculine) and thus for the way it defamiliarizes the sexualized female body and the desires it provokes by casting it instead as a body with a promiscuously capacious intelligence. Like the Brechtian actor, the polymorphous thinking body has the capacity simultaneously to act and to question the actions being performed, to be sexualized and to critique that sexualization.

Animating these theoretical influences is Vogel's sense of humor, which is perhaps her most distinctive trademark as a playwright. Specifically, a camp sensibility characterizes Vogel's comedy and her dramaturgy. Camp suits Vogel's formalism and her feminism, working as a defamiliarization strategy that emphasizes form over (or *as*) content and encourages a more oblique spectatorship. In "Notes on Camp" (1964), cultural critic Susan Sontag defines camp as both a way of seeing and a style; its main features are artifice, stylization, irony, playfulness, exaggeration, and excess.[32] Sontag writes, "To camp is a mode of seduction—one which employs flamboyant manners susceptible of a double interpretation."[33] Likewise, with *How I Learned to Drive*, Vogel wanted "to *seduce* the audience," and invite them to see "highly charged political issues in a new and unexpected way."[34] As a mode of perception, camp sees the relationship *between* things—between the erotic and the political, high and low, past and present, masculine and feminine—and Vogel's seductive strategy likewise draws audiences away from familiar, binary perceptions and toward more complex ways of seeing.

Esther Newton's ground-breaking anthropological study *Mother Camp: Female Impersonators in America* (1972) greatly imprinted Vogel as a graduate student.[35] Unlike Sontag's theorization of camp, which came out of a 1960s pop culture context, Newton's description of camp and drag practices emerged from her study of 1970s urban, gay subcultures. Newton defines incongruity, theatricality, and humor as camp's three main traits: "Incongruity is the subject matter of camp, theatricality its style, and humor its strategy."[36] Newton explains her choice of the word "mother" for the title: "camp humor ultimately grows out of the incongruities and absurdities of the patriarchal nuclear family; for example, the incongruity between the sacred, idealized Mother, and the profane, obscene Woman."[37] It is precisely these incongruities and these characters—the mother, the prostitute, the teenage girl, the "good" wife—that pervade Vogel's plays. In drag and camp, as in Vogel's plays, male/female, masculine/feminine operate as the most fundamental divisions structuring psychic and social development, both for those who fall within normative categories and for those who do not. Impersonators expose the incongruities of the heteronormative sex-gender system, which posits the relationship between male-masculinity and female-femininity as both natural and indissoluble, by wrenching it apart and parodying its codes and gestures. For the impersonators in Newton's study, as for Vogel the playwright, camp is "a strategy for a situation"[38] and in this way is not a fixed style but one that changes in relation to the social milieus within which it is performed. Vogel's characters impersonate roles given to them by a society still organized around the patriarchal family, and they perform a kind of drag that does not rely, as does gay male drag, on the incongruity of a male body concealed beneath feminine artifice, but rather on the incongruity within femininity, which defines women as sacred *and* profane and female bodies as idealized *and* degraded. Indeed, camp not only gives voice and visibility to queer sexualities but also works to defamiliarize heteronormative sexuality, highlighting the absurdity of conventional femininity and masculinity, as well as the culture that defines them. Camp shows us that these categories—homosexuality and heterosexuality—are neither rational nor natural, but rather arbitrary and shifting.

Vogel's camp is a method of defamiliarizing the normative, the everyday, the profane , and the discarded. Her plays are camp in their theatricality; in their blending of humor and pathos; in their exaggerated display of the conventions governing gender and sexuality; in their refusal of linear methods of organizing time; and in their deliberate confusion between heterosexual and homosexual, as well as sexual and not-sexual. Drawn, at times, with the broad brush strokes of farce (*The Mineola Twins, And Baby Makes Seven*) and, at other times, with a dark, fine edge (*Hot 'n' Throbbing, How I Learned to Drive*), Vogel's camp is a fusion of Lenny Bruce and Mae West—outrageous humor and exaggerated femininity—set in familiar contexts, like home and family. As the animating force of her dramaturgy of defamiliarization, Vogel's camp is perhaps most eloquently captured by Eve Kosofsky Sedgwick's formulation:

> To view camp, as among other things, the communal historically dense exploration of a variety of reparative practices is to do better justice to many of the defining elements of classic camp performance: the startling, juicy displays of excess erudition, for example; the passionate, often hilarious antiquarianism, the prodigal production of alternative historiographies; the "over"-attachment to fragmentary, marginal, waste or leftover products; the rich, highly interruptive affective variety; the irrepressible fascination with ventriloquistic experimentation; the disorienting juxtapositions of present with past, and popular with high culture.[39]

Responding as a feminist and lesbian to a male-authored canon, Vogel participates in just such "prodigal production of alternative historiographies," while the "juicy displays of excess erudition" and "ventriloquistic experimentation" of her characters, and the "juxtapositions of present with past, and popular with high culture" in her playworlds, position her plays as camp in the reparative mode. From *Meg* to *A Civil War Christmas*, her plays engage in a "communal historically dense exploration," bringing canonical and cultural history in reparative relation with the bodies they define. Simultaneously looking backward, reaching forward, and confronting the present, Vogel's plays engage in a three-way dialogue, unraveling and examining some of the central questions circulating in the dramatic canon, social history, and contemporary American culture.

Chapter Outline

The following chapters examine Vogel's ten published plays and are arranged around the topoi outlined at the beginning of this introduction: gender, sexuality, authority, family, fantasy, memory, and history. This arrangement is not meant to create isolated discussions that conclude at the end of each chapter. Rather, it is meant to highlight the conversation operating within Vogel's oeuvre, as well as the conversation between her plays and the canon that she inherited. Vogel's plays continually talk back to one another, posing similar questions but placing them in a new context and looking at them through a different lens. For example, she reveals, "*The Mineola Twins* is very much me rethinking *And Baby Makes Seven.*"[40] Reading *Twins* as a revision of *Baby* yields different interpretations than if they were viewed in isolation. Seen as plays in dialogue, they become two takes on the family drama in a late-twentieth-century period of social fragmentation. So while each chapter title signals a particular topic and focuses on a representative play(s) that examines it, the chapters and the questions they raise are in no way meant to be understood as discreet, but rather as part of an ongoing and overlapping conversation within Vogel's canon and between her work and the broader canonical and cultural history. Each chapter builds on the next to produce a multidirectional dialogue, which gains complexity, if not resolution, as each of her plays rewrites the next and as time and history bring new meanings to our interpretations of them.

Along with close analyses, there is a substantial amount of attention paid to the production and reception of Vogel's plays, especially the critical reception of New York productions. This focus is important in that it helps position Vogel's plays within the broader field of contemporary American theater. Perhaps even more centrally, the critical reception of Vogel's plays is integral to the very process of canonization that her plays are engaging with and questioning. The popular press, in particular the *New York Times*, shapes popular tastes and, in an important way, determines the canonical fate of a play—a bad review often ends the afterlife of a play. The production and reception detail that concludes the analyses of each play is meant to lay bare the political and social context underpinning the processes of canonization.

Chapter 1, "Gender and Authority," discusses Vogel's two earliest published plays, *Meg* (1977) and *Desdemona* (1977/1993). Obliquely addressing many of the conflicts and concerns of 1970s feminism, these plays place women center stage, exploring what is at stake in possessing—and usurping—canonical authority and examining the tensions within female homosocial situations that emerge out of class difference. *Meg; or, A Woman for All Reasons*[41] revises Robert Bolt's *A Man for All Seasons* (1960) to offer a different version of the life of Sir Thomas More, one told from his daughter's perspective. Here, Vogel raises such questions as: Who gets to tell history? Who is remembered, and how they are remembered? More's famously erudite and devoted daughter Margaret is, in Vogel's play, Meg—a willful and curious young woman and author of the story we see on stage. The play demythologizes both father and daughter, while suggesting the tendency of traditional historical narratives to make heroes of "great men," while casting women in supporting roles that amplify masculine greatness. *Meg* provides a valuable introduction to Vogel's work, particularly in terms of the way she portrays female characters as the subjects of history and their own lives. What becomes immediately clear in this early work is that, for Vogel, history is embodied and driven by desire.

In *Desdemona*, Shakespeare's most idealized heroine becomes exactly the whore Othello imagines her to be. Maybe worse. Neither idealized as a good and faithful wife nor honored as a martyr of male violence, Vogel's Desdemona is a product of the sexist fantasies that construct these and other such stereotypes of femininity in the first place. In contrast to Shakespeare's heroine, Vogel's Desdemona is a spoiled member of the upper class, who spends her time working at Bianca's brothel in order to alleviate the tedium of her aristocratic lifestyle. The play looks at the way female sexuality is structured in relation to social class, defamiliarizing the sexual stereotypes associated with upper- and working-class femininities. Here, Desdemona embodies the lasciviousness typically associated with the working class, while Emilia exemplifies the piety and fidelity of middle-class femininity. And while Desdemona romanticizes Bianca's brothel work as a life free from the bonds of marriage, Bianca secretly harbors aspirations of marriage and life in the middle class. As each woman jockeys for social position, it is clear that this position is ultimately determined by their material dependence on the men in their lives. Although the male characters never appear on stage, Shakespeare's play, it is understood, continues to unfold backstage, influencing Vogel's play and the conflicts among the three female characters. The ambiguous ending of *Desdemona* halts the inevitability of the tragic plot, but, in pointing toward Desdemona's presumed fate, also suggests the authority of dramatic forms, like tragedy, and canonical figures, like Shakespeare.

Chapter 2, "Reimagining Family," looks at *And Baby Makes Seven* (1984), a comic rewriting of Edward Albee's *Who's Afraid of Virginia Woolf?* that revels in the possibilities of fantasy and narrative revision to shape new forms of family. *Baby* revolves around the imminent birth about to take place in the lives of Anna and Ruth, a lesbian couple, and their gay best friend, Peter, who is the father of the child Anna is expecting. The women have a vibrant fantasy life from which they derive much of their sexual and domestic pleasure and through which they enact their anxieties about the impending arrival of the baby. Their fantasies involve playing the parts of three imaginary characters, which allow the women to devise elaborate plots and also to express feelings that might otherwise be deemed inappropriate. In preparation for the arrival of the "real" child, it is decided that the imaginary children must be "killed off" in a series of mock death scenes. And yet, the imaginary boys have the last word in the play, which suggests that fantasy is not opposed to reality, but rather another dimension of it. *Baby* underscores the public nature of private fantasies, while suggesting the pleasures to be had by weaving new plots from old narratives. Playfully displacing the authority of the Oedipal narrative with scenes borrowed from a broad range of cultural texts, from *Macbeth* to *The Exorcist*, *Baby* imagines how we might take perverse pleasure in reimagining the roles we play within family and everyday life, rather than unconsciously repeating the same story.

Chapter 3, "Revising Fantasy," focuses on *Hot 'n' Throbbing* (1992), a play that Vogel began writing in the mid-1980s and revised several times over the next two decades. *Hot* is darker than *Baby*, exploring the damaging potential of fantasy and the dysfunctional patterns reproduced within the heteronormative nuclear family. *Hot* offers a radical take on the relationship between sexuality, violence, and family structures, while interrogating a canon of texts that authorize violence and legitimize male authority over female pleasure. The play's protagonist, Charlene Dwyer, writes erotic screenplays for a feminist film company; she also has an abusive ex-husband who brings the play to a fatal end. While Charlene wants to create women who are the center of their own dramas, she is also inextricably enmeshed in a history of discourses that have defined female sexuality, discourses ventriloquized in the play by the male character, The Voice, and embodied by the female character, Voice Over. Charlene struggles to find a place within this history and a language with which to write erotic scenarios with different dynamics of power and desire. The play is a trenchant look at the connection among violence, sexuality, and canonical narratives, pointedly responding to male playwrights whose work, as Savran states, "romanticizes violence against women."[42] The tension between fictional representations of sexuality and violence and the actualities of domestic violence is left unresolved in the play, and the conclusion opens up troubling questions, rather than providing any clear answers.

Chapter 4, "Embodied Histories," looks at *The Oldest Profession* (1981/2005), a poignant portrait of five elderly prostitutes struggling in Reagan-era America, and *The Mineola Twins* (1996), a farce of Cold War–era America as told through the conflicted relationship between twin sisters. A revision of David Mamet's *The Duck Variations, Profession* displaces the metaphysical musings of Mamet's elderly duo by focusing on the devalued labor of five vulnerable women who are feeling the economic impact of Reaganomics on their lives and aging bodies. The women become increasingly at odds not only with the changing socioeconomic climate of New York City but also with one another, as they differ in their views of how to run their business—for maximum profit or communal harmony. Mamet's ahistorical play is given a historical context in Vogel's revision, and metaphysics is replaced by the material effects of poverty and displacement. The hostile present in *Profession* is contrasted with a mythic past remembered as a homey brothel in Storeyville, a place in which their bodies and labor are one and yet also a place that, in the end, seems only to exist in the stories the women tell one another.

Staging an accelerated history and striking a different tone, *Mineola Twins* is an over-the-top farce that spans the period of American history from Eisenhower to the Reagan/Bush administrations. Savran points out *Twin's* relationship to Brecht's *Seven Deadly Sins*, in its use of the split protagonist and dramatization of "psychomania," and to *The Good Person of Szechwan*, in the way it "links human labor, morality and gender . . . [and] underlines the fact that good and bad correspond to gendered oppositions in capitalist—and patriarchal— societies."[43] Vogel's satire allegorizes the political positions of left and right through the familiar sexual stereotypes of virgin and whore, while revealing the way any binary division, political or sexual, depends on its opposite pole for meaning and coherence. What is significant about *Twins* is that it tells political history through the bodies of women, as they come of age—and come apart—in a nation with increasingly polarized politics.

Chapter 5, "Memory Lessons," examines *How I Learned to Drive* (1998), a play about the forms memory takes and the lessons that emerge, for both the characters and the audience, out of their recollection. Vogel wrote *Drive*, in part, as a response to David Mamet's *Oleanna* (1992), an ideologically unbalanced, highly polemical play that was produced amid media frenzy over the Clarence Thomas–Anita Hill hearings and the national debate over sexual harassment laws. Vogel wanted, with *Drive*, to take the delicate subject of sexual abuse and unravel its complexity, historicity, and humanity. Describing *Twins* as "the burlesque version of *Drive*,"[44] Vogel suggests that these plays tell the same story, although in different registers. Published together as *The Mammary Plays* (1998), *Twins* and *Drive* are productively read as companion plays, as they span the same four decades of American history—1960s–90s—and stage two versions of female coming of age during this period, complete with period music and iconic fashion. However, while *Twins* is a sex farce staged in Technicolor, *Drive* is a minimalistic staging of a culture that relentlessly sexualizes young girls and women. L'il Bit, the play's protagonist, tells the story, recalling in disjointed order the memories of her relationship with her Uncle Peck. As with all of her plays, Vogel depicts people and subjects from multiple angles, challenging any easy distinction between victim and victimizer, perversity and normativity. Using a *Lolita*-esque pattern of seduction that unfolds from the point of view of the female, *Drive* shows both the tenderness and the pain of L'il Bit's relationship with Peck.

Chapter 6, "Stopping Time," examines *The Baltimore Waltz* (1992) and *The Long Christmas Ride Home* (2004), plays that implicitly interrogate a culture of homophobia, while simultaneously commemorating Vogel's brother, Carl. Vogel wrote *Waltz* as both a tribute to Carl and a fantasy fulfillment of a trip to Europe that the siblings never had a chance to take together. Her first nationally recognized work, *Waltz* defamiliarizes AIDS by presenting it as ATD (Acquired Toilet Disease), a heterosexual illness transmitted from schoolchildren to their teachers. Using a tripartite structure, with three stage worlds (fantasy, reality, and memory) and three characters (Anna, her brother Carl, and the Third Man), *Waltz* defies binary organizations of the world and binary categories that attempt to contain bodies and limit actions. The play also challenges the rhetoric of AIDS activism of the 1980s and 1990s that insisted on the "innocence" of AIDS "victims." In Vogel's play, Anna contracts ATD, coping with the news by going on a trip to Europe with her brother, Carl, and taking up promiscuity as her chosen therapy. Part fantasy travelogue and part parody of the classic film noir *The Third Man*, *Waltz* displaces the moral stigma of AIDS with a wildly imaginative and uninhibited sexual romp through Europe. We find out at the end, however, that it was Carl who was terminally ill, Anna's trip a fantasy imagined in the moment she found out her brother had died of AIDS. Fantasy and a circular structure imbue *Waltz* with a dreamlike quality, producing a playworld that is both politically charged and profoundly reparative in the way it transforms loss into a commemorative celebration.

The Long Christmas Ride Home (2003) is a poetic family drama that is at turns moving and unsettling. More somber and restrained than the lush theatricality of *Waltz*, *Home* takes a different route to examine a similar landscape: the movements of fantasy and memory, the reverberating impact of painful moments, the indelible lessons learned in childhood, and the marking of sexually deviant bodies in a homophobic culture. The play stages the multitemporality of the present, using the body as the site of historical encounter. Like both *Waltz* and *Drive, Home* is deeply concerned with the lessons of memory, contemplating the ways the past is continually reenacted in the present and how this recursive reenactment complicates understandings of unfettered forward movement into the future. *Home* also draws on the lyricism of Japanese drama and uses Bunraku-inspired puppets that stand in as the child versions of the adult actors, who orchestrate their movements, theatricalizing the process of remembering and the psychic divisions that emerge within a present haunted by the past. *Home* borrows the conceit of the family car trip from Thornton Wilder's *Happy Journey from Trenton to Camden* and the repeated ritual of the Christmas dinner in his *Long Christmas Dinner* to mediate on time and memory, repeated generational patterns, and the possibilities of forgiveness. With an unusual narrative structure that displaces individual voices and moves between different linguistic tenses and a stage design that uses the abstracted minimalism of Nō Drama, *Home* conjures a tone and atmosphere of ritual. As suggested by the play's epigraph, a poem written by Carl Vogel called "Floating World," Vogel's brother haunts this play as well, taking shape as the character Stephen. Part *shite* of Nō drama, part Stage Manager, Stephen is brought back to life by his sisters, Rebecca and Claire, every year on the day after Christmas, St. Stephen's Day. As celebrations of theater's capacity to bring the dead back to life and to make time stand still, *Waltz* and *Home* both use a circular structure, simultaneously stopping time and taking the audience on a round-trip journey, only to return them to the place where they began, but with perspectives inevitably changed by what they have seen along the way.

Chapter 7, "Haunted History," looks at *A Civil War Christmas: An American Musical Celebration* (2008). Markedly different from Vogel's other plays, *Civil War Christmas* is more directly historical, more densely populated with ghosts, and less centered on gender and sexuality. It is an epic play, a historical pageant, and a work of Dickensean proportions. Like Dickens's *A Christmas Carol, Civil War Christmas* is haunted, but the ghosts in Vogel's play are those of America's past. Set on Christmas Eve of 1864, the play weaves together a series of overlapping plot lines and characters—many of which are taken from historical documents and slave narratives—

punctuating them with period songs and narrated passages that fill in the historical details. Believing that America still lives in this moment—the eve of the end of the Civil War—Vogel wanted these stories to be part of a shared history and public dialogue, and her play invites audiences to revisit this moment annually and to feel its continued resonance in the present. (She also wanted to write a play that her nieces and nephews could see, without first having to go through therapy.)[45] In this, as in all of her plays, Vogel reminds us that theater is a vital public place to gather and witness stories—histories—that need bodies to be told.

CHAPTER ONE

Gender and Authority:
Meg and *Desdemona*

> The pressing issue for feminists becomes how to inscribe a
> representational space for women that will point out the gender
> enculturation promoted through the representation frame and
> that will belie the oppressions of the dominant ideology it
> perpetuates.
>
> —Jill Dolan, *Feminist Spectator as Critic*[1]

> I'm a believer in forms, Meg. I do not ask you or your husband
> to share my convictions; but do observe my conventions.
>
> —Sir Thomas More, *Meg*[2]

Vogel's early plays resonate as the work of a young graduate student
immersed in both the emerging discourse of feminist criticism and the
more established tradition of the western dramatic canon, comprised
(at that point) entirely of white, male playwrights. Conscious of both
the exclusions upon which the canon was built and the rich aesthetic
resources it offered, Vogel critiqued the conventions of the canon even
as she absorbed them. *Meg* (1977) and *Desdemona* (1977/1993) demonstrate the dramaturgical strategies that Vogel would continue to mobilize and refine throughout her career: a dialogic engagement with the
dramatic canon and with contemporary culture; an irreverent comic
impulse; a focus on female characters at the center of nonnaturalistic
playworlds; a juxtaposition of high and low, comedy and tragedy; and
a recognition of the relationship between social and aesthetic conventions, between the rules governing social relations and bodies and
those governing theater. As cultural theorist Raymond Williams

points out, conventions, in both senses, constitute the "real grounds of the inclusions and exclusions, the styles and the ways of seeing" of a given culture. Crucially, both social and aesthetic conventions "by definition are historically variable."[3] Vogel's plays foreground both the social inclusions and exclusions that conventions enforce, as well as their changeability; this double or dialectical movement is achieved through her conversations with social history and the bastion of convention: the dramatic canon.

Revising Robert Bolt's *A Man for All Seasons* and Shakespeare's *Othello*, respectively, *Meg* and *Desdemona* are situated in the early modern period, and both plays mobilize this temporal framing as a defamiliarization strategy that uses history to pose questions about the present. *Meg* and *Desdemona* use the past to register contemporary concerns raised by late-1970s second-wave feminism: women's exclusion from canonical history; the need to recover a women's history and women's stories; the need to claim canonical and social authority; the necessity and difficulties involved in claiming authority within discourses defined by and for men; and the challenges of establishing a collective feminist voice that can account for differences of class, race, and sexuality. While *Meg* demonstrates second-wave feminism's emphasis on reviving forgotten female figures in history and recovering women's oral histories, *Desdemona* suggests the conflicts that develop among women of different classes.[4] The plays work to champion feminist claims to authority, even as they complicate those claims by drawing attention to the intersection of gender, sexuality, and class. It was this latter challenge that made Vogel's plays an uneasy fit within the context of late-1970s feminism. She explains:

> Back then, when I was starting with things like *Desdemona*, even *Meg* or the *Oldest Profession*, it was seen as being very antifeminist because it was seen as presenting very negative images of women. Back then, interestingly enough, we weren't talking about class and gender or race and gender. It was very much that kind of new wave, National Organization of Women liberal feminism, and lesbianism was a dirty word.[5]

Not certain whether she was ostracized because she was "out as a lesbian" or because she didn't "see how one can separate gender from race, from economics,"[6] Vogel continued to write plays that linked gender and sexuality to class and constructed characters that enact the contradictions of a culture that positions women as antagonists to each other and to themselves. Not interested in celebrating women merely because they are women, Vogel saw more value in examining the conflicts within and among female characters that have learned the conventions of a male-dominated culture and canon so well that they see themselves as objects of an internalized male authority. As a student of drama, Vogel recognized the way female characters often acted as "puppets" for a male authorial voice, embodying a set of conventions developed by and for a male-centered playworld. Canonical female characters are, in effect, ventriloquists, speaking the words of male authority and acting in ways that complement the conflicts of the central male character. Aside from such important exceptions as Rosalind, Hedda, and Nora, the canon of early modern and modern drama is populated by female characters written to serve the interests of the male protagonists. And audiences over the ages have learned to focus on the centrality of the male conflicts and have internalized patterns of identification that make empathy for male heroes seem "natural." Since theater is both shaped by and shapes broader affective structures and social conventions, these habits of identification spill over into other contexts of spectatorship and into everyday encounters. These identification patterns also shape relations among women, as *Desdemona* suggests, casting them as objects competing for the legitimization of an authorizing male figure.

The first question Vogel asks when beginning work on a new play is: "What is the best structure to tell this?"[7] Using form to defamiliarize what has been naturalized in the present, Vogel illustrates that just as conventions change over time, so too can the social relationships that they structure change. The direct audience address in *Meg* implicitly poses the question: Who gets to speak? And the episodic structure of *Desdemona* disrupts the linear cause-effect plot of tragedy to ask: Are the women's desires and destinies thoroughly determined by the male-defined fantasies that govern a playworld like *Othello*? In both plays, female characters respond to male authority (both within and, implicitly, beyond the play-text), thereby inserting themselves into the stories—and the histories—that this authority constructs.

Observing Convention, Asserting Conviction: *Meg*

Meg centers on Sir Thomas More and his daughter, Margaret/Meg, and demonstrating a characteristic Vogel strategy, the play puts the female character in a position of authority. Here, Meg tells the story, demythologizing both her father's legacy as a Great Man and her own as his idealized daughter. She begins the play by opening an ancient-looking tome and reading in a tone of mock solemnity:

> Margaret More Roper was born in 1508, the beloved daughter of the reverent Saint Thomas More, martyr of the true Church—and died the obedient wife of William Roper, Esquire. . . . She submitted her brilliance in all things to her father and husband, thereby increasing her luster; and remains an example among women—as befits the daughter of a saint—saintly in compassion, humility, and obedience.[8]

In a plume of dust, Meg closes the book and introduces the audience to the other characters, who sit downstage: her father, Thomas More; her husband, William Roper; and Thomas Cromwell. Distinguishing between canonical history and the version she is about to narrate, she continues:

> Perhaps as unwilling schoolchildren, captive in a sunny classroom, you have heard or read of these three men—father, husband, and politician. Book after book are filled with words about their aspirations, their frustrations, their deaths. But all of that is another story—and not the story I tell you tonight. (7)

Metatheatrically foregrounding her role as storyteller, Meg employs the conventions of theater to complicate the conventions of history.

Typically remembered for her obedience, modesty, and erudition, Margaret More Roper is an example of history's tendency to flatten (idealize and/or demonize) female figures and cast them as supporting characters to a central male figure. However, Vogel's Meg complicates the idealized portrait we have come to know from traditional historical accounts. From the beginning, she is full of spirited energy, engaging her father in debate and mobilizing every "strategy" and "tactic" (9, 16) to persuade both her husband and her father in matters political, intellectual, and personal. Meg's modesty is reinter-

Figure 1: *Meg.* Jessica Jane Witham as Meg, Evjue Theatre, Madison, WI, 2010. Photo: Marie Schulte.

preted in Vogel's play as a lusty passion for Will Roper, her obedience overturned in the vow she writes and has Will recite to her: "I, William Roper, vow to be guided by my wife, Margaret More . . . in all matters civil, religious, and domestic" (8). Meg's revised vow is significant in the way it emphasizes the role of convention and authority in the legitimization of social institutions like marriage. And while she plays with these conventions, her father, Sir Thomas More, believes in their permanence and infallibility. In a pivotal exchange,

More tenaciously insists on the immutability of his beliefs, which, he claims, "are the conventions by which I have lived." Meg, who espouses a belief in the principles of openness and change, challenges her father by defiantly insisting, "The only convention by which we live is fear–(*Angry.*)" (62).

Meg illustrates the way history is so often transformed into myth and naturalized as the "way things are." As French theorist Roland Barthes puts it, "Myth does not deny things," but "on the contrary, it makes them innocent [and] gives them a natural and eternal justification."[9] It is by this process of naturalization that historical figures, such as Thomas More, and canonical texts, such as *Utopia*, have been mythologized, aesthetically elevated, and described with terms like "transcendence," "universality," and "truth." In contrast, *Meg* invokes the principles of historical perspective, change, and revision. With Meg as the narrator, More is recontextualized as the father in a family drama, rather than as the central figure of a history play. More himself asks Meg early in the play to "take over writing the family history," to which Meg replies, "(*Delighted.*) The family history! Could I?" Taking on the task with zeal, Meg begins facetiously with the following account: "The dominant force in the More household, around which the household revolved, was Mistress Margaret More . . . a saucy snippet" (16). Meg relishes her new role, playfully positioning herself at the center of the family story and of history. Her authority works in the play not to suggest that her story is more valid than ones that came before or that will come after. Rather, it underscores history as not a single story, but many different ones; the version you get depends on who does the telling. Neither the play nor its narrator makes any claims to truth or fact. From the start, the play is forthright about its own fabrications and takes pleasure in them.

From Meg's perspective, More is not an idealized hero, a saint, or a Great Man in the conventional sense. He is, rather, a stubborn thinker, a doting father, and a neglectful husband. In an intimate moment, Meg reflects thoughtfully to the audience, "There comes a time in life when father and daughter turn around and see each other as man and woman" (68). Here, the grand narratives of history are distilled to a poignant father-daughter story of growing up and letting go. What we see in *Meg* is a generational shift between More's unrelenting adherence to law and convention and his daughter's more pragmatic approach. For her, these laws and conventions need to be malleable enough to account for infinitely variable situations. Perhaps most significantly, Meg revises her father's martyrdom, wilfully refusing to attend his death. She refuses even to include his death as a scene in her play and so also averts any cathartic experience the audience might expect to have at the end of More's story. Too proud to play the role of the grieving daughter—"I will not make a public spectacle of myself—I can not do it" (72) —Meg encourages her husband to go in her place. And, of course, it is William Roper's story of More's life and death that became canonical history. What was authorized by William Roper—and Robert Bolt—as the history of a great man, author, and father was rewritten by Vogel as the story of a devoted daughter angered by a father who cared more for conventions than for his family. This "other story," however, is "a story never recorded" (73), not until 1977, that is. Although *Meg* is the least known of Vogel's plays, it continues to be produced at regional theaters around the country. It is a play that comments on the *how* of history: how history becomes consecrated as History, the forms it takes, and the voices it excludes. In her next play, *Desdemona*, Vogel uses what critic Amy Green aptly describes as a "seriously satiric feminist perspective"[10] to examine how sexual stereotypes and female relationships are structured through class and within a male-governed playworld. If Meg playfully usurps canonical history to tell us her story, Desdemona and her story remain determined by Shakespeare's authority, even as Vogel questions that authority by emphasizing the male fears and fantasies it legitimizes and the female conflicts it reinforces.

Fantasies of Female Sexuality: *Desdemona*

> I had been happy if the general camp,
> Pioneers and all, had tasted her sweet body,
> So I had nothing known. Oh, now forever
> Farewell the tranquil mind! Farewell content!
> Farewell the plumèd troops and the big wars
> That makes ambition virtue! Oh, farewell!
> —Othello, *Othello*, 3.3.355–60

Vogel wrote the first draft of *Desdemona* in 1977, and it was given its first staged reading at Cornell University in October of that year. It received a full production and a second-place prize in 1979 at the Actors Theatre's New Play Festival, the same year that Beth Henley's *Crimes of the Heart* took first place.[11] (Henley's play would go on to win the 1981 Pulitzer Prize for Drama.) However, it was not until 1993 that *Desdemona* received a full production at Circle Repertory in New York City. Theater audiences in the 1970s and 1980s were not receptive to seeing female characters behaving badly. They did not like seeing a promiscuous, overprivileged female protagonist treating her maid poorly. While the more difficult questions raised by feminism were tackled by performance artists, legitimate theater staged less disruptive female characters, like the suicidal protagonist of Marsha Norman's *'night Mother* (1983) and the likeably neurotic titular heroine of Wendy Wasserstein's *Heidi Chronicles* (1988). In this way, the broader structural inequities that the feminist movement addressed were reduced to the troubles of individual, white middle-class women. Vogel, in contrast, confronted such questions as: How is femininity constructed differently across classes? How do these differences effect relationships among women? How are women complicit in maintaining the very beliefs and actions that reduce their bodies to objects and subordinate their lives to male authority?

Even more to the point, *Desdemona* asks: What if Iago was telling Othello the truth about Desdemona's infidelity? How would that change our emotional response to the play? Would we champion her death? Why do we weep for Othello, instead of Desdemona? Vogel reveals her impetus for writing the play:

> In the 1970s, when I had read *Othello*, I was struck by the fact that my main point of identification, of subjectivity, was a man who is supposedly cuckolded, that I was weeping for a man who is cuckolded rather than for Desdemona. And, of course, at that point in the seventies, in terms of women's studies, there was all the virgin/whore analysis coming out, and it wounded me a great deal that Desdemona is nothing but an abstraction and that I didn't find any way of identifying with her.[12]

When genre, in this case tragedy, is seen from this perspective, we can understand the way it shapes our emotional expectations and, further, how our emotions are not private experiences, but rather products of our social conditioning. Satirically inverting the perspective of *Othello*, Vogel takes the audience backstage, pointing to the way theater conventions shape our emotional response to Desdemona's death. The play uses negative empathy to encourage identification with a Desdemona who is the embodied product of a fantasy of female sexuality reductively organized around the poles of idealized virgin/degraded whore. Shakespearean critic Lynda E. Boose argues, "the dangerous cultural binary of virgin and whore . . . acts not only as an external inhibitor but, even more problematically, as a set of stringent rules that culture has trained all women, even those who represent such widely different social classes as do the three women of *Othello*, to internalize."[13] Indeed, the bodies, choices, and actions of the play's three female characters are structured by this cultural binary. *Desdemona* underscores the female characters' limited agency by presenting a series of scenes that show a competitive and conflicted female homosocial environment, in which the male characters never appear, but from which they are also never totally absent. As critic Sharon Friedman explains, "The female world, though presented more subjectively, is still performing under a watchful, scrutinizing eye, awaiting judgment," and yet, "the spectator, perhaps for the first time, might stand outside it, recognize it, and resist its compelling vision."[14] In this way, *Desdemona* simultaneously defamiliarizes both the processes of canonization and the structures of spectatorship that canonical narratives produce.

Shakespeare is, arguably, the most imposing figure in the dramatic canon, his plays very often designated with those most legitimizing of terms—*timelessness* and *universality*. However, his status and the universal truths that his plays are said to contain are products of culturally and historically specific interpretative practices. As literary critic David Margolies argues, the timelessness and universality attributed to Shakespeare

> is neither a mark of excellence of the dramatist nor a neutral principle of interpretation; it is part of the ideological use of the plays. . . . Shakespeare is elevated above history; to challenge the timelessness of his plays is at once to call into question the whole ideology in which they are so deeply embedded.[15]

Vogel's revision of *Othello* highlights and undermines the aura surrounding Shakespeare, even though her characters never find an outside to the ideologies governing his text. As Jill Dolan writes in her introduction to *Desdemona in Amazon All-Stars: Thirteen Lesbian Plays*, "Vogel neatly overturns Shakespeare's moral universe, building a more complicated, autonomous, and satisfying experience (if secretive and doomed) for *Othello*'s women."[16] *Desdemona* does not recuperate Shakespeare's heroine in order to sanctify her. Rather, the play transforms her from an abstraction of Virtue to a material product of Othello and Iago's fantasy.

Desdemona has been alternatively exalted by critics as a model of feminine virtue and denounced an example of feminine disobedience. This contradiction suggests not only the changing attitudes surrounding "proper" feminine behavior but also the way canonical literature, especially Shakespeare, has historically served as a didactic tool that teaches moral values and offers ethical models. In the Victorian era, Desdemona embodied "the exquisite refinement, the moral grace, the unblemished truth, and the soft submission"[17] of the ideal feminine, whereas, in 1963, she was described as "hardly the perfect maiden according to Elizabethan ideals of feminine and filial conduct, and . . . not really the perfect wife according to the same code."[18] Vogel's Desdemona plays precisely within these fluctuations, defying her role as the embodiment either of Virtue or of filial disobedience. She is full of curiosity and desire, even as those desires remain circumscribed by the male figures—Shakespeare, Othello, Iago—who have authorized them.

As the quote that opens this section suggests, male authority over female sexuality in *Othello* is inextricably connected to social and political authority. Othello's "Farewell [to] the plumèd troops and the big wars / That makes ambition virtue!" draws a clear parallel between Desdemona's sexuality and Othello's political virility; whereas feminine virtue is associated with sexual purity, masculine virtue is anchored in political "ambition." Shakespearean critic Peter Stallybrass points out that, in Shakespeare's plays, "a woman's body could be imagined as a passive terrain on which the inequalities of masculine power were fought out."[19] Perhaps more importantly, it is not Desdemona's *actual* chastity that matters to Othello—indeed, "the general camp, Pioneers and all, [could have] tasted her sweet body," and he would have been undisturbed—but rather his *imagined* knowledge of her defiled body. The fantasy of Desdemona's sexual purity upholds Othello's mental, social, and political authority. By that same logic, her imagined infidelity destroys his sanity and authority. Desdemona's phantasmically pure body acts as the ground on which the hierarchies of male power are negotiated. What threatens this purity is its dialectical opposite—the body of the whore—and both are products of Iago's words and Othello's imagination. This duplicitous female sexuality is the deadly threat to male power in *Othello*. As Iago manipulates the semantic slippages between purity and contamination, virgin and whore, Desdemona's sexuality becomes increasingly uncertain and monstrous in Othello's mind. Unable to tolerate this ambiguity, he decides that she "must die, else she'll betray more men."[20]

While this deadly logic circumscribes *Desdemona*, Vogel's play focuses on the hostilities, the jealousies, and also the affections that circulate among the female characters. *Desdemona* incisively unravels the intimate exchange between Desdemona and Emilia in Act 4, scene 3, of *Othello*. The scene begins with Desdemona questioning Emilia about her stance on infidelity:

> DESDEMONA: Wouldst thou do such a deed for all the world?
> EMILIA: The world's a huge thing; it's a great price for so small a vice.
> DESDEMONA: In troth, I think I wouldst not.
> EMELIA: In troth, I think I should; and undo't when I had done it . . . who would not make her husband a cuckold to make him a monarch? I should venture purgatory for't.[21]

Here, Desdemona's sexual innocence and Emilia's sexual knowledge are underscored and linked to their respective class positions. This exchange naturalizes class-based constructions of female sexuality by attributing to the upper-class Desdemona qualities of honesty and chastity and placing the working-class Emilia in the role of sexual opportunist. Both women, however, defer elsewhere in *Othello* to what Boose calls the "presumptive whore," the "imagined other woman . . . whose existence must be theorized in order to carry the transferred guilt of the speaker's unacknowledgable fantasies."[22] Vogel, however, reverses the speakers of these lines and thus also the sexualities they construct. In *Desdemona*, it is Desdemona who guiltily asks Emilia, "have you ever cheated on your husband?" to which Emilia replies, "I'd never cheat—never—not for all the world I wouldn't." In an almost perfect echo of Emilia's line in *Othello*, Desdemona reminds her that "the world's a huge thing for so small a vice."[23] Working-class sexuality is, in Vogel's play, presented as chaste and devout, while aristocratic sexuality is restless and insatiable. And it is Vogel's Desdemona, not Bianca, who acts the part of the whore, the "imagined other woman" who gives shape to "unacknowledgeable fantasies."

Later in this same exchange between Desdemona and Emilia in *Othello*, conventional frameworks of passive female/active male sexuality are productively complicated by Emilia, who describes sexuality as a competitive game rather than an essentialized identity:

> Let husbands know
> Their wives have sense like them. They see, and smell,
> And have palates both for sweet and sour,
> As husbands have. What is it that they do
> When they change us for others? Is it sport?
> I think it is. And doth affection breed it?
> I think it doth. Is't frailty that thus errs?
> It is so too. And have we not affections,
> Desires for sport, and frailty as men have?
> Then let them use us well; else let them know,
> The ills we do, their ills instruct us so.[24]

In this provocative passage, Emilia articulates an alternative view of female sexuality, one that does not depend on the virgin/whore paradigm, but rather constructs an equivalence between male and female sexuality, comparing sex to "sport" and suggesting that women can and do enact an active desire coded as masculine. Sexuality is, within this model, not the essence of female identity, but a learned, mimetic performance. As Emilia points out, "the ills we do, their ills instruct us so." It is possible to read a homoerotic subtext in this passage, as well; Emilia's insistence that women can desire like men can be interpreted as saying, women can desire women like men desire women. Vogel's *Desdemona* playfully teases out this homoerotic subtext and develops similarly inventive metaphors for sex and sexuality, placing these in direct tension with class conflicts.

What began as a realist play in the late 1977 ended as an eighty-minute one-act play "written in thirty cinematic 'takes.'"[25] In the 1993 Circle Repertory production, the brief scenes were divided by bulb flashes followed by frozen tableaux, which allowed the audience to reflect on the interactions among the female characters as if they were, at once, historical portraits—a museum diorama —and also contemporary images—a film still. In her "Note to the Directors," Vogel writes, "*Desdemona* was written as a tribute (i.e. 'rip-off') to the infamous play, *Shakespeare the Sadist* by Wolfgang Bauer" (176). Bauer's brief 1977 play features the Bard as "Bill," a snuff-film maker, and the play unfolds in a series of short scenes reminiscent of S&M films. For example, Bill torments a character named Sonia by burning her with a cigarette, while taunting, "You don't like my poetry, you tramp, eh? Don't like it, you whore?"[26] Just as Bauer's play is divided into forty-nine takes with a forty-five-second blackout between each take, Vogel structured her play in thirty short scenes. Mimicking filmic jump cuts, *Desdemona* has a disjointed rhythm in which linear plot development is interrupted with juxtaposition and incongruity. Vogel encourages directors of *Desdemona* to "create different pictures to simulate the process of filming: Change invisible camera angles, do jump cuts and repetitions" (176), techniques she employed again in *Hot 'n' Throbbing*. Crucially and unlike Bauer, Vogel recommends that "there should be no black-outs between scenes" (176). What goes on between (as well as behind) the scenes of dramatic literature is as important as what takes center stage. While the form of Vogel's play disrupts the linear structure of Shakespeare's plot, if not its cause-effect logic, the set design by Derek McLane for the Circle Repertory production depicted a rough and ready backroom of the palace on Cyprus. Filled with material evidence of Emilia's endless chores, this setting displaced the private aristocratic space of Desdemona's chamber with the working-class space of domestic labor. Here, Emilia is the pious and faithful wife, Bianca the whore with the heart of gold, and Desdemona the impudent hussy, a word, it is worth noting, derived from *huswives*. Vogel's play makes the housewife a whore and the whore a woman who dreams of becoming a housewife. (The servant Emilia still does all of the work.)

Desdemona begins with a dumb show: there is a spotlight on the infamous handkerchief. Emilia enters, picks it up, stuffs it in her bodice, and walks off stage. This scene is quickly followed by a frantic Desdemona, searching for the lost handkerchief with the help of Emilia, whom we have just witnessed swipe it. As she punctuates her search with exclamations such as "Dog piddle!!" and "Goddamn horse urine" (178), it is immediately clear that this Desdemona—a lady who gives hand jobs in church pews and works Tuesday-night shifts in Bianca's brothel—is not the Desdemona of Shakespeare's play. Similarly, Vogel's Emilia is not the crafty working-class woman of Shakespeare's play, but a pious woman who loathes her husband, begrudges her work, and holds a conflicted affection for her mistress that is equal parts steadfast loyalty, class resentment and homoerotic desire. Bianca is a successful brothel owner, whom Desdemona idealizes as a liberated "New Woman," but who, in fact, secretly harbors hopes of trading her life in the brothel for a position in the middle class as Michael Cassio's wife. Further reinforcing the class distinctions among the women and reminding the audience that all female oppression is not created equally, a bored Desdemona is shown complaining that marriage is "purdah" (193), while a busy Emilia performs domestic chores continually throughout the play, from washing mountainous piles of laundry to peeling mounds of potatoes to brushing Desdemona's hair.

The social hierarchy among the women is established immediately by their accents: Desdemona's accent is "Upperclass. Very," Emilia's a "Broad Irish brogue," and Bianca's a "Stage Cockney" (175), a metatheatrical reference that gestures, perhaps, to the close associations between actresses and prostitutes throughout theater history. Desdemona is, at turns, mean, affectionate, and condescending toward Emilia, who hopes to be promoted to *fille de chambre*, an aspiration of upward mobility that Desdemona manipulates and mocks. Emilia despises Bianca on moral grounds, while Desdemona envies Bianca's economic freedom. As literary critic Marianne Novy points out, "Economics, ideologies, and lack of solidarity combine to confine women in this play."[27] The sexual and the economic are inextricable in this playworld, and over and over, *Desdemona* underlines the parallel structures of patriarchal marriage and prostitution. Whether she is a prostitute selling sex in a brothel or a faithful wife preserving her sexuality in exchange for material comfort, within a male symbolic system, a woman's sexuality is her greatest value and her greatest source of profit. The prostitute, Boose's "presumptive whore," is the hidden threat in all women, a reminder of female sexual agency within a social order that degrades such agency.

In *Othello*, Emilia insists to Desdemona that infidelity is of little consequence in the larger scheme of things: "The world's a huge thing; it's a great price for so small a vice." In Vogel's play, Desdemona adopts and revises Emilia's line when she returns from a lucrative shift at Bianca's brothel, saying flippantly to Emilia, "How large a world for so small a vice, eh, Mealy?" and adding, "I made more in twenty minutes than you do in a week of washing!" (208). In Vogel's play "great price" takes on literal meaning, referring not to punishment for a moral wrong, but rather to economic profit for a small investment of time. In an earlier scene, Desdemona describes her sexuality not in terms of moral value, but as a form of curiosity, a quest for worldly knowledge and mobility. She describes her brothel work as

> a desire to know the world. I lie in the blackness of the room at her establishment . . . on sheets that are stained and torn by countless nights—men of different sizes and smells and shapes, with smooth skin, with rough skin, with scarred skin. And they spill their seed into me, Emilia—seed from a thousand lands, passed down through generations of ancestors, with genealogies that cover the surface of the globe. And I simply lie there in the darkness, taking them all into me. I close my eyes and in the dark of my mind—oh, how I travel. (194)

The imagery in this extended metaphor suggests that mobility, agency, and knowledge are available to women primarily through their sexual relationships with men. This passage also reveals that women construct their own erotic fantasies; in the darkness of that room, Desdemona finds freedom in her fantasy of global travel. Desdemona's description of her yearning for worldly knowledge contrasts sharply with the play's constrained setting: "A back room of the palace on Cyprus. Ages ago" (175). An implicit analogy is drawn between the physical confinement of the female characters and their restricted agency and mobility. In contrast, the nebulous temporal setting of "Ages ago" ironically suggests that this is not a tale from an archaic past, but, rather, a strikingly contemporary story. Desdemona's evocative speech can also be read as a metaphor for the way a feminist reader might derive knowledge and inspiration from the texts in the dramatic canon—which are also "passed down through generations of ancestors"—reimagining them as a tool of female agency.

While Vogel overturns Desdemona's idealized status in the dramatic canon, she normalizes Bianca's role as prostitute, emphasizing the broader social function of her work. As Bianca puts it:

Aw have a place 'ere and Aw'm not ashamed t'own it. Aw'm nice to
the wives in town, and the wives in town are rather nice to me. Aw'm
doin' them favors by puttin' up wif their screwy owld men, and Aw
like me job! The only ponk Aw has to clean up is me own. (201)

Bianca's work is represented here as central to the healthy function-
ing of marriage and society. It not only performs a public service, but
it also allows Bianca to maintain the kind of independence that both
Emilia and Desdemona seek. As Desdemona sees her, Bianca is "a
free woman—a new woman—who can make her own living in the
world, who scorns marriage for the lie that it is" (194). And yet, although she takes pride in her work at the brothel and her service to
the community, she also dreams of a stable life with Cassio. Bianca's
hopes of moving into the middle class suggest that marriage promises a security more comforting and seductive than sexual and economic freedom. As Bianca insists, "All women want t'get a smug, it's
wot we're made for, ain't it? We may pretend different, but inside
ev'ry born one o' us wants a smug an' babies, smugs wot are man
enow t' keep us in our place" (214–15). Especially resonant in our
postfeminist twenty-first-century context, Bianca articulates wom-
en's powerful attachment to marriage and family as the primary plot
points around which to structure a life. While Vogel continually
complicates any easy or fixed definition of the female characters in
this play, what does remain consistent is that women's social power
comes either from their sexuality or from their husbands' rank. The
result is a playworld in which the women compete with one another
as objects of male possession. Emilia's description of the impossibil-
ity of true female friendships best elucidates the homosocial dynamics of this playworld. To Bianca, she says:

Don't be a fool hussy. There's no such creature, two-, three or four-
legged, as a "friend" betwixt ladies of leisure and ladies of the night.
And as long as there be men with one member but two minds, there's
no such thin' as friends between women. An' that's that. (200)

And these words ring true when Bianca finds out that the handkerchief Cassio gave to her as a gift was Desdemona's, and their friend-
ship ends in fisticuffs.

Significantly, the women do come together in a common cause.
Realizing that Othello is on to Desdemona's sexual shenanigans, the

women work together to fabricate the illusion of her chastity. In scene 2, Emilia scrubs sheets stained with what is supposed to be Desdemona's virginal blood but is, in fact, the blood of a hen that Bianca stole for their devious plot. The faux-bloodstained sheets enable a kind of female collaboration that adds dimension to the relationships among the women. As a visual object looming large on a laundry line backstage in the Circle Repertory production, the sheets worked as a hyperbolic emblem of a phony female purity, contrasting with the lily-white handkerchief and the proof of virginity it signifies in Shakespeare's play. The sheets hung as a blatant and bloody reminder of the material effects that emerge from such symbolic constructions of female sexuality. That the women work together to maintain the illusion of Desdemona's chastity underscores its fundamental importance to Desdemona's survival in both plays. This solidarity, however, cannot exist outside the male authority that defines female sexuality, and the women's failure to conjure the illusion of chastity suggests that, whether Desdemona was *actually* chaste or *really* a whore is beside the point. In the end, her sexuality remains circumscribed by a male symbolic and is not hers to define.

Shakespeare's closed moral universe permeates *Desdemona* from behind the scenes, effecting the bodies, desires, and relationships of the female characters. When Desdemona exits Vogel's playworld, she enters the playworld of *Othello*. In one such moment, Desdemona hears Othello call to her and so rushes off stage. The stage directions read:

(And then, we hear the distinct sound of a very loud slap. A pause, and Desdemona returns, closes the door behind her, holding her cheek. She is on the brink of tears. She and Emilia look at each, and then Emilia looks away.) (186)

This silent exchange of an empathic gaze quickly dissolving into fear and shame underscores the play's more poignant comment on female homosocial relationships. Desdemona and Emilia are barred from a moment of camaraderie and solace here—by class divisions and by the absence of a language for talking about male violence.

In the more comic scenes, *Desdemona* also imagines forms of pleasure and belonging among the women. In a parody of S&M, "*The beating scene*" audaciously shows Bianca teaching Desdemona the positions and gestures of "L and B" or what is known in "th' Life as a lam an' brim—first they lam you, an' . . . then you brim 'em . . . and then you give 'em wotever—an Adam an' Eve or a Sunny-Side Over" (210). Demonstrating a whole repertoire of possible sexual routines, Bianca emphasizes sexuality as role-playing to a naïve Desdemona and a horrified Emilia, telling them, "it's all fakement" (211). The high tragedy of *Othello* becomes, here, a bawdy burlesque of female desire, with women taking pleasure in instructing other women how to "fake it." As Desdemona *"perfects her synchronized moans, building into a crescendo, at which point she breaks into peals of laughter,"* comic release momentarily defers violent catharsis. She tells Emilia, who is busy reciting the Hail Mary, "It's smashing! . . . you really must try it" (212). Emilia's metaphoric description of sexuality as a game in *Othello* is here comically revised as an improvised game played among women. Female sexuality is dramatized here not as the essence of one's identity or as a patriarchal construction, but instead as bawdy theatrical entertainment performed with women as both actor and audience.

Desdemona's subtitle, *A Play about a Handkerchief*, points to the overdetermination of this prop and introduces the motif of "stealing" in the play: Emilia steals the hanky, Bianca steals a hen for its blood, Bianca thinks Desdemona steals Cassio from her, and Vogel steals Shakespeare's play. The handkerchief in *Othello* is a symbol and proof of female sexual purity. In Vogel's play, however, the handkerchief becomes a symbol, not of male control over female sexuality, but of betrayal among women as they compete for the sexual attention of men. In Vogel's playworld, the handkerchief is a "crappy little snot rag" circulated among the women, who are themselves defined as objects. And when Bianca removes the handkerchief, given to her by Cassio, from her bodice, the symbolic importance of this prop is immediately displaced by the more violent and visceral significance of the hoof-pick.

The hoof-pick operates as the visual and symbolic counterpart to the sheets and the handkerchief, which signify female sexuality defined as either chaste or defiled. As a phallic prop, the hoof-pick parodies male sexuality, while highlighting Desdemona's robust sexual curiosities. Fondling the hoof-pick, Desdemona fantasizes, "Oh me, oh my—if I could find a man with just such a hoof-pick—he could pluck out my stone," then proceeds to ask an unamused Emilia, "does your husband Iago have a hoof-pick to match" (182). In the play's climactic moment, Bianca wields the hoof-pick as a weapon against Desdemona when she finds out that the handkerchief Cassio gave to Bianca belonged to Desdemona. Enacting a darker kind of phallic parody, a jealous Bianca lunges at Desdemona with the hoof-pick, taking on Othello's role and even adapting several of the lines he speaks before smothering Desdemona. "Put out the light, and then put out the light," "Have you prayed tonight, Desdemon?" and "Down, strumpet!"[28] are revised by Bianca as: "You cheatin' hussy . . . Yer gonna snuff it, m'lady—so say yer prayers, yew goggle-eyed scrap o'a WHORE" (125–26). Vogel displaces Othello and Iago's imaginings of Desdemona's sexual infidelity with Desdemona's actual infidelity, staging the conflicts that erupt among the women when they become sexual competitors. The hoof-pick, as a metonymic representation of the male-driven playworld of *Othello*, acts as a masculine counterpart to the handkerchief, and as the women of *Desdemona* take possession of it, the obsessive focus on female chastity shifts toward the less obvious antagonisms among women that develop from such a focus.

Desdemona also points to the racist fantasies that have historically informed relations between black men and white women. In *Othello*, Desdemona states her blindness to Othello's race, insisting, "I saw Othello's visage in his mind."[29] In Vogel's play, however, Desdemona does not fall in love with Othello's rhetorical eloquence, but with his body. She overtly fetishizes Othello's skin color and the symbolisms attached to his race, making explicit the hypersexualization of the black male and the white women's complicity in this stereotype. Desdemona tells Emilia:

> I remember the first time I saw my husband and I caught a glimpse of his skin, and, oh, how I thrilled. I thought—aha!—a man of a different color. From another world and planet. I thought, if I marry this strange dark man, I can leave this narrow little Venice with its whispering piazzas behind—I can escape and see other worlds. *(Pause)* But under that exotic façade was a porcelain white Venetian. (193–94)

The numerous references to Othello's skin color and penis size throughout *Desdemona* suggest that, far from passive innocents, these women are active manufacturers of racist fantasies. In one of the more farcical moments, Desdemona naively wonders how

Othello is "constantly tearing his crotch hole" (205) of his underwear. The racially-inflected remarks continue when Bianca tries to allay Desdemona's fears that Othello might find out about her work—or even unwittingly visit her—at the brothel, saying that he wouldn't realize it was Desdemona he was sleeping with, since "the room's bleedin' black—blacker than he is" (209). Desdemona here becomes the authorizing figure of a racist fantasy constructed by a white symbolic. Her erotic attachment to Othello is structured by these fantasies, just as Othello's attachment to (and alienation from) her is structured by sexist fantasies. Teasing out the symbolic connotations of race and sexuality in *Othello*, Vogel positions the women in *Desdemona* as complicit coauthors of these stereotypes and the relationships they form.

Ultimately, male authority—social, discursive, literary—determines the female relationships in both Shakespeare's and Vogel's plays. Vogel's Emilia incisively states, "Women just don't figure in their heads—not the one who hangs the wash—not Bianca—and not even you, m'lady. That's the hard truth. Men only see each other in their eyes. Only each other" (220). Othello's imagined fears of Desdemona's infidelity are not *about* Desdemona, but rather about the relationship between Iago and Othello. While men operate in a self-perpetuating field of homosocial power, women form relationships with each other as objects subordinate to that power. Women's relationships, then, become the inverse of men's; they cannot see each other, but can only see the men for whom they are competing. Even when Desdemona admits to sleeping with Iago at the brothel and Emilia confesses to stealing the handkerchief and the two women achieve a moment of connection in their mutual forgiveness, they remain locked in the deadly logic that dictates the playworld. As Othello becomes increasingly agitated backstage (front stage in *Othello*), Emilia tries to allay Desdemona's anxiety by insisting that her husband would not "harm a sleeping woman," adding for reinforcement that she had just watched him "gather[] up the sheets from your bed, like a body and . . . and he held it to his face, like, like a bouquet, all breathin' it in" (223). Simultaneously, both women recognize this as an act of jealousy and understand that he has *"been smelling the sheets for traces of a lover."* In her most genuine line of the play, Desdemona says, "That isn't love. It isn't love" (223), which can be read as a direct response to Shakespeare's Othello, who justifies his murder as an act of "one that loved not wisely, but too well."[30] *Desdemona* ends with a series of very short scenes, images really, of Emilia brushing Desdemona's hair, counting the brush strokes, and counting down to the fate that they fear—and we know—awaits Desdemona. The play ends, however, on the ninety-ninth brushstroke. Ostensibly one brush stroke away from death, the play nonetheless halts the linear trajectory of *Othello* and its tragic conclusion. Desdemona, in Vogel's play, refuses her dramatic function in the tragic paradigm of catharsis and ends, heroes and victims.

Desdemona's 1993 New York premiere at Circle Repertory Theater was widely reviewed, both because Vogel had achieved a level of visibility among critics and audiences after her success with *The Baltimore Waltz* and because it is a play that takes on the most recognized dramatist in the western tradition. Responses were mixed. *Newsday*'s Linda Winer faulted the actresses' "terrible accents" and the play's lack of emotional heart, concluding nonetheless that "a little intelligent wondering on a provocative subject is a lot better than none."[31] Victoria A. Kummer responded positively to the play, writing that Vogel "is a playwright with an eye for the absurd, an ear for the bawdy, and a pen of surgical precision." Kummer makes a pertinent connection between Vogel's play and the Lorena Bobbit scandal that pervaded American media in 1993, writing, "there are probably more than a few men who will find something distinctly discomforting about the tenor of this play—the glee with which these women emasculate their men."[32] The hoof-pick that the characters toss around onstage would surely take on different meanings in light of Bobbit's late-night surgery on her husband. The *New York Times*'s Ben Brantley smartly describes the play as "an extended bit of intellectual vaudeville," concluding that the pleasure quickly "wears thin." Describing the bulb flashes demarcating scenes as "the visual equivalent of the clash of cymbals that follows a punch line in a vaudeville show," Brantley fails to comment on the more serious moments that this comedy is meant to accentuate. Ending with a damning ambivalence that brought the play to an early close, Brantley quibbles, "Though the play is often irritating, it isn't boring."[33] The *New York Post*'s Clive Barnes echoes Brantley's irritation, writing, "Her play, with its scatological detail, its coarsely modern (not to mention modernly coarse) language, and its author's determination to be naughty can be extremely annoying, but it is not—wait a minute—completely worthless." Barnes sees the play's "phony Shakespearean echoes" as its downfall and holds that the play succeeds only when those echoes fade and *Desdemona* can "develop a sleazy, steamy vitality"[34] on its own terms. It is unclear what kind of play Barnes wanted to see, but his review was the only one to suggest that *Desdemona* was dragged down by its association with *Othello*, rather than legitimized by it.

Some critics suggested that Vogel's Desdemona deserved what was coming to her. In his review for *New York* magazine, John Simon reveals more about his aesthetic tastes than about Vogel's play. Positioning *Desdemona* as a play "that parasitically lays its eggs in the host body of a classic," he dismisses it as a superficial derivative of *Othello*, which is "a play about the profoundest of human emotions."[35] Simon concludes his review by saying, "You might say this Desdemona is her own best Iago and deserves what she will get."[36] His review suggests two things: his belief in the sanctity of canonical texts and his belief that female promiscuity, accompanied by impudence, is deserving of punishment by death. Deadly logic, indeed. The *Globe and Mail*'s Kate Taylor echoes Simon, stating that Vogel's Desdemona is "too self-absorbed to raise much interest in others. Indeed, she is so obnoxious, you'll be longing for that brute with a pillow."[37] Missing the emotional impact of the tragic plot, Francine Russo of the *Village Voice* argued that "it's OK to rip off Shakespeare's characters, but Vogel can't get a free ride on his play's poignancy." Russo criticizes Vogel's play for its lack of genuine suffering: "The characterizations . . . don't make the transition to suffering, victims-in-kinship of male tyranny."[38] Vogel's play does not aim to make such a transition. The characters defy the category of victim and the suffering that comes from it, which is structurally evident in the play's refusal to end with Desdemona's death.

Usurping male canonical authority and placing female characters center stage, *Meg* and *Desdemona* are the work of a young playwright immersed in a canon weighted heavily toward British plays. In both plays, we can hear Vogel defining her own authorial voice. After these two plays, Vogel shifted her attention to the American dramatic tradition, responding to a canon of playwrights and a social history closer to home. Her focus from this point forward is on postwar America and the institutions, issues, conflicts, memories, and subjectivities that emerge in this period. Her later plays are at once more political and more personal; the juxtapositions are sharper and the subject matter more contemporary. The next chapter marks the beginning of Vogel's examination of family as the social and symbolic center of America culture—and American drama—and the epicenter of values, beliefs, and affective identifications of a heteronormative national culture. *And Baby Makes Seven* outs the American family as far from "normal." Family is presented here as an improvised performance, composed from fragments of cultural texts, which are rearranged into elaborate plots and reanimated by fantasy. In short, *Baby* is as much about the diverse forms that family can take as it is about theater and, in particular, Vogel's own playwriting practice.

CHAPTER TWO

Reimagining Family:
And Baby Makes Seven

> Whatever else any great American playwright has done, each
> one has created, and in turn become identified with, a personal
> vision of the American family. If anything, the measure of
> achievement in American drama has been a writer's ability to
> place a vivid family portrait within a larger societal frame—or,
> more to the point, to make the family represent not only the
> writer's inner life but a set of outer conditions.
>
> —Samuel G. Freedman, *New York Times*[1]

The family—as an idea, an institution, a symbol, a fantasy, and a social form—has provided rich material for American playwrights from
Eugene O'Neill to Tracy Letts. Dramatizing family dynamics offers a
microcosm through which to examine broader cultural values and
question national principles, such as freedom, individuality, opportunity, and happiness. Vogel insists, "It's important that the family be
put in its social context, that there is a world beyond,"[2] and she
works from an understanding that the public and private are not separate spheres, but interlocking, mutually defining social practices. In
her plays, the private (individual, psyche, home) is everywhere
marked as public (culture, narrative, nation), and reality and the everyday are infused with fantasy and the fictional. Revising Edward
Albee's *Who's Afraid of Virginia Woolf?*, along with myriad other
canonical plays and films, *And Baby Makes Seven* (1984) exploits the
possibility of reconstructing cultural narratives, along with the public fantasies and definitions of family they legitimize. Displacing the
more familiar script of the domestic drama with an intertextual col-

lage of famous scenes, lines, and characters, *Baby* depicts a family that makes it up as they go along, using fantasy and improvised performances to animate their domestic life. The play is set in Koch-era New York City and follows three soon-to-be parents—Anna, Ruth, and Peter—who are nervous about the impending birth of their child and who mobilize fantasy as a means of pleasure and a method for coping with the transition to a new kind of family life.

With its theatricalization of domestic conflict, use of broad comedy, and heightened emphasis on role-playing, *Baby* can be read as a burlesque of *Woolf*. Whereas Albee's emphasis in *Woolf* is on the power of language and illusion to dominate and deceive, Vogel's emphasis in *Baby* is on the capacity for language and fantasy to animate and reshape social relations. The imaginary son that George and Martha use as a discursive weapon is, in Vogel's play, embodied and performed—in triplicate—by Ruth and Anna. The women enact the roles of three imaginary boy characters; Ruth plays two characters— Orphan McDermott, a boy raised by stray dogs in the Port Authority Bus Terminal, and Henri Dumont, a French boy from Albert Lamorrise's film *The Red Balloon* (1956), while Anna plays the part of Cecil Bartholomew, a precocious nine-year-old who offers instruction and advice, to both the children and the adults. As displaced extensions of the women's adult personas, the three boys enable a mode of communication beyond the everyday, infusing spontaneity into their domestic life, acting as an outlet for the emotions and anxieties surrounding the birth, and authorizing the women to plot out new storylines.

Unlike *Woolf*, which portrays the boundary between truth and illusion as a vexed site of struggle and contest for authority, *Baby* depicts the boundary between reality and fantasy as polymorphously permeable. This difference can be understood by looking at the playwrights' opposing attitudes toward theatrical performance. Albee insists on the literary merit of his work, stating, "I will defend to my dying day my theory that an important play is rarely improved by performance," adding that a production is "collaborative as long as they do what the playwright is after."[3] For Vogel, the play's the thing. She sees a play as the product of multiple stages of authorship, putting it this way: "I am writing the script; the directors, actors and designers are writing the production; but the audience writes the play."[4] Vogel is excited to have her plays produced in new contexts—

whether *Desdemona* in Mexico or *The Oldest Profession* in Poland—and is interested to see what they will mean to a different set of collaborators and new audiences. While the play-text remains the blueprint for performance, the cultural context and social situation surrounding each production will elicit new meanings each time. And so whereas Albee claims a structuralist confidence in language as a meaning-making system, Vogel espouses a poststructuralist belief in the contingency of language and meaning; Albee's play demonstrates performative control, while Vogel's play illustrates theatrical inventiveness; Albee believes in the stability of his authority—his characters say what he means them to say—and Vogel's characters challenge the notions of autonomy, control, and regulation that such claims to authority imply. In short, whereas Albee sees live performance as a needless addition to the authority of his writing, Vogel contributes her authority to the larger project of making theater.

Baby was first staged in 1984 at the Eighteenth Street Playhouse in New York City, directed by Vogel. It was revised almost a decade later, produced by Circle Repertory and staged at the Lucille Lortel Theatre in New York in 1993. As Vogel was writing the first draft of *Baby* in the early 1980s, the pro-family movement had crystallized as a powerful cultural force, and the play remains a product of this era. In the 1980s, the values of the Reagan administration were taking shape as hegemony, and the culture wars were driving ideological wedges between the political left and right. It was a backlash period, during which the changes brought about by the 1960s and 1970s social movements—feminism, civil rights, and post-Stonewall gay and lesbian alliances—led to a reactionary reassertion of family values and the revival of the 1950s nuclear family as the key to a secure and prosperous nation. This conservative return to the golden age of family was most clearly defined by what it rejected—gay rights, feminism, divorce, and abortion rights—rather than by what it stood for. Emerging in reaction to the women's liberation movement, the gay rights movement, the invention of the birth control pill, and the landmark *Roe v. Wade* decision in 1973, the pro-family movement was (and is) an attempt by the Christian right to preserve the stability and sanctity of the family as a national institution. As one of its most visible spokespeople, Anita Bryant, a second runner-up for Miss America in 1959, launched her campaign to save the family in the late 1970s, primarily through ongoing attacks against homosexuals, whom she viewed as the primary threat to the traditional family. Her organization Save Our Children promoted the notion that gays were threatening the American family by recruiting and converting children to homosexuals. Bryant's hysterical homophobia and her hyperbolic display of conventional femininity was, for the right, a reassuring message that heterosexuality and masculine power were not, in fact, being threatened, and that the patriarchal family would indeed continue to be the realm in which heteronormative sexuality is reproduced. However, at the same time, many liberal feminists were also returning to the idea of marriage and motherhood as the primary purposes of a woman's life. Sociologist Judith Stacey argues that in "the Reagan period [there] was indeed a nostalgia for the modern family, and even for patriarchal kinship patterns, within feminism as well as elsewhere."[5]

In the twenty-first century, the nuclear family continues to hold strong emotional and ideological force in America, despite the fact that fewer and fewer families fit that definition. The persistence of family as an ideology and a public fantasy is due, in part, to the dearth of representations depicting other ways of creating family. With gay marriage being legalized in increasingly more states and television shows like *Modern Family* representing gay parenthood in the familiar context of the two-parent home in the suburbs, the family model is expanding to include different sexualities, if not different ways of living. It remains to be seen if the legalization of gay marriage in the United States transforms American culture into something more diverse and livable for many different kinds of lifestyles and family arrangements, or if it results in what social theorist Michael Warner describes as a division between the "Good Gay," who assumes a place within the status quo, and the "Bad Queer," who does not. Like the virgin/whore configuration, "the Good Gay is never invoked without its shadow in mind—the Bad Queer, the kind who has sex, who talks about it, and who builds with other queers a way of life that ordinary folks do not understand or control."[6] Within a heteronormative culture, marriage and family work to contain and define the sexualities of both the whore and the queer.

The shift toward a national heterosexuality is relatively recent, developing within a culture of anxiety that emerged in reaction to the changing norms of identity, sexuality, and family in the decades following the 1960s. It is here that Vogel's theater should be situated and read as a body of work that comments on the often unnoticed privileges, injustices, and hierarchies operating within a postwar heteronormative American culture. In their influential 1998 essay, "Sex in Public," Michael Warner and cultural critic Lauren Berlant develop a framework for understanding the contradictory processes of normalization that have "made heterosexuality hegemonic." They clarify that "we speak of heterosexual culture rather than heterosexuality because that culture never has more than a provisional unity. It is neither a single Symbolic nor a single ideology nor a unified set of shared beliefs."[7] Displacing understandings of heterosexuality as a thing with an essence, Berlant and Warner emphasize heterosexual culture, which includes a whole set of practices, values, and beliefs that structure the divisions between public and private and that regulate the activities of everyday cultural life. One of the central institutions of heterosexual culture is the nuclear family, and by policing the boundaries of what constitutes the proper family, the boundaries of proper citizenship are also policed: "The nostalgic family values covenant of contemporary American politics stipulates a privatization of citizenship and sex" and protects "the zone of heterosexual privacy."[8] It is precisely this "the zone of heterosexual privacy" that *Baby* both occupies and turns inside out, presenting sexualities not traditionally granted the rights of either privacy or proper citizenship, and situating them in the familiar context of home and family. As cultural narratives and fictional characters pervade the domestic sphere in the play, the social boundary between public/private is breached and the ordinary, the normative, and the intimate are outed as publically mediated fabrications of a heteronormative culture. *Baby* can be interpreted as a queer commentary on heteronormative family structures, making visible and audible what has been suppressed in culture and history and using campy humor as a style, strategy, and way of seeing. As Warner and Berlant write elsewhere: "Queer commentary has produced rich analyses of . . . the acknowledged and the disavowed . . . *the costs of closure and the pleasure of unruly subplots* . . . voicing strategies . . . jokes; identification and other readerly relations to texts and discourse."[9] There can hardly be a more succinct summary of Vogel's *Baby*.

In its frenetic intertextuality, *Baby* calls into question the very premises upon which textual authority is legitimized and demonstrates the methods by which it can be reworked as performative agency. Like *Hot 'n' Throbbing*, a play written during the same period, *Baby* is punctuated by literary quotations and popular culture references and animated by various registers of everyday life—from elaborate fantasy to mundane reality. And, like *Hot*, *Baby* revolves around questions of family, narrative authority, and the difficulty involved in writing new storylines. Ruth's insistence on the instability of authority and malleability of narrative stands in for Vogel's own strategy as a playwright who revises canonical texts and cultural attitudes. As Ruth insists to Anna, "I don't see why we can't change the . . . the narrative at this point."[10] Doing so, however, involves conflict, loss, and a collective belief in new forms—of family and fantasy.

As a bifurcated representation of Vogel, Anna and Ruth are prolific authors, master plotters, and imaginative collaborators. And like *their* author, Anna and Ruth use narrative to shape the meaning of their story. While Vogel's focus as a playwright is on narrative, at a certain point the emphasis shifts toward the importance of plot in the production of meaning. As literary critic Peter Brooks writes, "Plot . . . is the logic and dynamic of narrative, and narrative itself is a form of understanding and explanation."[11] Plots are "intentional structures, goal-oriented and forward-moving."[12] Plotting is disrupted—playfully, willfully—in *Baby* so that it is not directed by intentions toward ends and goals, but relished for its own sake. A pervasive strategy running through all of Vogel's plays, from *Meg* to *The Long Christmas Ride Home*, is the way her characters struggle to plot their own stories, to shape their narratives, to wrest authority, and to reorient the production and direction of meaning. Nowhere is this strategy made more explicit than in *Baby*, where the women weave wildly imaginative plots to entertain each other, to practice parenthood, and to gain a sense of agency in their lives. The play emphasizes plotting and narrative as the primary ways through which cultural meanings and values are constructed, and it compels us to imagine ways of revising plots and changing narratives in order to bring new meanings into our daily lives. Narrative, *Baby* suggests, shapes the meaning, value, and legitimacy of things like family, gender, and sexuality.

As coparents, Anna, Ruth, and Peter displace the customary couple that lies at the center of conventional comedies, while the familiar domestic setting is permeated by cultural narratives—from *The*

Exorcist and *Dr. Strangelove* to *Macbeth* and *Streetcar Named Desire*—that the women use to inspire their elaborate fantasy scenarios. Peter, however, is not as invested in fantasy as Anna and Ruth and so feels left out of their imaginary lives and extraneous to the experience of pregnancy, or as Ruth and Anna jokingly call it, "Woman Creating" (71). Peter thus insists that the arrival of the "real" (i.e., biological) child must result in the necessary "death" of the imaginary children. Fantasy, Peter contends, is incompatible with the reality of starting a family, and it is precisely this distinction between fantasy and reality that *Baby* interrogates by building a playworld in which fantasy is not opposed to reality, but rather is another dimension of it. Analogously, nontraditional families and unconventional genders are not imagined in opposition to some hegemonic norm, but are rather positioned as revised versions of these norms. In its reworking of the nuclear family, in its refusal to be bound by binaries of reality/fantasy, hetero/homo, sexual/not-sexual, and in its comic unraveling of traditional psychological frameworks for understanding gender and sexuality, *Baby* overturns many of the metanarratives and collective public fantasies that reinforce the nuclear family as the social and affective glue that binds together a heteronormative American culture.

As Vogel sees it, "where there's conflict, there's comedy."[13] Affirming the importance of form—narrative—in shaping meaning and generating comedy, Vogel says of *Baby*:

> I think the structure of the play *is* the meaning of the play. These three people are taking a journey, and it's a journey that a lot of people face at some point in their lives, which is that kind of insane crisis period just before you have a child, when you know your entire life will change but you're not sure how. . . . And there is that sense of high anxiety and great exuberance and hope, and fear. There is a sense of comic crisis in the structure of the play itself.[14]

The form of *Baby* is brilliantly conceived, with three death scenes culminating in the birth of the real child, a structure that reverses Vogel's trajectory as a playwright who gives birth to the play only by finding a way to end it. Bigsby describes *Baby* as "almost perversely metafictional," not only because of the many literary references but also because of the parallel it draws "between the creation of a text and the creation of the child."[15] Vaudevillian in tone and structure,

Baby resembles a sketch comedy routine, with the "straight" scenes between Anna, Ruth, and Peter interspersed with the more slapstick scenes, in which the children take over. Even in the children's deaths, there is comedy, as each one makes an exit in a kind of mock-tragic style. Indeed, as Bigsby contends, "The fact is that this trio constitute a comedy act."[16] Scene 4 uses slapstick to theatricalize the convergence between child-adult, everyday-fantasy, self-other. Ruth-as-Henri, in the kitchen fixing a peanut butter and jelly sandwich and singing a *"medley of Maurice Chevalier hits"* (79), is suddenly overtaken by Ruth's other persona—Orphan. As a *"Strangeglovian battle"* ensues between Ruth's two hands, *"each fighting for possession of the peanut butter and jelly"* (81), we see the contradictory nature of subjectivity performed as shtick. The scene delightfully reinforces that we are not always the sole author of our actions and that we internalize multiple and often conflicting impulses that disrupt any sense of stable selfhood. By acting out those contradictions, Ruth-as-Henri-*and*-Orphan translates psychic conflict into comic performance.

Ruth and Anna are ventriloquists, exploiting and performing the rupture between language and the speaking body and comically undermining the authority of the speaking subject as the originator of the words they speak. Ventriloquism, a form of communicative play that uses impersonation, role-playing, and jokes, enacts a physical and perceptual dislocation. Vogel mobilizes ventriloquism, here and elsewhere, to displace the individuality and autonomy of the speaker with the polyvocality of discourse. Anna and Ruth in *Baby* are literally (often hilariously) possessed by cultural texts and discourses and, in this way, act as cultural ventriloquists who recite texts even as they revise them. In *Baby*, the defamiliarizing effect of a voice spoken by an incongruous body underscores the fact that our identities are a patchwork of internalized identifications and thus can never be anything but contradictory and fragmentary. Moreover, the characters demonstrate how we might use cultural texts imaginatively to fashion more diverse kinds of identities.

Baby imagines how we might change the roles we play within family structures, rather than unconsciously repeating the same story. The play defamiliarizes everyday family relations, suggesting the perversity underlying performances of the ordinary and the normal. By using fictional frameworks to articulate and perform their sexualities, the characters in *Baby* undermine any claims to normative and stable identities, sexual or otherwise. They do not position themselves as marginal in relation to some imagined heterosexual norm. Instead, they explode the norm as itself the product of public fantasies, overturning the stability, privacy, and normalcy underpinning constructions of the heteronormative private sphere. Vogel has said of *Baby* that she hopes "we feel a sense of inclusion when we leave the theatre. I hope we . . . expand the boundaries of what we think parenting is. I always hope that the boundaries are a little . . . expanded at the end of any play."[17] In all of Vogel's plays, there is a sense of inclusion and expansion, a generosity as well as a reaching out toward less comfortable territories.

As Vogel has suggested, the three boys represent, roughly, the id (Orphan), the libido (Henri), and the superego (Cecil).[18] Acting out the affects and urges of Ruth and Anna, the boys also playfully subvert conventional beliefs in and appeals to the "innocence" of the child. These kids, like all kids *know*, and they "know more than adults would like" (112). *Baby* undermines traditional psychological paradigms of sexual development and family structures, suggesting that the Oedipal mother-father-child triad is no longer a sufficient model with which to conceptualize the American family. Similarly, the Lacanian Imaginary-Real-Symbolic is also proven to be an inadequate framework. Comically dislocating these psychic registers from their gendered associations, *Baby* shows that the Imaginary (associated with the mother) is just as anchored in the material, linguistic, and social as the Symbolic (associated with the father), just as the Symbolic is as permeated with the phantasmic as the Imaginary. More to the point, Vogel suggests that these three registers and the theories they support are themselves narratives—fictions—for understanding sexual and social development. Part of Vogel's strategy is to rework these narratives, change the storyline, specifically by overturning the hierarchy of reality (associated with the heteronormativity, the everyday) over fantasy (associated with the queer, the suppressed). As the "real" baby's birth date approaches, the imaginary children become more animated, asserting their right to "exist" and, by extension, asserting the real role of fantasy in everyday life. And yet these two registers are in continual tension, vying for legitimacy in relation to one another. Anna-as-Cecil comments to Ruth-as-

Henri about the behavior of the adults since the biological baby's conception, "They're not themselves. Ever since that baby," to which Henri replies, "Yeah. I hate that baby" (94).

Baby comically explodes conventional ideas not only of family but also of gender and sexuality. The play develops an understanding of gender not as ontology, but as a kind of cultural trope. As biologist Anne Fausto-Sterling writes, "If nature really offers us more than two sexes, then it follows that our current notions of masculinity and femininity are cultural conceits."[19] As Ruth and Anna slip seamlessly from feminine to masculine personas, from adult to child, the incongruities begin to dislocate our understanding of identity—gender, sexual, age—as "who we are" and portray it, instead, as a product of who and what we are imitating.

Although *Baby* is Vogel's most "out" play, its depiction of a lesbian relationship is neither a promotion of gay marriage nor an example of the "butch-femme aesthetic" that Sue-Ellen Case has argued offers an alternative to heteronormative realism. Case champions the butch-femme couple who "playfully [inhabit] the camp space of irony and wit, free from biological determinism, elitist essentialism, and the heterosexist cleavage of sexual difference."[20] According to Case, this "dynamic duo" establishes a feminist subject position that is "outside ideology."[21] If only ideology had such an easily attainable "outside." Vogel does not posit a place outside ideology, nor does she try to create female characters that are freed from biological determinism. Rather, she suggests that biology itself is laden with cultural significations and that our ways for understanding bodies on a biological level are always determined by and through language and ideology. Through a dizzying variety of comic role-playing, *Baby* exaggerates and externalizes the codes and narratives that shape our bodies, our fantasies, and our families. And by giving an embodied dimension to the imaginary children, the play brings fantasy into material visibility, challenging definitions of what counts as real and what does not and what counts as a "real" family and what does not.

Vogel confuses distinctions between homo- and heterosexual in the relationships among all the characters. In scene 2, for example, we find out that "no turkey baster" was used for their "real" child; after several attempts, Anna and Peter conceived the baby in a conventional sexual encounter that Peter describes as "pretty funny" and Anna describes as "also romantic." The couple made the encounters work—comically and romantically—by devising "little plots," such as "the Nubian boy spread on a Persian rug [and] the English schoolboy being disciplined" (73). Plotting and role-playing enable them to move *between* identities, allowing them to express desires that fall outside the homosexual/heterosexual binary. Anna, Ruth, and Peter also experiment with a threesome in an attempt to conceive a child, which further disallows reducing these characters a particular sexual identity. Likewise, when Ruth-as-Henri tries to seduce Peter, declaring, "I want to have your baby!" (66), any attempt to view sexuality as a fixed identity is comically subverted. The play is also intent on defamiliarizing moral responses to sexuality—which categorize it as either good or bad—presenting it, instead, as something positive, playful, and open to revision. Along with family, then, *Baby* suggests that sexuality and gender are merely fictions, "cultural conceits," albeit with real, material effects.

Perhaps Vogel's most radical move in *Baby*, as well as in her later plays, like *Hot 'n' Throbbing* and *Baltimore Waltz*, is in the way she complicates the distinction between the sexual and the not-sexual. As Eve Kosofsky Sedgwick argues, "the place of drawing the boundary between the sexual and the not-sexual, like the place of drawing boundary between the realms of the two genders, *is* variable, but is *not* arbitrary." These boundaries, Sedgwick suggests, regulate not only categories of gender and sexuality but also "the apportionment of forms of power that are not obviously sexual," such as "the means of production and reproduction of goods, persons, and meanings."[22] So in confusing the distinction between sexual and not-sexual, Vogel calls attention to the way this boundary structures relations of power and authority in almost every aspect of cultural life, including at home. That imaginary children are used to generate sexual fantasies among Anna, Ruth, and Peter, for example, disrupts conventional beliefs that children are not sexual, suggesting, instead, that sexuality is simply part of the experience of inhabiting a body. Moreover, the trio demonstrates a different model of relationship, one in which their affection for one another both is and is not sexual. Peter shyly discloses to Anna that, since their intimate encounters, he "miss[es] breasts," adding, "it's so alien to me. That softness" (73). Anna offers hers to Peter, saying, "whenever you get hit by the urge, you can always feel one" (74). When Ruth enters to find Peter stroking Anna's breast, she joins them, placing her hand gently on Anna's other breast. Smiling contentedly, with Anna's breasts as neutral territory, the three unite in a moment of touching intimacy. Their relationship both makes visible and renders porous the boundaries between heterosexuality and homosexuality, sexual and not-sexual.

When the children begin to dominate the household, however, the three parents agree that, as Ruth says, "We're going to tidy up the plots. No loose ends dangling. Starting tomorrow. We're going to kill them." Yet, as the one most committed to their imaginary life, Ruth also insists, "I want to get my last inch of fantasy out of them" (84). With more bravura than George's symbolic murder of his and Martha's son, the women "kill off" their imaginary children, one by one. These are the play's most effective scenes, animated by a complex affective structure that weaves broad comedy with loss and also a sense of genuine panic at the finality of the children's "death." When Ruth suggests to Anna that they "change the . . . the narrative," Anna replies, "We can't stop now. Not in the middle of the story" (105). There is a literal sense of fantasy taking on its own reality, its own logical trajectory, and its own set of meanings and values. As the women draw on a canon of famous final exits, the children's deaths work as a serious parody of tragic endings.

In the play's most poignant scene, Cecil and Peter have an inverted "father-son" talk, just before Cecil's death. Visually, there is additional comic dissonance, since Anna, here acting as the child, is also the very pregnant biological mother of the baby Peter has fathered. When Peter expresses to Cecil his anxieties about becoming a father, and about repeating the patterns that he learned from his own father figure, Cecil suggests, "just make it up on your own, this father thing, okay, Uncle Peter?" (113). In granting Peter the authority to devise his own parenthood story, Cecil also invests him with the power to imagine things differently, to think outside the Oedipal paradigm traditionally used to understand family and fatherhood. Being a parent is characterized here as a role that we learn and rehearse, and we do not need to perform it the same way over and over. Moreover, subjectivity is not something determined by past events but an ongoing creation that is made (and remade) in the present moment. Cecil tells Peter, "Anna modeled me a little bit on you" (122), suggesting that we can choose with whom we identify, we can choose whom we take as role models, and we can choose to incorporate into

Figure 2: *And Baby Makes Seven*. Left to right: Cherry Jones, Mary Mara, and Peter Frechette. Lucille Lortel Theater, New York City, 1993. Photo: Gerry Goodstein.

our selves the best aspects of those we love. That Cecil was "born," in part, from Anna's affection for Peter expands definitions of subjectivity and of parenthood and suggests the porous boundaries between identification and desire, creation and imitation. This exchange also reverses the parent-child hierarchy, showing that parents can learn from their children. Peter bonds with Cecil here, asking, "do you think maybe we could . . . change the ending? Deus ex machina? I'd really like it if you could stick around" (113). The child persona enables Anna and Peter to have an intimate exchange, in which Anna comforts Peter's fears of fatherhood and Peter feels closer to the women's imaginary life. Nevertheless, they decide to stick to their plan. Positioning an imaginary sword next to Anna's pregnant belly (a parody of heternormative sex), Peter lovingly "kills" Cecil, whose symbolic death prepares Peter for his new role as father.

Perhaps the most metatheatrical—and most humorous—moment in *Baby* is Orphan's melodramatic death scene. Coming home after getting groceries, Anna discovers Ruth-as-Orphan bound and gagged. After diagnosing Orphan with rabies, Ruth decides that it is time to put him down. Quoting *The Exorcist, Macbeth, King Lear, Romeo and Juliet*, Ibsen's *Ghosts, A Streetcar Named Desire*, and *Lassie*, Orphan expresses his primal fear of death, dissolving into a kind of psychosis: "Fuck Me, Jesus!" "Out, d-damned spot," "Mother, give me the sun," "that unwashed gggggrrr-grape has transported her soul" and "woof, woof, woof" (88) constitute an intertextual montage of popular and highbrow representations of possession, death, and madness. Indeed, Ruth's ventriloquism of classic and popular texts works as a burlesque of mad scenes, a parody of deaths and ends, and a comic dramatization of what it means to be possessed by cultural narratives. Sputtering every famous last line in the western canon, Orphan's death scene implicitly asks the question: Who gets the final word?

The reference to Blanche Dubois from Tennessee Williams's *A Streetcar Named Desire* is worth examining in some detail. Orphan channels the line, "that unwashed gggggrrr-grape has transported her soul,"[23] which Blanche recites as she is being taken away to the psychiatric hospital. Blanche's marriage to Allen Grey, who was both younger and gay, and her reputed promiscuity characterize her as sexually deviant, which gets translated in the play as a form of madness. As theater critic Anca Vlasopolos writes, "Blanche's fall from authority, her subjection, is masterfully captured by Williams in her being turned over to the supreme authority in charge of language, in charge of interpreting the past and predicting the future in the twentieth century: psychiatry, the scientific judgment of the soundness of the soul."[24] In contrast to Blanche's pathologized sexuality and psychology, Stella is the Madonna of traditional femininity, aligned with what is real, true, and sane. Blanche's antagonist, however, is not Stella but Stanley, the hypermasculinized counterpart to her hyperfemininity. As Blanche and Stanley battle each other for the love and loyalty of Stella, heterosexual desire wins out, and Blanche, having no place of belonging, is sent away. Ruth, Anna, and Peter could be read as a comic revision of Blanche, Stella, and Stanley. Anna and Stella, both pregnant, embody a conventional, maternal femininity; Peter and Stanley act as the antagonistic masculine force; and Ruth and Blanche represent unconventional sexual impulses and a tenacious belief in the reality of fantasy. However, Vogel's characters forge a sense of belonging together, as a queer trio.

The tension in *Streetcar* is, like in Albee's *Woolf*, between illusion and truth, masculine dominance and female submission. When Blanche sings the popular ballad "It's Only a Paper Moon," she expresses a definition of reality that encompasses rather than excludes illusion. As long as two people believe in the same illusion, the song says, "it wouldn't be make-believe."[25] Significantly, at the same time as Blanche sings her ballad, Stanley relates to Stella the "true" rumors of Blanche's affair with a seventeen-year-old boy. Blanche's worldview competes with Stanley's, even though his is no more rational or empirical. These distinctions between reality and illusion are crucial because they form the basis for defining the meaning of Blanche's sexuality and her sanity. Stanley's authority deems both illegitimate. In contrast, *Baby* dismantles distinctions between truth and illusion, along with the sexualities and psychologies they construct. Authority comes not from the power to distinguish truth from falsehood, but rather from the narratives one chooses to quote and enact. In *Baby*, identity is constituted through a theatrical collage of identifications and disavowals and enacted in an ongoing performance of citations and gestures.

Given Vogel's view that a play is never finished and fantasy never extinguished, it seems apt that the imaginary children come back to life at the play's end, asserting their reality even after the trio's baby is born. In Vogel's playworld, the imaginary children can and do coexist with the "real" child, and their persistent existence attests to the power of fantasy as the energizing undercurrent of daily life. As this family of seven moves between weaving fantasies and changing diapers, a new kind of chaos takes shape as the everyday. The closing tableau shows the three parents and their newborn son, Nathan:

(We see Peter, Anna and Ruth cradling Nathan in their apartment— one apartment among hundreds of their neighbors. The lights stream from adjacent windows where other families in privacy keep their own nightly vigils. The play ends as we hear Nathan's giggles and squeals). (125)

The reverse zoom contextualizes this new family within the larger cultural sphere, framing this scene as, at once, private and public. More precisely, the end uses theater as a space of public witness to a private moment, even as it also underscores the authority that goes into making those divisions in the first place. The concluding image does not replace a zone of heterosexual privacy with a zone of homosexual privacy. Rather, the final scene and the play show how public/ private, hetero/homo, fantasy/reality work mutually to define one another as either real or not, livable or not. Significantly, the play begins and ends with a creation story of sorts. Whereas the Prologue features the three boys talking squeamishly about "how babies come to be made" (63), the play's Epilogue offers a tale of how families come to be made—and remade—a cultural counterpart to the biological creation story that begins the play. As an image both intimate and shared, the closing tableau both returns to the beginning and points toward other plots waiting to unfold.

Quite fittingly, given its intertextual nod to *Macbeth*, Vogel refers to *Baby* as "the Scottish play," due to its troubled production history. This designation began with an early experience at LA Theatre Works, where the "artistic director chose the play to prove to his literary managers that it was a bad play, and chose a director who was hostile to the play." Despite a supportive cast, Vogel recalls, "There was a lot of homophobia expressed in the room,"[26] and the production, as a consequence, was disastrous, inviting homophobic responses from audience members, gay and straight. Mel Gussow reviewed both New York productions (1984 and 1993), both times unfavorably. In 1984, Gussow wrote that "the author does not know where to end her Gothic nursery tale" and that "the play swerves between heightened reality and mania."[27] In 1993, Gussow again called the play a "Gothic nursery tale," writing that it "operates on a single level and seems regressive, in several senses," and adding, "the work has not markedly grown over the years." Gussow does register a lukewarm response to the play's liberal quoting of "reverential sources" and admits that "Vogel strikes a responsive note" when "Thank Heaven for Little Girls" played in the background of the 1993 production.[28] In his harsh review of the 1993 production, Michael Feingold describes Ruth and Anna as resembling "two borderline psychotics." Feingold structures his review around a comparison between *Baby* and *The Baltimore Waltz*, which was staged in New York in 1992, stating that *Waltz* exemplifies "more creative uses for [Vogel's] sense of fantasy." He concludes with the hope that "her next play has less coyness, and a stronger sense of pain."[29] It isn't clear why a "stronger sense of pain" is an aesthetic requirement for *Baby*,

Figure 3: *And Baby Makes Seven*. Left to right: Emma Donson, Andy Jones, and Elly Jarvis. Arthur Miller Theatre, University of Michigan School of Music, Theatre, and Dance, Ann Arbor, 2010. Photo: Chris Dzombak.

or any other play, but it certainly suggests that pleasure for its own sake is not the stuff of legitimate drama. Or perhaps Feingold believes that, since Vogel is tackling a "gay issue," she should do so with more gravity. In contrast to these derisive reviews, Jeanne Cooper reviewed a 1994 staging of *Baby* in Washington, DC, concluding that "the comic energy and obvious humanity of the Freedom Stage Production are surely good medicine for Washington theater."[30] A 2002 review of *Baby* in Melbourne, Australia, offers a similarly positive take: "What makes *And Baby Makes Seven* fascinating is not its lesbian parenting, or its ménage à trois, but its brilliant unsettling of our notions, not of sexual boundaries, but of the 'real.'"[31] In a postmodern period where irony, apathy, and ennui seem the dominant modes, not only in theater but in almost all media and cultural production, the unironic tone of Vogel's play and its exuberant fusion of fantasy and everyday life is refreshing, if not always fashionable. And yet, as is often the case with Vogel's plays, *Baby* has found its most receptive audience decades after it was written. In March 2014, the curse was broken when the play was staged at New Ohio Theatre in New York City, just down the street from its premiere at the Lucille Lortel Theatre twenty years earlier. The production included a series of talk backs involving theater artists and scholars discussing Vogel's impact as a playwright and influence as a teacher. In the twenty-first century, audiences are ready to reimagine family, along with identities, values, and perspectives it forms.

Baby performs a reinterpretation of the cultural narratives—from dramatic texts to psychoanalytic models of sexual development to popular films—that structure the social identities and relations that we perform in daily life. As Judith Butler argues, "What happens at the level of cultural fantasy is not finally dissociable from the ways in which material life is organized."[32] Butler writes:

> The critical promise of fantasy . . . is to challenge the contingent limits of what will and will not be called reality. Fantasy is what allows us to imagine ourselves and others otherwise; it establishes the possible in excess of the real; it points elsewhere, and when it is embodied, it brings that elsewhere home.[33]

Baby takes up this "critical promise of fantasy" as its raison d'être. Vogel's theater, like fantasy, allows us to imagine family, home, and other forms of belonging in more diverse ways. While language and fantasy are used in *Baby* to create meaning and cultivate connection, we see a different relationship to language and fantasy in *Hot 'n' Throbbing*, which stages a darker portrait of the domestic sphere, in which fantasies are more volatile and canonical narratives more constricting.

Revising Fantasy:
Hot 'n' Throbbing

> The status of fantasy cannot be found within the framework of
> the opposition reality-illusion (imaginary). The notion of
> psychical reality introduces a third category, that of structure.
>
> —Laplanche and Pontalis, "Fantasy and the
>   Origins of Sexuality"[1]

> Fantasy is not simply a cognitive exercise, an internal film that
> we project inside the interior theatre of the mind. Fantasy
> structures relationality, and it comes into play in the stylization
> of embodiment itself. The body is not a spatial given [but part
> of] the web of visual, discursive, and tactical relations that
> become part of their historicity, their constitutive past, present,
> and future.
>
> —Judith Butler, *Undoing Gender*[2]

Like *Baby, Hot 'n' Throbbing* (1995/2000) reveals the public nature
of the private sphere, turning the family inside out to show the myriad words and images, values and beliefs that go into its making. And
like *Baby, Hot* shows the collective nature of individual fantasies.
However, while *Baby* imagines the possibilities of revising cultural
narratives and the families and fantasies they work to construct, *Hot*
depicts a kind of entrapment in canonical narratives and in fantasies
and family structures that have become destructive. If *Baby* uses
the generative possibilities of fantasy to remake family, *Hot* puts into
view the darker side of both fantasy and family. And whereas the
women in *Baby* perform a motley cast of characters from dramatic

literature and popular culture, the language and roles in *Hot* are not nearly as accessible or open to revision.

Hot takes place in a single evening, in the Dwyers' working-class townhome, where Charlene lives with her daughter, Leslie Ann (or Layla, as she prefers to be called) and son, Calvin.[3] Charlene is recently separated from her abusive husband, Clyde, and writes for Gyno Productions, a film company that produces feminist erotica. The action of *Hot* alternates between two competing and overlapping playworlds, "the stage lights and the red lights—reality, constructed as we know it, and a world that sometimes resembles the real—as we fantasize about it." The highly stylized theatricality of the red-light area contrasts sharply with the mundane realism of the Dwyers' "living room in a townhouse that cost $79,900 ten years ago. On a 9% mortgage, no deposit down."[4] These two realms— fantasy and reality—are far from separate, however. Fantasy intersects with and influences the "real world," shaping the desires and thoughts of the characters in it. The play asks: Who authorizes the fantasies that define gender and sexuality, bodies and pleasures? What happens when women try to author their own fantasies? Is there a vocabulary for that? By invoking the canon of literature— from Herman Melville to Vladimir Nabokov to Henry Miller—Vogel stages the history of male-authored fantasies of female pleasure, showing the way these canonical narratives shape our imaginations and teach women how to cast themselves as objects of masculine desire—and to find pleasure there.

The remaining two characters in *Hot* are The Voice and the Voice Over (V.O.). The Voice is both an embodied, male character and an omniscient voice who narrates passages from canonical texts, such as James Joyce's *Ulysses*, Vladimir Nabokov's *Lolita*, and Shakespeare's *Othello*, which both pervade and interrupt Charlene's own narrative voice. The V.O. is a female character who enacts—more particularly, overacts—and directs the erotic screenplay that Charlene is writing. As a sex worker, the sexily clad V.O. represents women's most commodified role on the popular American stage—the stripper. She enacts the hypersexualized female body in popular culture, while The Voice embodies literary history and dominant culture. Charlene is negotiating her place between these two traditions, trying to become an author of female pleasure and desire within a history that persistently positions women as object and spectacle.

In the 1999 Arena Stage production in Washington D.C., The Voice was played by Craig Wallace, an African American actor, while the V.O. was played by Sue Jin Song, an Asian American actress. The casting further complicated the roles these characters perform with the racialized sexual fantasies conjured by the actors' bodies. Stereotypes of a passive Asian femininity and a hypersexualized black masculinity—both stereotypes constructed by a racist white imagination—operated, at times, in dissonant tension with their roles onstage. At other times, their roles exaggerated those stereotypes. Jin Song's V.O. appeared as a kind of dominatrix, an image that conflicts with the "lotus blossom" image of Asian femininity but that reinforces the "dragon lady" stereotype. Wallace's deep bass gave a resounding sense of authority to the passages he read as The Voice, and his imposing physical presence amplified his role as strip club bouncer. With these two actors reading and enacting the canonical narrative and popular images that structure sexuality, the (predominantly white, middle-class) theater audience was reminded of their own cultural fantasies being staged.

Vogel began the first draft of *Hot* in 1985. Witnessing a violent domestic dispute in her hometown of Providence, Rhode Island, Vogel began collecting newspaper reports on other such incidents from the *Providence Journal*. Within a year, her file was filled to overflowing. When Vogel applied for and received a grant from the National Endowment for the Arts (NEA) to write the play in 1994, she knew she would juxtapose domestic violence and pornography as a way of challenging the censorship of art in the United States. In 1990, NEA chair John Frohnmayer vetoed the grants to four performance artists—John Fleck, Holly Hughes, Karen Finley, and Tim Miller, aka "The NEA Four"—on the basis that the explicit homosexual and feminist content in their performance pieces did not benefit the public and so was deemed obscene. Since then, all future grant holders have been required to sign a pledge promising not to create art that offended the community. In her "Author's Note" to the 1997 playtext, Vogel writes, "I was interested to learn that 'obscene' came from the Greek, for 'offstage.' Violence in the Greek theatre was kept offstage."[5] That "obscene" has become a word signifying a sexual image or act put inappropriately *into* public view suggests that modern divisions between private and public have shifted in relation to the divisions between heterosexuality and homosexuality that they structure. The play's epigraph exposes the zone of heterosexual privacy that censorship protects: "*Hot 'n' Throbbing* was written on a National Endowment for the Arts Fellowship—because obscenity begins at home." In the play's 1994 American Repertory Theater production, directed by Anne Bogart, this epigraph was the play's subtitle, making it clear that obscenity, and the zone of heterosexual privacy that it preserves, would be placed front stage.

In the mid-1980s, not only was the topic of domestic violence entering public discourse, but the pornography debate was also in full swing. Anti-pornography feminists denounced all pornography as intrinsically bad and harmful to women. Andrea Dworkin, for example, writes that "pornography is the orchestrated destruction of women's bodies and souls; rape, battery, incest, and prostitution animate it; dehumanization and sadism characterize it; it is war on women[;] . . . it is tyranny."[6] This definition of pornography, which conflates sex with its representation, leaves no room for more varied, nonviolent forms of pornography. The anti-pornography position of some feminists was shared by the Meese Commission on Pornography, a 1986 report released by U.S. attorney general Edwin Meese that sought broader definitions of pornography and stricter anti-obscenity laws making more types illegal. The report served a conservative agenda to restore the moral fabric of American cultural life by controlling the production and distribution of pornography. As "a first amendment feminist" worried about the alignment of feminism and theater with right-wing conservatism, Vogel is concerned about "what we censor in this country," and she recognizes that censorship often works to limit the agency, authority, and pleasure of women and those outside of the dominant culture.[7] Charlene Dwyer, a single mother who writes erotic screenplays for a living, agrees: "It's only pornography when women and gays and minorities try to take control of their own imaginations. No one blinks an eye when men do it."[8]

Judith Butler offers a way of approaching pornography that does not lapse into either the linguistic essentialism of anti-pornography feminists or a radical relativism that leaves even extreme forms of pornography, such as snuff films, unchallenged. In relation to pornography's repetition and circulation of graphic, sometimes violent, sexual images, Butler argues for a feminist reading of pornography that resists the literalization of this imaginary scene, one which reads it instead for the incommensurability between gender norms and practices that it seems compelled to repeat without resolution. . . . To read such texts against themselves is to concede that the performativity of the text is not under sovereign control. . . . This raises the possibility of *resignification* as an alternative reading of performativity and politics.[9]

To challenge the realism and reality of pornography is to reveal its scripted language and fantasy structure. Here lies "the possibility of *resignifcation*" that *Hot* stages, as it uses dramatic form to disrupt the realism of family and fantasy and moves toward developing a new language of female pleasure and sexual agency. By staking a claim to narrative authority—to producing the stories that shape public imaginations—women writers can actively shape the dynamics of desire and structures of fantasy. Narratives such as E. L. James's erotic romance *Fifty Shades of Grey* (2011) show that women-authored eroticism can achieve popular success. However, there is little new in *Fifty Shades* and its sequels. The sexual dynamic of James' novels simply rehearses the same masochistic fantasies with which women have traditionally been taught to identify. (That middle-class women around the world devoured these books shows how deeply invested female heterosexuality is in fantasies of male domination.) Imagining more diverse scenes of sexual pleasure, in which women are active, desiring agents, will make possible more diverse roles for women and men in everyday life. As Charlene puts it, echoing the Ruth in *Baby*, "You have to believe you can change the story line."[10]

As suggested by the quote from psychologists Jean Laplance and J. B. Pontalis opening this chapter, fantasy should not be understood through the modalities of truth or illusion but as a *structure*—a form. Laplance and Pontalis write, "Fantasy is not the object of desire, but its setting. In fantasy, the subject does not pursue the object or its sign: he appears caught up himself in the sequence of images."[11] Rearranging the sequence of images reorients our identification with the narrative constructed. In *Hot*, fantasy is staged as part private domestic drama, part public spectacle. Charlene struggles to find a language with which to articulate female pleasure and erotic desire, only to be overtaken by a fantasy not of her own making. As *Hot* emphatically shows, fantasies do not exist in some isolated realm of private thought or private space; rather, our fantasies are shaped by cultural attitudes, images, and narratives, and they also shape the *materiality* of our daily lives and social relationships in ways that undermine distinctions between private and public, individual and collective.

Hot is built around juxtapositions—between sexuality and violence, body and voice, fantasy and reality, high culture and low culture, masculinity and femininity, public and private. The stage design makes visible what is typically kept private—the domestic sphere and erotic fantasies—and makes it available for public viewing. The notes for the set state, "The red light arenas and the living have this in common: They are stages for performance, for viewing" (6). This stage design positions the audience as voyeurs, complicit in the action that unfolds. Further reinforcing our cultural habits of viewing and image consumption, the Arena Stage production included several televisions sets, which played scenes from horror films, boxing matches, and classic Hollywood love stories. The screen images permeated the late-1980s playworld with a visual archive of cultural representations of sex and violence, which, at times, conflicted with the action on stage but at other times offered a more romanticized version of the stage action. Leslie Ann and Calvin are described in the character list as "voyeurs, as teenagers are, hooked on watching—TV, Nintendo, music videos, parents" (5). Significantly, only Leslie Ann and Calvin take part in both playworlds, interacting with, imitating, and learning from both. Moreover, popular music, from Janet Jackson's *Control* to Frank Sinatra, pervades both stage worlds as a kind of shared public consciousness. As the audience was taking their seats in the Arena Stage theater, for example, Blondie's "One Way or Another" played, filling the theater with the affective codes of popular culture before the playworld itself was even introduced. The two stage spaces and the characters in them are in constant tension—the stripper and the single mother writing erotic fiction to make ends meet, the girl dancing erotically and the daughter being praised by her dad for her sexual appeal, the horror film and the play's final scene in which Charlene is killed by her ex-husband. Vogel represents pornography and domestic violence not as obscene (off stage), but as a spectacle for public witness.

The play opens with "a growing red light" under which the audience sees "Leslie Ann dressed in very tight pants and a halter top," making suggestive stripper or vogue-ing movements," as Charlene sits at her typewriter. The V.O. narrates the play's first lines, which are the words that Charlene types: "She was hot. She was throbbing. But she was in control. Control of her body. Control of her thoughts. Control of . . . him . . . He was hot. He was throbbing. And out of control. He needed to be restrained. Tied down. And taught a Lesson. But not hurt too much. Not too much. Just . . . enough" (9). As Charlene shifts the power dynamics of heteronormative relations, positioning the man as dominated erotic object, she also questions her authority to revise this script. In her definition of social power, literary critic Carolyn G. Heilbrun articulates the play's primary concern: "Power is the ability to take one's place in whatever discourse is essential to action and the right to have one's part matter."[12] As she tries to assume a place within the discourse of pornography, Charlene's words and thoughts are continually infiltrated by the screen images positioned on stage, the canonical passages narrated by The Voice, and seductive moves performed by the V.O. Cultural discourses—both written and performed—conflict and converge with Charlene's erotic voice, suggesting the way our imaginations, far from being within our control, are structured by a history of images and narratives. *Hot* is deeply concerned with the complexity of women's claim to authority—control—especially over representations of sexuality. The play explores the limited autonomy of women's erotic imaginations, their limited capacity to imagine themselves as sexual subjects, and the material implications of these limitations in everyday life. As Charlene's authority as a pornographer is placed in dissonant tension with her authority as a mother, the play destabilizes conventions of both motherhood and female sexuality in far-reaching ways.

Hot oscillates between familiar images of a mother worrying about her children and less familiar images of a woman writing pornography. When Charlene expresses worry to Calvin about what Leslie Ann does when she goes out with friends, the audience sees Leslie Ann join the V.O. under the red light, where, together, they "do a slow, expert teasing dance for an imaginary male clientele" (25). Like any teenager, Leslie Ann learns her sexuality both inside and outside the home, rehearsing and performing the seductive postures and movements of heteronormative femininity. While practicing her sexuality, Leslie Ann also provides material for Charlene, who watches the striptease "mesmerized" (26) and then later works this theatrical display into her film script. Calvin, too, watches Leslie Ann and the V.O., and he "parallels their movements" (25), suggesting that he is not only the consumer; in an increasingly sexualized marketplace, he must also learn how to perform these seductive moves.

The V.O. both invites a voyeuristic gaze and also problematizes that gaze with her narrative voice. As a "sex-worker" and Charlene's "inner voice," the V.O. is both the embodiment of erotic discourse and the narrator of Charlene's screenplay. Throughout the play, the V.O. also acts as both a performer in and the director of Charlene's screenplay, initiating scene changes by commanding, "CUT TO." Both the V.O. and The Voice give a material presence to history—the history of the literary canon, of popular culture, and of female sexuality—and a body to the cultural voices we internalize as knowledge. Film scholar Kaja Silverman writes, "Western metaphysics has fostered the illusion that speech is able to express the speaker's inner essence, that it is 'part' of him or her,"[13] which reinforces notions of a unified subject in control the language she speaks. Realist theater, with its emphasis on psychology and subtext, perpetuates this illusion that a character's words articulate an inner, individual truth. In contrast, *Hot*, like *Baby*, continually undermines any notion of language as original, individual, private, and immaterial, and instead invokes the collective nature of individual identities and the history of language and discourse.

Juxtaposing high and popular culture, domestic and erotic, words and bodies, *Hot* mobilizes a camp sensibility to deconstruct the sexual iconicity of heteronormative femininity and defamiliarize the nuclear family as the wholesome, sacred, and stable center of American culture. Queer critic Andrew Ross defines camp as a "rediscovery of history's waste" and, subsequently, *"the recreation of surplus value from forgotten forms of labor."*[14] Camp retrieves historical objects and modes of production in order to remake their use-value and cultural function. As a single mother who writes feminist pornography, Charlene recreates surplus value from two typically discarded forms of labor—sex work and motherhood—while using this labor to produce different representations of female sexuality and pleasure. The play as a whole also recycles images from horror movies, popular music, and television, encouraging the audience to read these cultural artifacts as the very material structuring heteronormative fantasies.

While *Baby* reconfigures the structure of the nuclear family, *Hot* both shows the ways the nuclear family functions to reproduce heteronormative genders and sexualities and reveals the perversity underlying that normativity. Here, in this seemingly ordinary family, the mother finds inspiration for her erotic writing in her daughter's and son's burgeoning sexuality; father and son watch their daughter/sister dance erotically under the red fantasy light; the son masturbates while watching his mother smoke a cigarette and as Michael Jackson's "Beat It!" pulses in the background; and the sister yells at her younger brother for watching her undress from behind the bushes. Making the family a spectacle for public witness and situating it within the wider culture, *Hot* reveals the ubiquitous and intersecting ways we learn and perform our sexualities, both inside and outside the home. And linking voyeuristic practices in the private sphere to those same kinds of practices in the public sphere, the play shows how sexuality resists and continually spills over the boundaries we construct between private and public.

Distinctions between public and private sexuality are further complicated through the play's juxtaposition of the literary and visual representations that teach us how to perform our sexualities. Calvin masturbates into his baseball mitt, while the V.O. reads from *Moby-Dick*, for example, an incongruous image that links the sexual and discursive and puts the seemingly private acts of reading and masturbating into public view. Male voyeurism and female objectification are foregrounded when Clyde and Calvin watch Leslie Ann, who stands self-consciously under the red light, imitating the seductive moves that the V.O. performs. Father and brother watch "with glazed attention" as The Voice narrates Cleo's striptease dance from Henry Miller's *Plexus*. And just as Clyde teaches Calvin how to offer a dollar bill to the V.O., who enacts the part of Cleo, The Voice reads the final line from Miller's passage: "it was tantalizing, especially to a sixteen year old who had still to know what it feels like to make a grab for a woman's bush" (49). The convergence of father-son bonding and high pornography confuses the normative and the perverse and underscores the way young men are trained as aggressive sexual consumers. Later, Clyde gives Leslie Ann five dollars, just as any father would, which further highlights the value of bodies and desires in a heterosexual economy. The juxtapositions are startling and bold. Female and male sexuality are "normalized" within the nuclear family in much the same way as in popular culture, with the female body coded as sexually consumed object and the male as sexual consumer and voyeur. While women learn to become eroticized objects in this fantasy narrative, young men, in a heterosexual culture, learn to become active, often violent consumers. Earlier in the play, Clyde tells his son Calvin to watch out for his sister, because "that body of hers . . . you know what I mean? You got to control her. Girls' bodies at her age . . . they should be *licensed*" (48). The subtext of this lesson is that women's sexuality is to be contained and displayed for male pleasure. Coached by their parents as well as by the cultural texts that surround them, Leslie Ann and Calvin learn to perform their sexuality and gender. By situating family within the wider context of cultural production, *Hot* shocks the audience into a reconsideration of the inviolability of this central unit of American culture.

The play's emphasis on narrative and writing suggests the way form—genre—relies on aesthetic conventions to shape and teach the social conventions governing normative genders. In a brief yet telling exchange, Calvin reveals his admiration for Charlene's detective character. He states, "I really like the detective, mama. He's cool," to which Charlene replies, "I'm kinda proud of him" (21). It is easy to forget that this sweet exchange between mother and son concerns the pornography that the mother is writing and that the son is apparently reading. Calvin's admiration is both an expression of his genuine praise for his mother's writing talents and a suggestion of his identification with and incorporation of the type of masculinity that the detective represents. Film critic Frank Krutnik explains the allure of the detective figure in film noir, while pointing out the way this figure is embedded in broader cultural myths:

> The "hard-boiled" private eye represents an "Americanisation" of the classical detective. The world through which he moves and which he seeks to order is comparable to the mythologized Frontier of the Western, a world of lawlessness . . . and dominated by assertive masculine figures of self-appointed authority. The lawless context of the "mean streets" world legitimizes the private eye's own aggressiveness in pursuit of his mission to establish a regime of truth.[15]

As the author of the fiction, Charlene reworks the "regime of truth" and the "self-appointed authority" embodied by the noir detective, parodically revising his masculine aura. The Voice narrates Charlene's version of the detective:

> What the TV dramas don't show you is that we spend most of our days sitting on our butts, drinking stale coffee. And when you do get to the crime scene, the trails and traces are so stupid a kid could tell you who done it. And the action has come and gone long before you turned up. And so you feel like one limp dick. (33)

While domestic spaces are hotbeds of fantasy production in *Hot*, generic film fantasies are transformed into mundane scenes of boredom and impotence.

Leslie Ann likewise learns her sexuality from the genres of popular culture. During a sleepover, she nervously tells her friend about her sexual fantasies, echoing the scenario that her mother's screenplay attempts to reverse: "Do you think of them, like, 'hurting' you? Well, I don't mean like hurting you, but like, you're tied down and you can't stop them and they do things to you that hurt you, that make you scream but you can't . . . and it makes you get hot only it's 'cause it's not for real?" (57). This masochistic position of sexual powerlessness that Leslie Ann finds erotic is one that women are encouraged to identify with as spectators of commercial film, readers of canonical fiction, and consumers of pornography. Women learn to identify with and find pleasure in these fantasies of powerlessness, in part, by convincing themselves of their unreality, even as they are internalized as familiar and habitual. However, as film critic Linda Williams argues, "There is thus a real need to be clearer than we have been about what is in masochism for women—how power and pleasure operate in fantasies of domination which appeal to women. There is an equal need to be clearer than we have been about what is in sadism for men."[16] Significantly, the girls are watching a horror movie when Leslie Ann describes her fantasy. Williams highlights the "rhetoric of violence" in horror films, pointing to the way the spectators' bodies "jerk," a movement discursively linked to both "tear-jerker" and "jerk-off,"[17] female emotional excess and male sexual pleasure. Williams defines pornography, horror, and melodrama collectively as "body genres," since they all feature a female body in various states of emotional excess—tears, screams, or orgasm—and she examines the system of sensations evoked the bodies of spectators who consume these genres. Williams explains, "in each of these genres the bodies of women figured on the screen have functioned traditionally as the primary *embodiments* of pleasure, fear, and pain," and this lack of proper aesthetic distance from a female body in varying states of ecstasy marks these genres culturally as low.[18] Invoking both porn and horror, *Hot* underscores the way women's bodies have served as sites of male desire and violence and the way female spectators have learned to identify with and adopt this dynamic as their "natural" sexuality.

Revealingly, literary critic N. J. Stanley uses the word "horror" three times in his critical essay on *Hot*. In one such instance, he writes, "Charlene's earlier, self-serving explanation in defense of her writing doesn't absolve her from our horror when we realize that she uses her own children as models for her fantasizing."[19] That Charlene needs "absolving" of the sins of writing pornography seems directly related to her role as mother. More telling is Stanley's claim that Charlene is "self-serving" for choosing a career as an erotica writer, suggesting again that the maternal model she ought to embody is the desexualized Madonna, the moral center of the patriarchal family. Charlene's decision to write pornography is self-serving only if one defines motherhood as a kind of selfless, sexless martyrdom. As Charlene explains, she prefers imagining "beautiful, strong bodies touching each other" to working for minimum wage at a hospital: "Cleaning up messes. Bodies and mess" (53–54). Since women have historically been reduced to messy body matters (birth, bleeding) and the work that involves messy bodies (mothers, nurses), Charlene's writing offers an opportunity to rewrite the narratives that continually cast women in these roles. As a writer, she can use her discursive authority to imagine and create fantasies of female *pleasure*. However, this is no simple task, or one that Charlene achieves. And yet *Hot* succeeds in identifying the authority that media and literature have in defining our pleasures and desires.

The play's metafictional overtones highlight the difficulties Charlene has in articulating her own narrative authority. As a film writer, Charlene is in a position of creating a different set of images and a different kind of spectatorship. As an *erotic* film writer, Charlene is positioned as producer of the very plots and stories that stimulate and define female sexuality. Literary critic Brian Richardson refers to Charlene's incorporation of the intercepting voices into her text as "materialist metatheater," which he defines as "a creative, nonviolent recursivity [that is] an alternative to the more deeply ingrained verbal habits and behaviors of the culture at large."[20] This reading suggests that Charlene controls and directs the language she uses. However, the "cultural at large" is everywhere present in the play, continually conflicting with the words Charlene writes, redirecting her narrative at every turn. And while her engagement with the historical discourses that have authorized female sexuality decenters their authority—a decentering performatively enacted by The Voice's fragmented recitations—Charlene often cannot find her own voice within this discourse.

The passages from Miller, Melville, Nabokov, and Joyce are not merely chunks of text inserted for a fragmented, postmodern effect. Rather, they illustrate the dynamic relationship between high and low cultural forms, the mind and the body of culture, so to speak, reminding the audience that these texts shape the bodies, thoughts, and lives of these characters; they are part of the air they (we) breathe. In short, the intertextual references underscore the material implications of practices of canonization. *Ulysses, Lolita,* and *Plexus* are all part of a modernist literary canon that consists, in part, of male writers attempting new ways of articulating and authorizing sexual desire—male and female.

Vogel is not suggesting we dispense with these texts; she is encouraging a critical engagement with them, as with all historical objects that we inherit. In *Hot,* she is concerned with finding new ways of representing female sexuality and new ways of talking about violence, which might then enable other ways of imagining and enacting desire. As she relates to Bigsby, "We are still using a legacy, a language, if you will, of male pornography while trying to transform it into female erotica."[21] Early in the play, Charlene searches for variations on the word "throbbing," and the V.O. offers "Pulsating," "Heaving," "Pulsing," while the Voice suggests synonyms with more violent connotations: "Beating" and "Battering" (22). This parsing of the words associated with eroticism suggests the way violence is embedded in the language we use to define sexuality. Literary critic Shoshana Felman explains that eroticism is a product of language: "the scandal lies not so much in the fact that that the linguistic is always erotic, but in the much more scandalous fact that the erotic is always linguistic."[22] And so if the language changes, what we find erotic also changes. *Hot* reveals how language and representations are often structured by and around male authority and desire, and the play asks: How does this gendered authority over language and representation shape the bodies and sexualities that it defines? How much room is there for change?

This indissoluble relationship between language and the bodies it defines is theatricalized through the characters of The Voice and V.O., who recite and perform the history of discourses that have gone into defining sexual desire. These characters not only embody this discursive and performative history (canonical literature, stripping) but also displace the speaking or writing subject as the origin of discursive authority. The Voice and the V.O. enact the historical body of language with which Charlene inevitably has to negotiate, and Charlene's authorial power emerges from the capacity to initiate material effects through her writing, in terms of both bodily pleasure and economic profit. Charlene explains to Clyde the satisfaction that writing gives her in quasi-biblical, materialist terms: "And I write down these words. And the words become flesh. *(Beat)* And the pay's much better" (55). Charlene describes her writing as "saving my sanity" (55), as it offers a way of gaining authority over her thoughts, words, and material circumstances. The performative authority enacted by writing, that is, has material implications.

When Clyde bursts into Charlene's house, drunk and lonely, he makes a spectacle of himself by performing a parody of female sexual display. As he sashays into the living room, Clyde announces, "I'm here to audition. To Give You. New material. The E-Rot-icly UnEmployed. . . . Ta-DA!! And Now! The Burlesque Theatre of Langley Park! Presentin'! SEX—ON—WELFARE! . . . BWAH-BWAH-BWAH!!! . . . bum-bum BWAH—bum-bum. . . ." (30). In this parodic performance, Clyde is both mocking Charlene's new career and underscoring his own humiliation. Charlene responds to his burlesque by calmly getting a gun and shooting him in the buttocks. Here, the relationship between the female stripper and the phallic male gaze is inverted so that Clyde mocks his own erotic failure, while Charlene responds to this spectacle with a parody of self-defense. As cultural historian Rachel Shteir writes in a passage relevant to this scene, "the history of striptease is one of men and women failing together and apart." Here, Clyde parodies striptease—the social ritual that

Figure 4: *Hot 'n' Throbbing*. Left to right: Colin Lane and
Lynnda Ferguson. Arena Stage Theater, Washington, DC, 1999.
Photo: Joan Marcus.

most explicitly performs the dynamics of heteronormative desire. As Shteir writes:

> What is interesting about striptease is that it flaunts female sexuality—and male sexuality too—in spectacular forms, along the way making fun of those forms. . . . Confronting Americans with private act in a public space, the best stripteases wove together the mask of humor with corporeal unmasking, intellectual dazzle with physical prowess. At its most archetypal, striptease embodied great theatre's antic spirit—albeit in a limited way—with the "polymorphous perversities" and roguish transgressions that all great theatre contains.[23]

Striptease can be read as both a theatricalization of everyday heteronormative relations and a metatheatrical comment on the pleasures of looking that theater allows. With his striptease, Clyde places himself in a position coded as feminine, reflecting both the humiliation he feels due to his lack of economic success and the threat he feels in regards to Charlene's writing job.

Clyde is conflicted by Charlene's new writing career, both turned on and threatened by her newly claimed narrative authority. In a vulnerable moment, he tells Charlene, "you taught me about desire" (41). And yet he also mocks her work, poking fun at the mascot for Gyno Production—Rosie the Rhino—who, in pink pasties and a G-string, playfully parodies female objectification. Clyde expresses his disdain for Rosie, saying, "A Rhino in a G-string does not inspire me," to which Charlene replies, "it's supposed to be funny . . . for women" (36). Rosie the Rhino suggests the possibilities available for revising the language and images structuring female desire. But she does not make sense to a male gaze seeking to be pleased or flattered. As a working-class, white man who does not meet the ideal of the economically successful and socially powerful American male, Clyde maintains his claim to masculine power through physical force and verbal humiliation. He is described in the character list as "over forty. Holes in dungarees. Almost a beer belly," and Vogel insists that whoever plays this role has "to go gangbusters. . . . The bigger the asshole you are, the more we'll love you. Trust me on this" (5). Indeed, Clyde's hyperbolic performance of a failed masculinity induces a kind of empathy, as he seems powerless over his words and actions. His performative repertoire seems limited, lacking gestures of reciprocity or empathy. In his increasingly erratic performance, we can see him flailing for some other way to "do" his gender. Oscillating between sexual parody and mockery and sincere attempts at communicating with his ex-wife, Clyde seems to be, like Charlene, in search of a new script.

In the following exchange, Clyde seems genuine in his desire to listen to Charlene. Here, he listens to Charlene describe her writing practice in terms that illustrate the play's leitmotif:

> CLYDE: . . . So where do all these words come from?
> CHARLENE: I don't know. When I really get going, it's like a trance—it's not me writing at all. It's as if I just listen to voices and I'm taking dictation.
> THE VOICE: "Case 103 continued. Subject, however, experienced constant excitation, due to what the subject described as inner 'voices' usually urging him to erotic acts."
> CLYDE: Doesn't that spook you? I mean, whose voices are these? Who's in control?
>
> V.O.
> But she was in control.
>
> CHARLENE: Well, they're the characters speaking, or the script itself. I mean, it's me, but I have to get into it. At first it spooked me a little. But now I know when I hear them, it's a good sign. And I am in control. (37–38)

The writer does not possess the words she uses; they possess her. Control over language is presented here as a complex historical struggle that shapes bodies and lives. As The Voice narrates a case study from famed nineteenth-century sexologist Richard Von Krafft-Ebing's *Psychopathia Sexualis* (1886), which effectively categorizes all but the most conventional forms of sex and sexuality as pathological, Charlene "is taking dictation." It is not clear who is speaking, who is authorizing her script, and in this ambiguity *Hot* reveals both the complexity and the possibility of women's claims to narrative authority. In the above exchange, the V.O. interjects, inserting her embodied voice into the historical discourses invading Charlene's consciousness and complicating the division of sexualized body/literary voice. However, the question remains unanswered in the play as to whether the V.O.'s words contain any truth value or if her body is her only claim to power.

Narrative control is, in the play, inextricable from control over one's body, its pleasures, desires, impulses. In defense of her choice to write erotica, Charlene insists, "I am not a pornographer. I write erotic fiction designed for women" (39). Charlene further explains her writing strategy to Clyde by emphasizing the centrality of language, rather than physical acts, in women's erotica: "For one thing, desire in female spectators is aroused by the cinema in a much different way. Narrativity—that is, plot—is emphasized." In a passage that suggests something of Vogel's own playwriting strategy, Charlene adds, "Most importantly, we try to create women as protagonists in their own dramas, rather than objects. And we try to appreciate the male body as an object of pleasure" (39–40). The challenge is finding a language that does not return to the same script of male domination and female submission. When the audience finds out that Charlene has a restraining order against Clyde and that he has cut the phone lines before barging into the house, their history of violence, the erotic screenplays Charlene is writing, and the passages read by The Voice converge.

In the final section of *Hot*, the fantasy world and domestic space converge as a spontaneous erotic encounter between Charlene and Clyde turns violent. Clyde confesses that he came to see Charlene after realizing he did not have enough money to afford a prostitute. This confession leads to a more humiliating disclosure that he is no longer sexually turned on by "the usual . . . uh . . . escapes." His usual fantasies are interrupted by the thought that perhaps "some woman is writing them . . . or she's someone's mother" (65). As Charlene's newly cultivated authorial power begins to invade Clyde's erotic imagination, he becomes impotent. Out of compassion for his vulnerability, Charlene offers to play the part of prostitute—for the bargain price of $18.37—and indulges Clyde's sexual fantasy. Yet the combination of Clyde's humiliation, his emotional vulnerability, and his discomfort with Charlene's new writing career lay the ground for the sudden shift from sexual desire to violence that provides the climax of the play. The precise shift from eroticism to violence occurs when Charlene assures Clyde that she has protection. The Voice asks, "What is she doing with condoms in the house?" (67). This concrete suggestion of Charlene's sexual agency crystallizes Clyde's feelings of powerlessness and failure. As feminist critic Lynne Segal writes, "The last thing men . . . 'want' the women in their lives to be—whether wives, daughters, friends, workmates, lovers, or whatever—is the ubiquitously sexually desiring, universally sexually available, creature of much pornographic fantasy."[24] We are not far from *Desdemona* here. Heteronormative male sexual and social power, it seems, has much invested in maintaining distinct boundaries between the realm of sexual fantasy and the realm of domesticity. Indeed, it is a boundary built to secure and protect the power to define women's bodies as the objects of male pleasure and authority. As fantasy and reality converge, however, Charlene and Clyde seem suddenly to be caught in scripts and performances that neither is able to control. Here, language and fantasy take on an unsettling authority of their own, and in an eerie echo of Charlene's explanation to Clyde of the power she feels writing, the V.O. states, "And the words become flesh" (67).

Charlene's Gyno film turns into Clyde's dark fantasy, a snuff film in which Clyde enacts a role and a script that he seems simultaneously to direct and to have no control over. The camp effect in this scene emerges from the stark contrast between high and low, performativity and theatricality, sexuality and violence. The tone of the scene is best described by queer critic Kathryn Bond Stockton, who defines a "dark camp" that "keeps the violent edge of debasement visibly wedded to caprice."[25] The volatility of the scene is amplified and denaturalized by the exaggerated words and gestures of the actors' performances. Unable to heed the V.O.'s warnings to "Get out of the house!" (70), Charlene now seems to be under the command of The Voice, who has usurped the V.O.'s filmic directive, "CUT TO," with his own commands of "Jump Cut." This initiates retakes of scenes that get progressively more violent, and it is clear that Charlene is no longer in a narrative of her own writing or a fantasy that she has the power to shape. As violent snuff film replaces feminist erotica, Calvin and Leslie Ann watch the unfolding scene from outside the sliding glass doors. The kids face the audience, while the audience becomes implicated in the stage action as complicit voyeurs. The violence escalates, and Clyde beats Charlene in a stylized slow motion, lip-syncing a script spoken by The Voice: "You. Goddamn. Whore. . . . You're the one making me do this, Charlene" (71, 73). Shifting the authority of his violent acts back to Charlene, Clyde, it is clear, is out of control. The ventriloquism and "elaborate pantomime" (71) of the scene work to separate body and voice, act and agent, the speaker and the history that his words carry. As a melodramatization of the "stylized repetition of acts"[26] that make up heteronormative masculinity, the exaggerated theatricality also distances the audience from the brutality and thwarts the cathartic response traditionally associated with tragic ends. The scene's stylized theatricality removes the action from its realistic setting in a working-class living room, expanding its meanings and implications beyond the private sphere and into the realm of public fantasy. We are all familiar with Clyde's words; they are not his alone.

Clyde strangles Charlene as The Voice reads Molly's soliloquy from James Joyce's *Ulysses*. Juxtaposing violent image and erotic language, contemporary culture and canonical history, obscenity and art, the narration of Joyce's authorization of Molly's pleasure resonates dissonantly in relation to Charlene's flailing body and the helpless warnings of the V.O. It is a moment of tremendously disturbing proportions. Joyce's creation of Molly as narrator has been held up as an example of Joyce's masterful ability to "accurately" voice female sexuality and also denounced as chauvinistic. Literary critic Lisa Sternlieb points out that "Joyce's ventriloquy has been read alternatively as mindless misogyny . . . [and] as a rare example of *l'écriture féminine*, a woman writing her own body."[27] Critics who judge this representation of female sexuality as either *true* or *false*, artful or obscene, miss the point that Molly is a *character*, with no actual control over her own pleasure or its expression. It is our interpretations of Joyce's *writing* that define Molly. With each reading, Joyce is invested, again and again, with the canonical authority to voice and define female sexuality, whether we see this as obscene or virtuosic. By interpolating canonical texts, *Hot* suggests how canonical writers like Joyce shape our fantasies and provide the language with which we define our own desires. As Clyde tightens his grip on Charlene's neck, The Voice whispers Othello's deadly poetry: "Put out the Light and then Put out the light" (73). And Charlene's silent and lifeless body becomes the sign of this authority.

Three different endings, which directly follow this moment, have been staged in productions of *Hot*, suggesting Vogel's difficulty in finding a way out of the cycles of violence it represents. The ending at the American Repertory Theatre in Cambridge, Massachusetts, in April 1994, under the direction of Anne Bogart, suggests a generational repetition of the violence between Clyde and Charlene. Leslie

Ann enters, sees her dead mother, then walks under a spotlight, where she strips to the music of the "stripper theme." But this spectacle is devoid of eroticism, as "she does not bump or grind."[28] The stage directions read, "If this were a film script, we would see The Girl age before our eyes."[29] Leslie Ann takes off her clothes and dons her mother's, taking her mother's place at the computer and typing the words that begin the play: "She was hot. She was throbbing. But she was in control. Control of her body. Control of her thoughts."[30] This ending suggests that there is no way out of the cycle of violence just witnessed.

The second ending emerged from a conflict of opinion between Vogel and long-time collaborator and artistic director of Arena Stage, Molly Smith. Vogel sought to find a way out of the disturbing cycle suggested by the first ending and so wanted to flash forward to Leslie Ann as a university professor, giving a lecture to her students on the relationship between sexuality and violence. However, Smith wanted a more cryptic ending, with Leslie Ann coming in to find her mother's dead body, freezing in a tense pose of fear and anger. The V.O. responds to her fear in a soothing, maternal voice, saying, "It's okay. It's all right," and Leslie Ann's body relaxes. This ending depicts a soothing if helpless maternal presence, disembodied and divested of her discursive power. Vogel was unhappy with the decision to stage it that way; its very ambiguity, to her, seemed irresponsible toward audience members who may have experienced abuse. This conflict of opinion marked the end of the professional relationship between Vogel and Smith.

The third ending, the one staged at Signature Theatre in 2005, with Les Waters directing, flashes forward ten years, to show Leslie Ann as a literature professor and Calvin as a Hollywood screenwriter. This ending invokes German playwright Heiner Müller's technique of the synthetic fragment, which condenses time and juxtaposes images, ideas, and themes, in place of the logic and structure of linear plot. This version, Vogel's preferred ending, plants the seeds of futurity and points to new ways of writing about and performing sexuality. As a university professor, Leslie Ann has entered a different discursive history—critical, scholarly discourse—in order to claim authority over the canonical and cultural narratives that haunted her mother's consciousness. This ending emphasizes the possibilities of change that can come out of an intellectual engagement with the past, a critical questioning of the ideas and images that have been passed down, and a revision of the texts that continue to inform our bodies and imaginations. Moreover, this ending suggests ways of cultivating dialogue and awareness that move beyond moral categories of good and bad and the reductive and immobilizing roles of victim and victimizer. The play ends with Leslie Ann instructing her students on their *Moby-Dick* essays: "I expect you to be in control of your arguments, in control of your words, and in control"—and then Leslie Ann and her mother's voice say in unison, "of your thoughts." The stage directions read: "*Leslie Ann Dwyer freezes at the sound of her mother's voice*" (75). This moment of maternal haunting sheds light on the play's epigraph: "Some plays only daughters can write" (48). This maternal echo perhaps signals a new legacy—although by no means an uncomplicated one—of discursive tools passed down from mother to daughter, tools with which to rework a history of discourses that have consistently excluded their voices. As Butler writes:

> The voice that emerges "echoes" the master discourse, but this echo nevertheless establishes that there is a voice, that some articulatory power has not been obliterated. . . . Something is persisting and surviving and the words of the master sound different when spoken by one who is, in the speaking, in the recitation, undermining the obliterating effects of his claim.[31]

Although no one can claim full authority and control over their words and thoughts, since those words are part of a history that both precedes and produces individual subjects, participating in a discourse inevitably changes its contours and claims. *Hot's* third ending offers the most hope for altering the script of sexual violence, as Charlene's writing and Leslie Ann's teaching "undermine the obliterating effects" of the master discourse of pornography. The continued revisions of *Hot* are Vogel's attempt to find a true ending to the play, one that neither forecloses on the possibilities of change nor promotes a naïve optimism. The multiple endings also suggest that, for Vogel, a play is never finished and that, yes, it is possible to "change the storyline."

Vogel reveals that many artistic directors refused to stage *Hot*, since they thought it would be too disturbing for audiences, "the same audiences," she points out, "that pack *Pulp Fiction.*"[32] Reviews of *Hot* ranged from defensive to confused. *Washington Post* reviewer Lloyd Rose was remarkably resistant to the Arena Stage production of the play and its dialectical struggle between changing the script of sexual violence and reenacting more firmly entrenched, familiar ones. Indeed, Rose missed the play's central questions regarding family, fantasy, sex, and violence, positioning *Hot* instead as a male-bashing counterstatement to Mamet's *Oleanna*. He writes:

> In the center of this play there's some genuine, risky ugliness—the female suspicion that masculine strength will always ensure masculine control; that a woman's tender emotions—her socially approved love and compassion—are her worst enemies; that there's something fundamentally, unalterably wrong with men. Vogel slaps these nasty fears smack in the audience's faces. "Hot 'n' Throbbing" ought to be on a double bill with David Mamet's fear-of-feminism "Oleanna."[33]

Hot does reveal "some genuine, risky ugliness," but it does so in a way that provokes discussion about the "nasty fears" presented, not in a way that places blame. As the O.J. Simpson trial became a media frenzy, just two months after the premiere of *Hot,* and as film was developing its own aesthetics of violence, theater critics did not have a vocabulary for discussing stage violence that was neither sensationalized nor romanticized, as in the plays of Sam Shepard and David Mamet, but rather problematized. *New York Times* critic Jason Zinoman described the 2005 Signature Theatre production as "too busy, an academic exercise so overstuffed with ideas and theatrical tricks that any trace of humanity has been crowded out."[34] In his *New York Post* review, Frank Scheck quipped that "*Hot 'n' Throbbing* could more accurately be described as cold and uninvolving," warning that anyone "looking for cheap thrills at this play by Paula Vogel . . . will be disappointed."[35] The only critic to contextualize *Hot* was Alisa Solomon, who in her *Village Voice* review explained that the play was responding in part to the NEA obscenity trials. Solomon praised Les Waters's direction of the dualistic and dueling stage worlds, which she saw as "creating a productive sense of dislocation in both realms." Solomon understood the deliberate tension between farce, fantasy, and an "edgy sense of real," referring to Vogel as "one of America's most daring and complicated dramatists."[36] In *Hot,* Vogel holds sexuality and violence, private and public, fantasy and reality in dialectical tension, juxtaposing the history of images and texts that structure our imaginations, provide the setting for our desires, and teach us how to perform our genders. While *Hot* dramatizes the structure and historicity of fantasy, the plays discussed in the next chapter, *The Oldest Profession* (1981/2005) and *The Mineola Twins* (1996), stage female characters at the center of postwar American history and politics.

CHAPTER FOUR

Embodied Histories: *The Oldest Profession* and *The Mineola Twins*

Women have lived in a world in which they apparently had no history and in which their share in the building of society and civilizations was constantly marginalized. . . . Most importantly, women have been denied the power to define, to share in creating the mental constructs that explain and order the world. Under patriarchy the record of the past has been written and interpreted by men and has primarily focused on the activities and intentions of males. Women have always been, as have men, agents and actors in history, but they have been excluded from recorded history.

—Gerda Lerner, *Why History Matters: Life and Thought*[1]

The Reagan revolution not only has suffused "the personal" with political meanings well beyond those imagined in the "sexual revolution" of the 1960s, but it has . . . helped to create some extremely limiting frames for what properly constitutes the practice of U.S. citizenship.

—Lauren Berlant, *The Queen of America Goes to Washington City*[2]

As feminist scholarship over the last three decades has made clear, women have, within the grand narratives of History, traditionally been cast as marginal supporting characters, omitted altogether, or associated with a feminized popular culture. As the continuing work of feminist, critical race, and queer studies demonstrates, there are other ways of telling history, other ways of organizing time. These alternative historiographies remind us that there is more than one way of telling history and more than one history to tell. With *The Oldest Profession* (1981/2005) and *The Mineola Twins* (1996), Vogel contributes two takes on postwar American history, with women acting not as props but as the main players. Since both plays look back on a not-so-distant past, they can be read as history plays, of sorts, that position women as active citizens and central shapers of American culture. Moreover, these comedies stage something similar to the work Lauren Berlant performs in *The Queen of America Goes to Washington City*. Berlant writes, "*The Queen* does a diva turn on citizenship, attempting to transform it from a dead (entirely abstract) category of analysis into a live social scene that exudes sparks, has practical consequences, forces better ways of thinking about nationality, culture, politics, and personhood."[3] *Twins* and *Profession* enact precisely this kind of diva citizenship, as the female characters expand the practice of citizenship, even as their lives are circumscribed by "the processes of valorization that make different populations differently legitimate socially and under the law."[4] The characters' roles as citizens are often at odds with their sexualized bodies, and Vogel negotiates this tension by making sex and sexuality a form of civic engagement in these plays. And so while the characters' sexually saturated bodies are foregrounded as the products of a culture obsessively focused on sex and female bodies and a right-wing political discourse focused on women's reproductive functions, their roles as politically engaged citizens undermine this reduction of women to sexualized/reproducing bodies, setting into motion a productive dissonance between women acting as representatives of the national body politic and as critics of American culture's privatization of sex and citizenship.

Discarded Labor, Diva Citizenship: *The Oldest Profession*

Equal parts Beckett, vaudeville, and *Golden Girls, Profession* is a play situated between comedy and crisis and structured by repetition. The 1980s playworld is defined by the political, cultural, and economic climate of Reagan-era America, with the bodies and stories of its characters acting as a commentary on the enduring social effects of this administration. Set in a period when Medicare was under threat, individualism on the rise, and productivity the primary goal of human labor, the play invokes the history of sex work to reflect on the effects of late capitalism on the bodies, lives, and relationships of five elderly prostitutes. The women live and work together in a sort of family business, an oddly homey collective whose forms of labor, community, and aging bodies are not recognized as a vital part of the national body politic. In an attempt to reconcile themselves to a hostile present, the women in *Profession* hark nostalgically back to their life in the brothel in a place called Storeyville, which stands as a counterimage to the "nostalgia-based fantasy nation" of an American public "directed toward the family sphere."[5] The play both sexualizes and politicizes the bodies of these women, while at the same time overtly sexualizing the body politic. Presenting sex acts as civic acts, *Profession* poses the question: Why are women's bodies made to bear the sexual meanings of a national public, even as they have historically been barred from that public as its proper citizens?

Vogel points to three reasons for writing *Profession*: she wanted to try a play using repetitive form, to write a tribute to her grandmother, and to revise Mamet's *The Duck Variations* (1972).[6] The subtitle, *A Full-Length Play in Six Black-Outs*, suggests that form *is* content here; each blackout both divides the scenes and signals one of the character's deaths. As each scene opens with one less woman on the stage, a note of urgency seeps into the otherwise comic play. Vogel modeled the character Mae, in *Profession*, after her grandmother, who passed away just before Vogel wrote the first draft in the mid-1980s. This homage was shocking to the artistic director of the Actor's Theatre of Louisville, Jon Jory, who ended up refusing to produce the play.[7] In a decade of Blanche Devereaux and *Cocoon*, Jory was still unsettled by a play depicting elderly women with active libidos. That dissonance is, in fact, partly what the play works to generate; staging hookers who could be your grandmother calls into question the stereotypes surrounding both. Interestingly, Mamet also found inspiration for *The Duck Variations* "from listening to a lot of old Jewish men all my life, particularly my grandfather."[8] *Profession* revises Mamet's two witty, elderly male characters as five spry old women in the Life. Vogel rewrites Mamet's ahistorical playworld as a historically specific, embodied playworld, in which five women oscillate between political and nostalgic discourses, using stories to construct a sense of community, security, and hope amid an inhospitable society. This aged quintet attempts to regain a sense of belonging in their Upper West Side neighborhood, to maintain ownership of their bodies and the capital they generate, and to create a feeling of security in a 1980s America turned cold by capitalist self-interest.

Profession depicts an America in crisis. At the center of this crisis are five women whose status as senior citizens (assumed to be both sexually and socially nonproductive) and work as prostitutes (productive sexually but whose labor is not legitimized socially) makes them doubly marginalized. The play thus works a double defamiliarization. First, it works against the desexualization that typically accompanies being a senior citizen, by transforming this stage of life into one of social virility. The sexuality of these old prostitutes becomes an extension of their vitality as civic subjects *and not* an expression of their function as either sexualized or reproductive bodies. Second, prostitution is defamiliarized as a profession built on nurturing, compassion, and love, rather than corruption, disease, and social deviance. When we learn several minutes into the play that these women are prostitutes, we have already associated them with images of home cooking and past loves. Fusing the affective connotations of home and grandmotherly love to the history of a commodified female sexuality produces a refracted image of the national body politic.

While earlier versions of *Profession* were produced in the 1980s and 1990s, by its 2005 Signature Theatre production in New York City, *Profession* had become a history play, looking back to the Reagan era and its implications in the present political, social, and economic life of the nation. Theater critic David Krasner points out, "the 1980s . . . saw the AIDS epidemic, the Reagan administration, and continuing obstacles to minority participation in the economy. The anarchy and liberation of the 1960s gave way to rampant individualism and acquisitiveness even within the most liberal segments of society."[9] The material effects of these changes are evident in the clothes, food choices, business strategies, and living conditions of the five women. The historical context of *Profession* was emphasized in Signature Theatre's production with its stark street-scene setting and pointed references to Mayor Koch's efforts in the 1980s to "clean up" Times Square. These efforts, along with Mayor Rudolf Giuliani's housekeeping in the 1990s, resulted in the hypercommercialization of midtown Manhattan and the subsequent displacement of many prostitutes and strip clubs to the outer corners of the island. Vying for space in this competitive market, the women of *Profession* seem

Figure 5: *The Oldest Profession.* Left to right: Patricia Lopez, Mary Louise Burke, Katherine Helmond, Carlin Glynn, and Joyce Van Patten. Signature Theater, New York City, 2005. Photo: ©Carol Rosegg

out of place, displaced by the "alley prostitutes," who are part of the "whore diaspora" incited by gentrification, and outpriced by the rising cost of living. Inserting prostitution into the most enduring national myth—the American Dream—Mae questions the work ethic of the street prostitutes: "Where the hell is their pride? Where the hell is their ambition? This is America, where any girl can start in the alley and work her way up to Madam."[10]

Profession begins with the women sitting on a "long bench on 72nd and Broadway, New York City," on a "sunny day shortly after the election of Ronald Reagan in 1980." (13). Along with this specificity of time and place, the characters are each precisely drawn. Vera is "the youngest, 72. Loves the sun." She is anxious about the rising cost of living in the city, especially her rent and food bill at Zabar's; Edna, seventy-four, is "a good time girl. Best Friend of Vera. Loves her work." Lillian thinks the government owes her some support after her years of public service; in contrast, Ursula, a fiscal conservative and quasi-Reaganite, is "Germanic, bossy, set and determined. Believes in rules, promotion, work ethic" (130). Although seventy-nine, Ursula thinks that "Social Security has no place in a free market" (135). Mae, the former madam of their brothel in Storeyville and now CEO of the group's street business, is described as "83. A self-made woman" (130). Mae is the most nostalgic of the bunch and seems the most out of place in this competitive economic climate. Even so, she is hardened to this new context, taking out "a large, gleaming wicked hat pin" to defend their territory from the "cheap amateur whores [who] don't know how to act like ladies" (138). The women's increasing social invisibility produces a palpable vulnerability in the play. The brothel in Storeyville, where their bodies were valued and their work gratifying, becomes a necessary myth that contrasts with their stark New York City reality, where their bodies are invisible and their labor no longer of value. However, the women's memories also present snapshots of American social history, from their Organization Man client from the 1950s, Mr. Jonathan, who "was just so handsome in his gray flannel suit," to their complaints in the 1980s about cuts to social services amid the "Me Generation" (134). These references situate the women in a broader social and historical narrative, and we get a sense of character and context that is not reducible to either the desexualized stereotypes of matronly old women or the hypersexualized stereotype of the prostitute.

Prostitution works in the play as a metonym for different modes of production in American society, as well as the different ideologies supporting them. And the five women represent the alienated labor force. Lillian, a believer in Keynesian economics, sees their work as a public service that is integral to the health of the nation and deserving of government subsidies. Mae's method of handling the business reflects a socialist-minded model, where income is distributed evenly and expenses are shared collectively. In contrast, Ursula espouses a capitalist belief in top-down organization, maximum profit, and increased productivity. As the women strategize about how to make ends meet, Ursula suggests a kind of post-Fordist model of production, in which they limit time spent with clients, shorten lunch breaks, and specialize their services. In order to remain competitive with the younger street prostitutes, Ursula suggests advertising their services in the back of the *Village Voice*, which, she argues, would boost and diversify their clientele, who are quite literally dying out. She also insists they raise their rates and collect payment—in cash—immediately after services are rendered. Ursula articulates her business model thusly: "We should up our fees. Change to a price list. . . . We have to increase the rate of turnover, and make the girls more time efficient" (142). And she justifies her conservative business plan by invoking their duty as citizens: "Remember, President Reagan has called on all Americans to reduce the deficit, and to balance the budget. We can start here. . . . No more two hour lunches" (148). Mae suggests that, rather than using a mass-production model for their business, which dehumanizes their relationship with their clients, they should, instead, run their business like an extended family. They could trim their allowances, rather than their time with clients. Having retired at eighty-three, Mae even volunteers to go back to work, rather than making the others work longer hours. Ursula has no patience for Mae's old-fashioned ways, stating adamantly, "we're not going to stay in the Life, Mae, unless you stop living in the past! It's a New Age: We've got to get off our fannies and sell!" (141). Living and working in this "New Age" neoliberal economy, the women in Profession become increasingly alienated from their labor, from each other, and from their place of belonging.

In a 1980s free-market economy, the labor traditionally associated with women's bodies—prostitution, motherhood, domestic work, caregiving—became increasingly invisible and devalued. The 1980s saw the rise of the feminization of labor, with the number of single mothers going up, along with the number of women working in low-paying service industry jobs. Grounded as they were in an entrepreneurial ethos and emphasis on progress, the 1980s were an especially unwelcoming social climate for older women, past their reproductive stage and subsisting on Medicare. And yet when Ursula, champion of neoliberalism, realizes that her strict new business policies are not supported by the rest of the women, she feels betrayed: "After all these years, to find out I've been working alongside communists." When Vera responds, "We're not communist. We're . . . labor" (165), an ideological battle ensues. While Ursula champions an approach that transforms their bodies into products of mass production, the other four retain a belief that their bodies and labor are theirs to claim. This is a highly political claim, given that sex workers' bodies and work have historically been coded as abject and illegitimate. *Profession* dramatizes sex work as not only legitimate but central to a healthy society; it also shows the way our bodies are not entirely "ours," but a product of our social milieu.

History emerges in the play most powerfully through the embodied memories of the characters—smells, tastes, and the sensual pleasures associated with their most cherished clients. Memories of food and home pervade the play, underscoring the incongruity between the grandmotherly appearance of the characters and their work as prostitutes. Vera opens the play with the recollection of the delicious "bit of lemon sole" (131) that she had for dinner the night before, sharing the first of several fond food memories. The play's food motif suggests the embodied nature of memory and also introduces the feelings of nurturing and comfort so lacking in the present circumstances. Vera's descriptions of sole, berries and cream, and red beans and rice cultivate a homey feeling, while connecting the materiality of memories and affect to the materiality of economics and social life. The women's embodied recollections link their individual bodies with the collective social body of which they are a part.

Life at the Storeyville brothel is recalled most vividly through Mae's stories of happier times and happier clients. As the voice of nostalgia in the play, Mae looks to the past for refuge from the unfriendly present:

> Remember the house where we all first met? A spick-and-span establishment. The music from Professor Joe in the parlor; the men folk bathed, their hair combed back and dressed in their Sunday best, waiting downstairs happy and shy. We knew them all; knew their wives and kids too. . . . There was honor in the trade. . . . My father went to Storeyville when I was a girl. Mother used to nod to Miss Sophie in the street before Mass in the Quarter. (139)

Here, prostitution is a familiar, vital part of American culture and family life, inextricable from its most sacred institutions. Mae's memories of the brothel are full of all the warmth and security typically associated with home. Harking back to a golden era in which there was professional integrity in the trade, Mae wonders, "where's the pride in the name prostitute? It's all gone downhill since the government poked their nose in our business and booted decent and self-respecting businesswomen out of Storeyville" (139). Outrage and indignation in the play are offset by nostalgia and the creative powers of memory to construct imagined places of stability and belonging. One of the play's most poignant moments comes when Mae starts to lose her memory (a revision Vogel made for the Signature Theatre production). Confessing to Vera that she's "losing it," Mae, with her fading memory, suggests that the past is no longer available to her as a strategy for coping with the present. This moment also acts as a metonym for the nation's memory loss, the collective "forgetting" of members of society who are old, ill, poor, or otherwise deemed worthless.

Nostalgia is evoked in the play as longing for a (mythic) time when prostitutes were part of the family life of the nation and a (hoped-for) time when senior citizens are not cast aside as unproductive, socially invisible members of society. From the Greek *nostos*, "return home," nostalgia can work as both a personal and a collective process through which memories are selected and reassembled to construct a certain image and understanding of the past. Nostalgia can take many forms and be used for different purposes. Historian James E. Combs points out that "Ronald Reagan made nostalgia into a political art."[11] By "exalting the model of the past," Combs argues, "nostalgia makes it over into something that we may have lost." In this way, "nostalgia politics is . . . a denial of history, and even more fundamentally, a denial of process."[12] And yet, in *Profession*, nostalgia works as a generative counterfiction to an increasingly sentimentalized political discourse, a useful fiction that generates a felt relationship to a past perceived as more secure than the present. The nostalgia in *Profession* makes no claims to truth, nor does it "deny history." Instead it draws from a different archive—one grounded in stories and memories—in order to create a feeling of belonging in the present. The women in *Profession* translate Reagan-era nostalgia into a yearning for a home based not on nuclear family values, but on the comfort and community of brothel life.

In *The Future of Nostalgia*, theorist and media artist Svetlana Boym defines two types of nostalgia. The first is "restorative nostalgia," which "signifies a return to the original stasis, to the prelapsarian moment," relies on notions of truth and tradition, and "evokes a national past and future." The second type is "reflective nostalgia," which "is more concerned with historical and individual time, with the irrevocability of the past and with human finitude." Both types reinforce that nostalgia is a longing not for a place, but for a time.

More precisely, nostalgia is a certain attitude or feeling toward time. The focus of reflective nostalgia is "not on the recovery of what is perceived to be absolute truth but on the meditation on history and the passage of time." As if describing the characters in *Profession*, Boym describes "nostalgics" who "resist the pressures of external efficiency and take sensual delight in the texture of time not measured by clocks and calendars."[13] Reflective nostalgia can be understood as a simultaneous retrospective looking backward and prospective looking forward and as a productive collaboration between personal and collective memories that creates "a double exposure, or a superimposition of two images—of home and abroad, of past and present, dream and everyday life."[14] In this formulation, theater itself becomes a nostalgic space, in which past and present come together in collaborative dissonance. It is not insignificant that the women in *Profession* yearn for a place called Storeyville, a place composed of stories and revived as "a superimposition of past and present, dream and everyday life." Nostalgia can be deployed as an ideological tool that uses the past to legitimize or escape the present, and it can also be mobilized to generate fictional narratives that foster a sense of belonging in the present.

This sense of belonging is a fiction cultivated by the women in an era where capitalist values of productivity, profit, and mass production have replaced less standardized forms of work and where street prostitution has replaced brothel life. In his essay "Central Park," cultural theorist Walter Benjamin describes the destruction of the aura of the prostitute in mass-production:

> Prostitution opens up the possibility of a mythical communion with the masses. The rise of the masses is, however, simultaneous with that of mass-production. Prostitution at the same time appears to contain the possibility of surviving in a world (*Lebensraum*) in which the objects of our most intimate use have increasingly become mass-produced. In the prostitution of the metropolis the woman herself becomes an article that is mass-produced.[15]

Benjamin goes on to state that with the mass-produced whore "the brothel never forms the background, as the street so often does."[16] Although Benjamin romanticizes pre–Industrial Age prostitution, his distinction is useful in the way it highlights the two socioeconomic eras and kinds of sex work evoked in *Profession*: one in the alienated capitalist present, signified by the new generation of street prostitutes, who work alone and compete for clients; the other in an idealized Storeyville past, where community and home still exist and body and labor are one. The mass prostitute does not have time to invest in emotional connection with her clients; the brothel prostitute's whole work revolves around this very task. The mass prostitute is displaced in modern society; the brothel prostitute makes her home in a brothel.

Not only does Vogel bring prostitution center stage as a legitimate form of labor, but she also brings to the foreground the prostitute left backstage in Arthur Miller's *Death of a Salesman*. One of Lillian's oldest clients in *Profession* is Mr. Loman, a gentleman who insists on paying in silk stockings and thinks America is still at war with Japan. In a reverent nod to Miller's most famous hero, *"There is a respectful silence as the women realize that Mr. Loman has lost his marbles"* (145). Bringing the prostitute out of the shadows of Willy Loman's failed life and into the spotlight, Vogel casts her as the kind-hearted Lillian, who Ursula claims "stays in bed with Mr. Loman much too long" (142). In Vogel's play, the prostitute's story is central, while Loman's more familiar story forms the backdrop to the drama of these five women. In some ways, *Profession* is to *Death of a Salesman* what *Desdemona* is to *Othello*: a comic glimpse behind the scenes of an iconic tragedy. While Shakespeare's idealized heroine/imagined whore is transformed by Vogel into an actual whore, Miller's abstract symbol of Loman's lonely failure becomes in Vogel's play an embodied, multidimensional character (and an actual whore).

Theater critic Deborah R. Geis elaborates on *Profession*'s intertextual nod to Arthur Miller's *Death of a Salesman*, writing, "Vogel's exploration of the politics of commodification draws explicit connections between Willy's failed career and the complex emotional trajectories of these women who have sold their bodies for a lifetime."[17] While Geis is right in drawing this connection, there is an implicit moralizing of prostitution in her suggestion that the women of *Profession* were forced into the Life and are therefore sexual victims. The play does not moralize sex work, but rather situates it at the center of a social history of labor in postwar American culture. Prostitution is a legitimate job in *Profession*, and the women recall many happy years working in the trade. Thus, although Geis rightly states, "What is important here is that we get [*Death of a Salesman*] from the prostitute's point of view," she also insists that, "despite Mae's glowing account of the past, we can never get too far away from the notion that the prostitute's bodies are being bought and sold."[18] The play, in fact, means to bring us *closer* to that notion. Geis's moralizing interpretation, perhaps more suited to a naturalistic play, comes precisely from the ideology that positions these women and their work as marginal. A more productive way of approaching the play and its characters is through a materialist analysis of the economic and political systems that position these women—because of both their age and their profession—at the bottom of the social hierarchy, increasingly invisible and yet exposed. Juxtaposing two economically prosperous and highly mythologized periods in American cultural history—the 1950s and 1980s—*Profession* shows who is left out of that economy and mythology. While Loman's obsolescence occurs amid the shift from industrial capitalism to a Fordist assembly-line model of production, the women of *Profession* struggle to find a place amid the socioeconomic shift from Fordism to post-Fordism, which is characterized by specialized markets, products, and jobs; a growth of white-collar workers; and the feminization of the workforce.

Perhaps the most salient link between *Profession* and *Salesman* is the interpenetration of past and present, individual and collective memory, in both playworlds. C. W. E. Bigsby points out that, in Miller's play, "past and present are causally connected (a narrative logic implying moral coherence)," as well as operating as "consistent realities informing and deforming one another."[19] Whereas the past is reconstructed in both Miller's and Vogel's plays as a refuge from a hostile present, the linear temporal logic implied by the cause-effect "moral coherence" in Miller's play is displaced in *Profession* by a repetitive structure that mimics the relentless logic of late capitalism. This structure suggests the inevitability of these women's demise within such an individualistic socioeconomic system, which considers even abject poverty to be volitional. Linking the history of capitalism to the history of prostitution, *Profession* questions how material conditions shape women's bodies and are shaped by embodied female labor. We empathize with these women who sit together on a New York City bench, alienated from society, from each other, and from a profession in which they once took pride and pleasure.

Aside from the women's departures, the most visible signals of crisis in Signature Theatre's production came in the gradual decline of the women's physical appearances, especially their costumes. Whereas at the beginning of the play, each woman's personality is signaled through the distinctive style of her well-tailored suit, toward the end, when only Edna and Vera remain, they look dowdy and disheveled, a faded leopard print on Edna's boxy trench coat the only reminder of better times. Individual style is replaced by the generic signs of poverty. The women's situation takes on an added urgency as their numbers diminish, the sense of community suggested at the beginning now replaced by desolation. When only Edna and Vera remain, they realize with desperate immediacy their lack of worth in a culture that privileges the new and the young. Their options are: look for work at MacDonald's or get married.

However, there is life after the Life. In the Signature Theatre production, as each woman departed from the group, she removed her street clothes, donned luxurious lingerie, and took her place in that big brothel in the sky, performing a classic cabaret number as a ritual of remembrance and return. As each woman returns to Storeyville, its mythic quality is reinforced, and the lines between history and memory, past/passed and present, are further blurred. These are poignant moments, in which the audience recognizes that there is no place for these women in America's future. Lillian's rendition of Mae West's "I'm No Angel" and Edna's cover of Nina Simone's "I Want a Little Sugar in My Bowl" position the women within a different kind of cultural history, one in which women's bodies are valued and not commodified, one where they can be sensual without being sexualized and produce pleasure and not prurience. Joining Lillian in brothel-heaven, Mae says warmly, "It's great to be back, Lillian. I am home,"[20] and sings her final number, "Say, Mr. Fix-It Man." The interscenes underscore the play's nostalgic impulse, a longing for home that grows with each woman's departure.

After the play's penultimate blackout, we see Vera alone on stage, lying on the bench and trying to shield herself from the elements with a worn-out trench coat and newspaper. This image of poverty, so common on urban streets, is jarring here, since we have seen Vera in better times and listened to her stories of past flames and home-cooked food. Old and alone, Vera now skittishly digs through the garbage for a half-eaten sandwich. This stark moment is juxtaposed with the rest of the women, still visible at the side of the stage, secure within the brothel, singing "Sunny Side of the Street." This concluding image does not reify the past, but rather stages a dialectical relationship between past and present, history and memory. Here, reflective nostalgia is mobilized to defamiliarize the present, rather than to idealize the past, and to evoke a feeling of community and belonging lost in our contemporary moment. *Profession* exposes the vulnerability and erasure of two degraded social groups—prostitutes and the elderly—and the final blackout, which leaves none of the women visible, renders this erasure unsettlingly absolute.

With an absent artistic director and an uncommitted director, the Signature Theatre production of *Profession* was challenging for all involved. However, fittingly given the play's emphasis on female labor, it was the "divine actresses"—Marylouise Burke, Carlin Glynn, Katherine Helmond, Priscilla Lopez, and Joyce Van Patten—who staged the play. A difficult production process emerges when, Vogel contends, "directors . . . are doing it as a job rather than believing in the journey." She adds, "it's really a conflict of vision." Positive production experiences—such as Anne Bogart's *Baltimore Waltz*, Molly Smith's *The Mineola Twins*, Les Waters's *Hot 'n' Throbbing*, Mark Brokaw's *How I Learned to Drive*, and Tina Landau's *Civil War Christmas*—happen when directors act as "leaders, supporters," who both "embraced the play and made it their own with emotional vulnerability, courage, and passion." In these productions, the director, actors, designers, and playwright fought together "for the play to be the best it could be, rather than fighting [for] power over the room."[21] A successful staging of a Vogel play, it seems, requires collaboration and commitment to the process, rather than to predetermined end results.

Reviews of *Profession* were decidedly mixed. The *New York Times*'s Ben Brantley seemed surprised to find that "even in panty-flashing bordello drag, none of these hookers comes across as mere jokes," going on to describe Vogel as a "venturesome dramatist [who] provides a transforming theatrical wit, compassion and tolerance that keeps even queasy theatergoers hooked." However, Brantley concludes that "form is uneasily dictating content" in this "draggy production."[22] *Daily Variety*'s David Rooney stated his opinion more bluntly: "the play doesn't add up to an awful lot."[23] Both critics seem to yearn for a more naturalistic drama that has characters with inner psychological conflicts that might explain (away) their external suffering. That is not Vogel's play. *Profession* does not tell a universal, timeless story, but rather aims to make a pointed comment on the material effects of economic and political ideologies. The history it stages—which is America's history—matters, as do the bodies that bear its traces.

Fast Cars and Maidenform Bras: *The Mineola Twins*

Decades ago Susan Sontag pointed out that tragedy has never fit comfortably within the American dramatic tradition because its deterministic worldview goes against the national disposition, which leans heavily toward optimism and belief in progress. Comedy, however, with its emphasis on "conscious self-manipulation," "invulnerability" to serious suffering, and "role-playing," has been one of most productive and vital popular forms in American culture, resonating with a national character built on experimentation, mobility, and change.[24] Not only does comedy's depiction of a mutable world suggest the possibility of transformation, but it also foregrounds the experiences of the ordinary person, rather than the nobility, which speaks to the democratic impulse in American culture. From Mark Twain to Charlie Chaplin to Tina Fey, comedy has often served as the mode of American social critique. And yet comedy is by no means gender neutral. When writing *Mineola Twins*, Vogel wondered, "Would it be funny if women told the jokes?"[25] She contends, "comedy is very hard for women to do," since it "is traditionally a critique of society, and we still have problems accepting critiques from prodigal daughters, as I call them."[26] In all of her plays, Vogel uses comedy as a technique that both brings audiences closer and disorients their perspectives. Sometimes campy, often clever, and always disarming, Vogel's humor is the most recognizable trait of her playwriting. The humor in her plays is sometimes edged with something darker, however. She explains, "Whether I'm writing a comedy or a tragedy, they come from the same source. This is what I'm worried about. This is what I'm fearful about."[27] Comedy in Vogel's plays comes from a place of incongruity and irreverence, of questioning; it is not meant to reinforce the audience's assumptions, but to overturn them.

The Mineola Twins is Vogel's only farce. However, it also reworks some of the same questions asked in her earlier plays. As Vogel points out, "*Mineola Twins* was created by me thinking, 'Okay, I wrote *Hot* '*n' Throbbing*, it's time for me to laugh.'"[28] She has also suggested, "*The Mineola Twins* is very much me rethinking *And Baby Makes Seven*."[29] All three plays take the family as the central social unit, even as they question how family is seen and constructed. *Twins* might be best described as a family comedy within a political satire and a history of white, middle-class femininity within a social history of postwar American culture. The play uses the theatrical device of the split protagonist—in this case twin sisters—to allegorize a nation divided between political right and left and a female sexuality divided (still, again) between virgin and whore. Satirizing America's postwar fixation on apocalyptic endings and sex, *Twins* takes the audience on a thirty-year romp from the 1950s to 1989, presenting women as both products and producers of history, popular culture, and politics.

The signs of popular culture abound in *Twins*, and the play's protagonists, Myra and Myrna Richards—identical "except in the chestal area"—embody these signs. The twins perform sexualities that are morally coded as "good" and "bad," and yet their bodies contradict this sexual/moral encoding. Myrna, the virginal "'good' twin," is "stacked," while Myra, the promiscuous "'evil' twin," is "flat as a pancake."[30] Their incongruous embodiment suggests that the social body (an object constructed by history and culture and the condition of subjectivity) can be at odds with the lived body (the experience of subjectivity). As a broad comedy that does not hold back on boob jokes, *Twins* is emphatically a play of the body and a bawdy play. As Vogel states, "Breast jokes are rife with cultural anxiety about female sexuality."[31] Indeed, breasts signify simultaneously as sexual and maternal, unconsciously evoking the two feminine "types" that our culture prefers stay clearly differentiated—the sexualized woman and the idealized mother. The set design of Joe Mantello's 1998 New York production visually amplified the breast theme by superimposing onto the stage curtain an enormous image of a woman's torso clad in a Maidenform bra. This iconic symbol of 1950s femininity loomed over the play action, setting the farcical tone and accentuating the jokes that pervade the play. As Myra and Myrna come of age in postwar American popular culture, they present a vivid image of a divided postwar femininity, perhaps best captured in Revlon's massively successful 1950s "Fire and Ice" campaign: "In every good woman there is a little bad."

Popular music from each decade acts as the play's soundtrack, reminding the audience of the social messages conveyed through popular culture and retained as embodied memory. This once-resonant music can, decades later, bring back the affective energy of an entire social moment. Vogel suggests, "It would be nice to score this production with female vocalists of the period—Teresa Brewer, Doris Day, Vikki Carr, Nancy Sinatra, etc. These singers were on the Top Ten; as a country, we should not be allowed to forget this."[32] Media scholar Susan J. Douglas explains that popular culture of this period began offering women "different personas, some of them strong and empowering and others masochistic and defeating," from which to choose. For example, girls could sing along with "My Guy," "I Will Follow Him," and "Baby It's You," or, alternatively, they could rally around "Don't Make Me Over" and "You Don't Own Me."[33] Vogel argues that popular music is "important as a way of saying 'This was gender in 1960.'"[34] Like Vogel's satiric history in *Twins*, Douglas offers "a different sort of archaeology of the 1950s, 60s, and 70s," by excavating "remnants of a collective female past not usually thought of as making serious history."[35] In a description befitting the manic twins, Myra and Myrna, Douglas describes the experience of young women coming of age in the 1960s: "Pulled in opposite directions—told we are equal, yet told we were subordinate; told we could change history, yet told we were trapped by history."[36] Myrna and Myra embody this contradictory message, performing the divided politics and paranoia of postwar America.

Set in the middle-class Long Island community of Mineola, a landlocked neighborhood sandwiched between the hectic diversity of Queens, New York, and the eerie calm of Long Island's more affluent suburbs, the play blasts through three eras, each signaled by skirt lengths, wig styles, and current hot-button issues. The first set of scenes takes place during Eisenhower's administration in the 1950s; the second period takes place during Nixon's post in the late 1960s; and the last scenes take place in 1989, just as Bush Senior takes over from the Reagan administration. In the 1950s, the twins are polarized according to their sexuality; in the 1960s, they are divided by their political beliefs; and in the late 1980s, they are separated by their cultural values and lifestyles.

The play's high-energy action is punctuated by sci-fi-infused, surrealistic dream sequences. The subtitle, *A Comedy in Six Scenes*,

Four Dreams, and Six Wigs, reveals the play's tone, formal symmetry, and imaginative theatricality. Vogel frames the play as both a political satire and an epic battle of warring twins:

> I have been extremely upset at the Republican right taking over our Government. So I thought, okay, let's go back to the 50s, with its quintessential combination of comedy and terror. As a culture then, we went into science fiction, invaders from Mars, instead of looking at those who were invading us from within. . . . We used our fear of aliens to mask our terror at what was the heart of America. I used the image of twins that war: Jacob and Easu, a blood hatred between them. It's where we are emotionally as a country.[37]

Replacing warring brothers with battling sisters, *Twins* conjures the affective energy of an increasingly polarized and conflicted postwar America, from the Cold War panic of the 1950s and 60s, to the revolutionary activism of the 1970s, to the culture wars of the 1980s. The femininities embodied by Myrna—the "good girl" who dreams of becoming a wife and mother—and Myra—the "bad girl" who rebels against sexual mores and social institutions—work in the play as extensions of America's political polarization.

The play performs this polarization by having the same actor play both twins, a bipolar expression of a single body politic. In the 1998 New York premiere of *Twins* at Roundabout's Laura Pels Theatre,[38] Swoozie Kurtz played Myra and Myrna, winning an Obie award for her virtuoso performance of a schizoid femininity. Like a popular culture version of Divine in John Water's *Female Trouble*, Kurtz stormed through four decades, handling the countless changes in costume, character, mood, and political context with dazzling skill. However, unlike Divine, Kurtz was a female impersonating femininity. The female drag in *Twins* is a fusion of camp and female masquerade. Film critic Mary Ann Doane defines female masquerade as double mimesis that "designates the distance between the woman and the image of femininity."[39] This mimetic distance is comically exaggerated in *Twins* so that the acts, signs, and gestures of white, middle-class heteronormative femininity are hyperbolically performed and rendered absurd. Skirting around gender binaries by having a female actor impersonating femininity, *Twins* deploys a drag that relies on the incongruity between feminine artifice and female bodies, between female spectacle and female agency, and between cultural images and affective impulses.

In its episodic structure, its double-role casting, and its use of history as a theatrical device, *Twins* is Vogel's most Brechtian play. However, the play also has a feminist focus not found in Brecht. Elin Diamond explains that while "Brecht's account of the *gestus* alerts us to the vectors of historical change written into dramatic texts, . . . he makes scant provision for gender in representation or as the ground of social struggle."[40] Diamond develops a gestic feminist theory that "would 'alienate' or foreground those moments in a playtext in which social attitudes about gender could be made visible." This visibility is achieved through the defamiliarizing "not . . . but," a fusion of the Brechtian *gestus* and Derridian "differences within."[41] The theatricality of "not . . . but" enables the spectator to see in the actor's words and gestures choices not made and the differences *within* identity. In this way, the "not . . . but" mobilizes performance to denaturalize gender and sexuality, exposing the acts and gestures as historically constructed and variable. As noted in the introduction, the Brechtian "not . . . but" is deployed in Vogel's work as a kind of "yes and!"—a spontaneous, supplementary impulse that initiates an ongoing cultural dialogue. *Twins*, as a whole, enacts this supplementary impulse, as a farce inserted into the grand narrative of postwar American history. Like the "not . . . but," the "yes, and!" casts each gesture and action as part of a broader social situation. However, the "yes and!" articulates the broader canonical conversation that Vogel is participating in as a playwright and a feminist.

Vogel suggests two ways to do the play: "1. With good wigs. 2. With bad wigs." "Personally," she writes, "I prefer the second way" (97). The various wigs that the twins wear signal a certain type of femininity, as well as a distinct historical period. Together, the wigs function as a kind of *gestus*, linking femininity as a masquerade to the historical and cultural forces that construct it. The other characters in the play include: Jim and Sarah (played by the same actor), who are the romantic partners of Myrna and Myra, respectively; Ben and Kenny (also played by the same actor), who are Myra and Myrna's respective sons; and two mute male characters, who move furniture, play psychiatric aides, and act as wardrobe assistants. Helping to explain the apocalyptic fears and erotic energy that animate the play and the historical period it covers, Vogel writes, "With the single exception of Sarah, all characters should be played in a constant state of high hormonal excitement" (96). The final casting element includes, like in *Hot 'n' Throbbing*, "The Voice." However, unlike in *Hot* where The Voice acts as an omniscient mouthpiece of male authority, here The Voice is the shared consciousness of the twins. It is both sisters' voices—or rather "the amplified prerecorded version of the actor who plays Myra and Myrna." It is their shared consciousness, formed from the history and culture within which they act: "Either brainwashing or subliminal seduction, it's the way the sisters talk to each other. In dreams" (97).

Mantello (who originated the role of the Third Man in Vogel's *The Baltimore Waltz*) exploited the theatricality of *Twins* to achieve a kind of campy cartoon aesthetic that, in many ways, captures the way the 1950s and 1960s are often remembered—as one-dimensional Technicolor images and stereotypes. In this production, the twins' extreme political and sexual roles—far left/far right and good virgin/ evil whore—contrast with the more fluid political and gendered dispositions of the supporting characters. The cross-gender casting of the secondary characters promotes this fluidity. Whether man, woman, or boy, Mo Gaffney (as Jim/Sarah) and Mandy Siegfried (as Kenny/Ben) played all of their parts without ever fully "becoming" the gender of a character. They even flaunted their cross-gender role-playing by performing their costume changes on stage, in front of the closed curtain. During these interscene strip shows, Siegfried and Gaffney physically switched roles, making visible the performative codes and signs of gender. With the help of the two mute male assistants, they visually transformed from one gender to another and one sexuality to another. To heighten the theatricality of this gender switch, both actors paused in the middle of their transformation to remain briefly in an androgynous state. Wearing only generic undergarments and hair covers, each performed a little solo dance, the movements alone signaling the gender they were performing. For example, as Siegfried changed from Kenny to Ben, her dance movements were characterized by the sharp, jerky movements associated with a youthful masculinity. These masculine movements contrasted with Siegfried's own biologically female body, which she momentarily foregrounded by mimicking the motions of classic striptease and exposing her midriff. Just as quickly, she resumed the role of "boy," rolling down her t-shirt to cover her midriff and changing the rhythm of her movements to signal the confident and cocky struts of a teenage boy. Siegfried's brief striptease reminded the audience not only that gender is formed out of learned, performed acts and gestures and attitudes, but also that we look at these gendered performances differently depending on the bodies performing them. The play, as a whole, denaturalizes gender and gives the seemingly natural, neutral postures of masculinity and femininity a historical context.

Myra and Myrna can be read as a parody of the America Dream defined as a fantasy of material success, carried out with an attitude of unwavering optimism, and achieved through fierce competitiveness. Doris Day's "I'll See You in My Dreams" scores this parody, and as her signature song blares from the jukebox, Myrna discloses her Dream to her boyfriend Jim:

> Once I've learned stenography and typing—when my rising young executive-husband comes home with work from the office—he can put his feet up on the hassock while I take dictation. We'll have a son, and by the time he's three or four, we can afford a three-bedroom house in Great Neck with an office downstairs. Then we'll have a dog, and maybe a daughter too—(109–10)

Myra's rebellious revision of the Dream sets up the sisters' contrasting worldviews and dispositions. Also to Jim, Myra proclaims:

> There's never been a movie made that's even close to how I'm going to live. I'm making it up from scratch. No marriage. No children. No suburbs. Just freedom! (122)

Opposing her plans, Jim insists, "But you're a girl! You can't do that!" (122), and their gender debate culminates in Jim's essentialist conclusion:

> Men are defined by what they do–their actions in the world. It's different for you—you're a girl. There are . . . absolutes in their world for girls. Girls don't do, they just are. (125)

Drawing on the tenacious correlation between active-masculine and passive-feminine that has traditionally characterized gender roles and relations, Jim's reductive argument encapsulates the gender conformity we associate with the 1950s, even as it is visually undermined by the obviously female actor playing his role. Jim dates both twins, though for different reasons, defining them according to their sexual dispositions, which, for women, are also moral dispositions. Myrna's chastity provides a stable moral ground of "absolute goodness" (115), while Myra's defiance and sexual promiscuity provide him with physical satisfaction.

The manic tone of the playworld swings between frenzied desire and panicked paranoia. Lust and paranoia, it is suggested, are the primary affective modes of political engagement in postwar American culture. In the 1950s, Myrna says of her sister: "she . . . scares me" (106). In the late 1980s, liberal Myra expresses a similar sentiment about her right-wing son, Ben, confessing, "he . . . scares me" (175). In *Twins*, the threatening other, in turns out, is very, *very* close to home. As the twins react against one another from their teenage years to middle age, they each stake their patriotic claim—"We will never give this country back" (166, 176). Driving one another to exhaustion, the sisters perform an obstinate form of citizenship grounded in reactionary fear, rather than productive dialogue. The only way they are able to communicate is subliminally, irrationally—in their dreams.

Dreams were a recurrent theme of 1950s popular culture, emerging from the popularization of Freudian psychology and the enthusiasm of a growing consumer culture. Media studies scholar Juliann Sivulka writes, "Whether it was a dream house, Dream Whip, dream kitchen, dream cake, or 'Dream Lover,' the opulence and technology of the decade optimistically suggested that many of these dreams could come true."[42] Of course, manufacturing dreams works productively to drive a consumer culture built on desire, while also sustaining the promise of the American Dream: if you can dream it, then, with enough hard work, you can obtain it. Mobilizing the concept of dreams as a marketing campaign, most famously in Maidenform's "I Dreamed . . ." advertising campaign, championed fantasy fulfillment and fueled the imagination of women who might otherwise have felt stifled by domestic life. The emphasis on dreams also worked to create a dual image of femininity—the glamorous dream woman and the everyday housewife. Both personas were available to all women, it was suggested, provided they don the right bra, the right shade of lipstick, and the right hair color. *Twins* burlesques this mass marketing of a dream femininity and, by extension, a dream nation, with a farce that pits what the dreams promised—prosperity, beauty, sexual allure, and security—against the emotional climate they created—anxiety, fear, competition, and paranoia. Using an aesthetic befitting dreams, *Twins* resists mimesis and realism in favor of a frenetic surrealism.

Nightmares were also an undercurrent of the 1950s and 1960s. Science fiction films proliferated in this period, targeting and titillating a youth audience who absorbed the redundant plots and simplistic morality as a kind of postwar worldview. As film critic Peter Biskind explains, "the Manichean Us/Them habit of thought . . . was an occupational hazard of the cold-war battle of ideas."[43] Sci-fi operated as an escape valve for expressing cultural anxieties surrounding not only Communism and the Bomb but also social tensions such as racism and homophobia. The basic premise of these films, however imaginatively recycled, remained fairly consistent: a terrifying alien invader threatened the safety and stability of the family, community, nation, and/or globe. Depending on the political leanings of the film producers, the alien was either something to be purged at all costs (the right's version) or befriended as a peaceful ally (the left's version). The appeal of both kinds of sci-fi films is in the way they contained fears and anxieties about "the other" within the conventions of genre. The anxieties regarding an alien invader reinforced divisions between America and the world, as well as between left and right. It is precisely these anxieties, divisions, and reinforcements that *Twins* unravels. The play exploits the tension between security and paranoia, fear and eroticism, while satirizing the codes of gender and sexuality that were constructed to uphold a sense of political security and stability. Using the titillating terror of the Bomb as the animating energy of the playworld, *Twins* puts into motion both connotations of the word *bomb* in this era: an enemy threat and also a "very sexy woman."[44]

The play's second dream sequence, entitled "Myrna in the Hospital. Myrna in Hell," blends dream and nightmare to theatricalize the affective dissonance of postwar American consciousness. Set in mental hospital, where Myrna has been committed by her sister, the scene fuses the conventions of the Hollywood musical and the horror film, with Myrna wearing a wig à la Bride of Frankenstein and swinging the arms of a straitjacket with the grace of Ginger Rogers in heels.

Her sidekicks are two mute male orderlies, who try to fasten her into the straitjacket as they dance alongside her in perfectly choreographed time. The juxtaposition of dreamy musical and horror is accentuated by Myrna's monologue describing a scene in which she murders her sister and stages it as a suicide. Beginning in the future tense and then shifting to the present, Myrna temporally displaces her murder fantasy in a dreamlike way, explaining how she braces her father's rifle "at a jaunty angle" so that her sister's "big toe jams the trigger while her mouth sucks the double barrel—just like old times with the football team." The black humor culminates when Myrna says to her sister, "This is real, you asshole, this is happening" (143). As the sound of a beating heart thunders through the theater, Myrna pulls the trigger, and a bouquet of flowers explodes from her sister's neck. The slapstick horror emphasizes Myra and Myrna's absurdly violent codependence; they cannot escape the other, cannot destroy each other, and cannot survive without each other. Four decades later, this has crystallized into a national political disposition of distrust and opposition.

The play uses farce, ironically, to suggest that we need to take more seriously women's central roles in culture and history, rather than dismissing their contributions as inconsequential. Douglas asks why "girls and women come across as the kitsch of the 1960s—flying nuns, witches, genies . . . go-go-boot-clad dancers in cages,"[45] while figures like James Dean, Elvis, and Marlon Brando are considered important figures in social history. In *Twins*, Vogel takes the kitsch of the past forty years—along with its feminized connotations—and fuses it with politics. The effect is camp. More precisely, the effect makes visible the kitsch-camp hierarchy. Eve Kosofsky Sedgwick distinguishes camp-recognition, which is a performative act of consecration, from kitsch-attribution, which is a devaluing judgment. Sedgwick differentiates kitsch and camp in the following way:

> Unlike kitsch-attribution, camp-recognition doesn't ask, "what kind of debased creature could possibly be the right audience for this spectacle?" Instead, it says, *what if*: What if the right audience for this were exactly *me*? What if, for instance, the resistant, oblique, tangential investments of attention and attraction that I am able to bring to this spectacle are actually uncannily responsive to the resistant, oblique, tangential investments of the person, or of some of the peo-

ple, who created it? And what if, furthermore, others who I don't know or recognize can see it from the same "perverse" angle.[46]

All of Vogel's plays pose this performative "what if?": What if we looked at this from a different angle? What if women were at the center of this history? What if we placed history and politics in a different register? The "perverse angle" in *Twins* encourages us to see women as both subjects and objects of history, as both makers of culture and products manufactured by an American marketing industry, and as both the authors and butts of boob jokes. It is no wonder that Myrna and Myra are odds with the social world, with each other, and with themselves.

Cultural signifiers such as Ford cars and Maidenform bras in *Twins* reveal the social forces at work in the construction of postwar middle-class heterosexuality. As a feminine symbol of masculine power, the automobile is perhaps the most resonant icon of the 1950s, symbolizing affluence, mobility, freedom, and autonomy. Working as a marketer of Ford cars in *Twins*, Jim talks excitedly about the new model that he is involved in developing. He tells Myrna:

> I'm pledged to secrecy—but you've never seen anything like this car!
> ... And wait till you see the grille on this baby—well, I helped a little to come up with the design—it looks just like . . . like—*(Jim gets flushed)*—Well, I can't say. Guys are going to go crazy over this buggy.
> (109)

The symbolic parallels between the smooth yet articulated curves of the grille of a 1950s car and the smooth yet articulated curves of a woman in a Maidenform bra have produced enduring symbolic connections between sex and cars. And yet it was not only men creating images in the 1950s and 1960s (as *Mad Men* would have us believe) and then selling them to female consumers; women participated in the production of these images and held powerful positions in the advertising industry. As Sivulka points out, the three most successful ad campaigns of the 1950s—Revlon, Clairol, and Maidenform— were written by women. And to "the automotive industry, women represented the largest, most powerful market in the world." Women were hired to offer "input on color harmony, luggage space, seat ad-

Figure 6: *The Mineola Twins*. Left to right: Swoosie Kurtz and Mo Gaffney. Roundabout Theatre, New York City, 1999. Photo: Joan Marcus.

justments."[47] As Jim tells Myrna, "The firm's even hired this poetess to come up with lyrical names—like Fiesta or Bronco or Ford Epiphany!" (109). As a young man, Jim is driven by his libido and his love of cars, whereas the twins' sexuality and ambition are more tightly constrained. Wanting more than what the 1950s promised to women, Myra hopes her "next decade is better than this one" (125).

Leaving the 1950s behind, *Twins* moves swiftly forward to 1969. Here, the twins and the country are dealing with Nixon, Vietnam, the explosion of social movements including feminism, and the ever-present threat of the Cold War. Jim has become a failed organization man, and the sisters are becoming increasingly politicized and paranoid. Myra is a radical antiwar activist, while Myrna is a Long Island housewife with a philandering husband and a nervous condition stemming from her time spent in the psychiatric ward. Myrna retaliates for being committed by her sister by giving the police information on Myra's whereabouts. Consequently, Myra does time in jail for her countercultural behavior. Here, she "discovers" lesbianism, eventually moving in with Sarah. Whether crazy or criminal, the sisters become increasingly divided as the decades pass. Crucially, the play is not arguing for a unity of opposites, a reduction of two into one. Rather, it points to the need for dialogue between the warring factions. The Voice reminds the audience that the twins share an unconscious dialogue, however conflicted and terror filled it is. The play works to raise that dialogue to the level of consciousness, thereby highlighting its comic absurdity and implicit violence.

By 1989, amid the aftermath of two Reagan administrations and a decades-long Cold War, competition and paranoia have developed into a national disposition. The looming Maidenform bra that opened the play is, in scene 5, replaced by a looming image of George H. W. Bush. These visual cues in Mantello's production mark a shift from women as products of popular culture—with femininity marketed as image, commodity—to women participating in the political conflicts of a divided nation. The first Bush term, or more precisely the end of two terms of the Reagan administration, marks a point of extreme political polarity in American social history. As the culture wars deepened the divide between right and left, the reassertion of family values worked to exacerbate distinctions between normative and deviant lifestyles. American studies scholar Sharon Monteith explains that the tactic of the right in the 1980s was to persuade the American people that "conservatism [would bring] a return to cultural norms following the 'disharmony' of the sixties."[48] Moreover, with a deregulated free market, "family values," like those of the 1950s, became a highly regulated image and commodity that was marketed to consumers as the renewed American Dream.

With more and more women in the 1980s asserting reproductive rights and entering the workforce, the political fissures in this period focused, perhaps not surprisingly, on women's bodies and on the reassertion of family values. *Twins* demonstrates the way politics often plays out through women's bodies, their choices, and their daily lives, provocatively pointing to the way "women" become a political "issue" when significant social changes begin to occur. Since the midcentury, as women began to enter the public sphere en masse and assume more agency over their bodies, conservative images and narratives in popular culture reacted by relentlessly reinforcing their functions as either sexual objects or maternal caregivers. The right continues to challenge the legality of abortion, claiming the fetus's right to life, even as it champions military expansion and the death penalty. As manic citizens, the twins play out these contradictions and parodically embody the absurd collapse of politics, personal "values," and popular culture in contemporary America public life.

By the Bush administration, the twins' domestic lives have become the reverse of their political values. Myra has settled into a comfortable domestic life with her lesbian partner, Sarah, and son, Ben. Sarah's relatively natural presence and the congruity between character and actor playing her (both female) create a canny realism. These casting and acting incongruities work to denaturalize heteronormativity, while making homosexuality seem ordinary. Ensconced in her domestic life with Myra, Sarah, ironically, comes across as the play's straightest character. And while Myra was the radical in the 1960s and 1970s, the conservative Myrna, now divorced, has joined the Reagan-era feminist backlash and become a right-wing radio shock jock à la Rush Limbaugh. As an icon of the American right, Myrna decries the influences of multiculturalism and "tofu-eating-feminazi-fetus-flushing," calling for the reinstatement of true American "cultural values" (167). Her son, Kenny, perhaps predictably, has turned rebelliously to the left, looking to his freewheeling aunt Myra for guidance, while Myra's son, Ben, looks to Myrna as his right-wing role model, adopting her book on family values, *Profiles in Chastity*, as his life manual. The polarization in this period is almost complete.

The play's climax comes when Myrna plants a bomb in the abortion clinic at which Myra works. Realizing that her sister is inside, The Voice-as-Myrna frantically warns her sister to "get to the door NOW" (182). Unlike the Voice Over's helpless warning to Charlene in *Hot*, The Voice in *Twins* has more authority here. As the unifying force of the sisters' schizophrenic subjectivity, The Voice (of culture, of history, of consciousness) is the only thing they share. This shared Voice, however, emerges only when the threat of annihilation creates an atmosphere of frenzy; it is only then that the sisters listen to each other. Suggesting the need for more deliberate, productive dialogue, the play's final dream sequence shows Myra *"summoning up all of her courage"* to say to Myrna, "And I really wish . . . I wish we could be closer" (184).

The play ends with a dream sequence in which the domestic

space is invaded by apocalyptic nightmare. The scene opens with the sisters' voices talking to each other and longing for some kind of reconciliation. This is Myra's dream, and it is interrupted by a *"crash and flash of light"* (184), which replays the "real-life" disaster that took place in the previous scene when Myrna bombed the abortion clinic. Sarah awakens Myra from her fitful dream, reassuring her jokingly, "We almost blew up, just like any other happy nuclear family." (185). Recalling a time when free-floating fears were not part of everyday life, Myra says nostalgically to Sarah, "Sometimes I miss the fifties," adding, "In the fifties we were scared of Boris Karloff. We weren't scared of riding the Long Island Railroad or working in clinics" (185). Although the play ends on an unsettling tone that highlights the (still) deeply conflicted nature of American politics, it also depicts a new family scene, with the image of Sarah and Myra lying together in their bed. As Sarah says, "Sleep tight, honey," to Myra, The Voice replies, "Sweet Dreams" (187), and Doris Day belts out, more ominously now, "I'll See You in My Dreams." The American Dream is, in *Twins*, revised as part sci-fi film, part domestic drama, and part campy comedy.

Since critics were already familiar with Vogel through *The Baltimore Waltz* and *How I Learned to Drive*, *Twins* was seen as an unsophisticated attempt at political farce. Vogel had wished to have the "ha-ha funny" tone of *Twins* produced before she dug in with *Drive*, which implicitly says, "This is how it feels on the inside."[49] However, the reverse happened, with *Drive* premiering in New York first—to wide acclaim—and *Twins* following its trail of praise, only to be received as a frivolous follow-up to its more serious and sensitive predecessor. Ben Brantley warns that spectators familiar with Vogel's work via *Drive* will "have difficulty recognizing her voice here," and he criticizes Vogel for "manipulating cultural clichés" in *Twins*, without "necessarily ris[ing] above them."[50] He contends that "much of [Vogel's] gender-twisting satire would undoubtedly seem stale to a downtown audience who have sat through more advanced variations on the same themes by performers like Lypsinka and Five Lesbian Brothers." Comparing Vogel's rousing burlesque to the edgier lesbian theater downtown, Brantley fails to take *Twins* on its own terms, as a legitimate political farce that is closer to Christopher Durang than Split Britches. Brantley dismisses the sisters as caricatures who are "never much more than the sums of their slogans and fashion accessories."[51] Vincent Canby of the *Times* thought that "the politics of the play are fairly rudimentary,"[52] and the title of his review alone—"The Mad History of Women as Told by Twin Barbies"—suggests a dismissal of the play as a kitschy take on pop culture. Reducing Myrna and Myra to replicas of the world's most ubiquitous doll and describing the play as an insane "history of women," Canby betrays a sexist snobbery. Women's history in America is, for Canby, reducible to commodified images of popular culture, while satiric humor, written and enacted by women, can only be "rudimentary." One wonders, however, if there was resistance to watching women in drag, acting as both comedians and representatives of political positions and national values, as opposed to sexual icons—Barbies. Perhaps Brantley and Canby could not reconcile seeing the Mineola sisters as political representatives, while at the same time listening to them hurl crude jokes at one another.

Michael Feingold of the *Village Voice* pointed to the play's "femaleness" as a feature that "some male critics will no doubt resent." For Feingold, the success of the play was in the "triumphant performance" of Swoosie Kurtz. "Kurtz," Feingold writes, "is definitely the show." Perhaps the most damning comment came in Feingold's comparison to of Vogel's work to Wendy Wasserstein's most successful play: "*The Mineola Twins* is a simple, loosely strung narrative, a sort of low-rent *Heidi Chronicles* times two."[53] Comparing Vogel's satiric portrait of a schizophrenic American femininity to Wasserstein's realist representation of a flailing female protagonist suggests the limited vocabulary available to critics for talking about plays written by women, especially female-centered ones. Able only to relate Vogel's play to another female-authored play with a female protagonist, Feingold's comparison betrays the limited imagination of critics, who could see plays by women only in relation to the ghetto genre of "women's theater."

Despite the critiques, *Twins* has been produced regularly over the past decade and a half, becoming increasingly relevant as more women participate in the political sphere and in popular culture parodies. In a well-received 2007 production in Baltimore, the play was described as a story about "these schizophrenic times" told "through two women." One reviewer wrote, "*The Mineola Twins* is a comedy, and now that boomers are getting more reflective, it also deserves to be classified as part of an expanding genre: the critical history of postwar self-absorption."[54] The play's popular success and political relevance have trumped its initial presumed lack of sophistication. While Monica Lewinsky and Hillary Clinton were the duo that many critics referred to after the play's 1998 New York production, in 2008 Hillary Clinton and Sarah Palin were the cultural touchstones. Thanks to Tina Fey's and Amy Poehler's imitations of Palin and Clinton on *Saturday Night Live*, women, politics, and comedy have become quite a relevant combination. And as the right continues to search for its "Hillary," the line between "real" politics and social satire becomes increasingly difficult to distinguish. The twins are, like Fey and Poehler, meant to be imitations, not realistic characters; they are allegorical representations of a polarized national disposition, not realistic, moral examples of good/bad teenage girls, wives, or mothers. *Twins* works when Myra and Myrna are taken seriously as social satirists and national representatives. And in these first decades of the twenty-first century, with the convergence of politics and popular culture fairly complete, they are an increasingly pertinent pair.

Vogel contends, "I actually take what I do as a playwright very seriously. I'm always asking, 'What should we do? What should playwrights do?' Go back and look at what the Greeks did. One could not be a Greek playwright and write a tragedy without writing a satiric comedy on the same subject."[55] If *Twins* presents a farcical vision of the split within American politics and American femininity, *How I Learned to Drive* gives us another picture of the past four decades—the rupture between the body and voice within female subjectivity. Published together as *The Mammary Plays*, *The Mineola Twins* (1997) and *How I Learned to Drive* (1998) work dialectically as two sides of postwar American social history. Vogel reveals that she wrote *Twins* and *Drive* as companion plays—a kind of macrocosm/microcosm of late-twentieth-century American culture. She "wanted the plays to travel the same time period, from the end of the 1950s to the end of the 1980s," with "one play . . . looking at the culture from the outside and one . . . exploring how the culture feels on the inside."[56] The exterior, pop aesthetic of *Twins* works as the counterpart to the more minimalist style of *Drive*. Both plays, as Vogel suggests, present a "history of white, middle-class femaleness."[57] While *Twins* uses fake breasts and wigs to highlight the myriad ways these body parts have been the focus of a cultural fixation on sexualized female bodies, *Drive* uses a female narrator to tell us something about inhabiting such a body. In *Drive*, the frenetically divided Myra and Myrna reemerge in L'il Bit, who tells a complex story of her internal division between objectified body and subjective voice, a split negotiated through recollected memories, reactivated affects, and retraced roadways.

CHAPTER FIVE

Memory Lessons:
How I Learned to Drive

> Theatre . . . is the repository of cultural memory, but, like the
> memory of each individual, it is also subject to continual
> adjustment and modification as the memory is recalled in new
> circumstances and contexts. The present experience is always
> ghosted by previous experiences and associations while these
> ghosts are simultaneously shifted and modified by the processes
> of recycling and recollection.
>
> —Marvin Carlson, *The Haunted Stage:*
> *Theatre as Memory Machine*[1]

How I Learned to Drive is Vogel's most celebrated play and the work
that earned her international recognition as an important voice in
American theater. In contrast to the broad caricatures in *Twins*,
Drive is a precisely sketched story of a young girl's coming of age—
and coming apart. While critics have defined *Drive* as a sensitive depiction of "child abuse"[2] and even "a love story,"[3] Vogel says, "I actually describe *Drive* as a comedy," adding, "Of course it's not, but the
first half very much functions as comedy. At some elemental level, it
is who I am. . . . Maybe it's a survival strategy. Some people say that
this comes from Jewish genes."[4] Juxtaposing comic scenes with moving and at times disturbing ones, the play interrupts, at every turn,
conventions of spectatorship and identification. Vogel wrote *Drive*,
in part, as a response to the uneven representation of sexual harassment in David Mamet's 1992 polemical play, *Oleanna*.[5] In contrast
to the linear naturalism of *Oleanna*, which makes its conclusion
logically inevitable, *Drive* has a recursive structure that defies reso-

lution. *Drive* is not a psychological portrait of sexual abuse, nor is it concerned with getting at the truth of the present by uncovering the trauma of the past. Rather, the play looks closely at the process of remembering, examining the imprints and traces of the past that turn up as memories in the present. In particular, it looks at the way memories are continually reshaped and revised to construct present meanings, perspectives, and subjectivities.

In *Drive*, as in her other plays, Vogel is interested in looking at "how we are trained to desire."[6] As she states:

> A lot of people are trying to turn this into a drama about an individual family. To me it is not. It is a way of looking on a microcosmic level at . . . how we are taught at an extremely early age to look at female bodies. One of the tag lines I had in my head when I was writing this play was, it takes a whole village to molest a child. . . . At what age are we sexualizing our children in a consumer culture to sell blue jeans and underwear?[7]

Drive shows how our sexualities and our subjectivities are not "ours," but rather the products of culture and history. It shows a culture that separates sexual and social being and teaches young women to see their sexuality as something to flaunt and also to hide, something that defines them and yet is not theirs to define. With popular images and music punctuating the playworld, we are continually reminded that this is not the private confession of an individual protagonist, but a public staging of a sexually fixated culture.

Although *Drive* is a play that seems to open itself to psychoanalytic interpretations and analyses of its main character, it is more productively approached as a play that mobilizes memories to pose questions about the present. In its first New York revival since its world premiere at the Vineyard Theatre in 1997 (with Mark Brokaw directing), *How I Learned to Drive* was mounted at Second Stage Theatre in January 2012, with Kate Whoriskey directing. This production had a vintage red Buick sitting center stage, which stood in sharp contrast against the backdrop of a very blue sky. With two chairs comprising the rest of the set, the stage design assumed an almost surrealistic quality, with the car signifying as the vivid material remains of memory, writ large. Reviewing the 2012 production, Ben Brantley described it as "a wry and poetic memory play."[8] Similarly, *Variety*'s Marilyn Stasio called it "an expressionistic memory play."[9]

Vogel has described *Drive* as "a history play," explaining further, "It's a way of using history to see what we are naturalizing now."[10] Dramatizing history as memory, the play stages the last four decades of the twentieth century from the perspective of a now forty-something woman, L'il Bit, who looks back on her adolescence and, specifically, her relationship with her Uncle Peck.

Literary scholars Alan Shepard and Mary Lamb succinctly explain the significance of memory in the Vogel oeuvre and its relationship to broader, national history: "Vogel makes her characters preoccupied with the topos of memory itself as well as the memories recollected on stage. . . . As they open up symbolic spaces that house some piece of their history, they vicariously engage us in their efforts to tell the memories anew in light of the personal and national changes that form the backdrop of the action."[11] As L'il Bit retraces the affective imprints her memories have left on her life, we see the changes those memories bring to the present as she recalls them. Likewise, her memory lessons teach the audience the social history surrounding her adolescence—the sensory landscape, evoked through images, songs, popular culture references, and also the political landscape, evoked through Peck's service in World War II and L'il Bit's factory work and "string of dead-end jobs"[12] during the Nixon recession in 1970. Both Peck and L'il Bit drink to cope with feelings of isolation within their social milieu, and their individual struggles are implicitly linked to the battles America was waging overseas.

Focusing on memory moves us away from reading L'il Bit's story as the psychological journey of an individual protagonist and toward a broader understanding of the way memory renders conceptually and experientially porous the boundaries between individual and collective, past and present. French philosopher Gilles Deleuze describes memory as the point of contact between self and world, "a membrane which puts an outside and an inside into contact, makes them present to each other, confronts them or makes them clash. The inside is psychology, the past, involution, a whole psychology of depths. . . . The outside is . . . the future, evolution."[13] This dramatic encounter of inside (memory) touching outside (world) characterizes the fundamental encounter of all theater and is especially significant in *Drive* as L'il Bit's memories confront and clash with the memories of the audience. Not at all individual, private, or secret, memory is both the world turned inward—the world experienced as self—and the world turned outward—the self staged as world. Remembering also enacts a unique temporal convergence, as the remains of the past in the present (Carlson's ghosts) get recollected and recreated as the future. Historian Jonathon Boyarin also points out that "memory is neither something preexistent and dormant in the past nor a projection from the present, but a potential collaboration between present consciousness and the experience and expression of the past."[14] Adding that "identity and memory are virtually the same concept,"[15] Boyarin explains that it is through memory that subjectivity is constructed. Subjectivities are perpetually being remade through the process of remembering, since "memory is not only constantly disintegrating and disappearing but constantly being created and elaborated."[16] This is precisely the drama of memory- and self-remaking that *Drive* stages, as L'il Bit recollects pieces of her past, turning memories of shame and alienation into present forgiveness.

Drive employs a nonchronological structure, using detours and reverse movements to mimic the workings of memory, to reorient structures of empathy, and to map out a different temporal terrain of sexuality and subjectivity. L'il Bit remembers her past with the distance of a director observing a rehearsal, and her detached recollections characterize this not as a story of sexual abuse, but rather as a performance of memory's role in shaping subjectivity and embodiment through particular arrangements of time and attitudes toward the past. The play displaces the conflict-climax-resolution pattern of realist drama with an associative pattern that uses juxtaposition to forge connections between the lessons of sexual development and gender training and the contradictory consequences of those lessons. Lessons in heteronormative femininity, L'il Bit realizes, involve seeing your body not as your own and not as a source of pleasure or agency. Moving between exposure and concealment, L'il Bit gives shape to her memories and forms them into a newly made self, a self made legible through the structuring power of narrative, the indelible impressions of affect, and the reparative possibilities of performance.

As in *Twins*, popular culture of the 1960s, 1970s, and 1980s is woven into all aspects of *Drive* as a way to situate the characters as social subjects within a specific cultural and historical context. In her "Author's Note," Vogel suggests, "The vaudeville sections go well to the Tijuana Brass or any music that sounds like a *Laugh-In* soundtrack," adding that music "rife with pedophilish (?) reference," such as "Little Surfer Girl" and "This Girl is a Woman Now," might be chosen (5). The broad comedy of *Twins* is not so far away from *Drive*. The popular music situates L'il Bit's memories within the broader cultural memory, infusing the troubling subject matter with a pop culture aesthetic. Moreover, by setting this story to a 1960s pop music soundtrack, Vogel further undermines the moralizing or therapeutic impulses that would play this story as tragedy or confessional drama. *Drive* encourages the kind of complex, contradictory perspective that political correctness seeks to smooth over. As Vogel insists, "In my sense of the political, you can never be politically correct. To be political means to open up a dialogue, not to be 'correct.'" She wanted, with *Drive*, "to see if audiences would *allow* themselves to find this erotic; otherwise, they only see victimization without empowerment."[17] If the spectator finds the relationship erotic, they are immediately implicated in Peck's seduction of L'il Bit and perhaps then compelled to reflect and empathize rather than demonize.

Drive draws, in part, from Vogel's fascination with Vladimir Nabokov's *Lolita*, which she has read more than a half a dozen times since high school.[18] Like *Lolita*, Vogel's *Drive* is a story of seduction, a picaresque tale, and a satiric examination of American culture. Unlike *Lolita*, *Drive* puts the young woman in the driver's seat, giving her the narrative voice through which to direct the story. Teaching audiences to identify with female protagonists is part of Vogel's ongoing strategy as a playwright. As she points out, "women have been trained to empathize with male subjects," whereas "men have not learned how to empathize directly with a female character."[19] To retrain both men and women to identity with female characters is to open up new ways of seeing gender and of being in relationship. Blending empathy, humor, and suffering, Vogel brings into often uncomfortable focus the implications of the "Lolita" myth—the myth of a female sexuality that is both innocent and cunning, available and active—placing this myth in direct tension with the stigmatized pedophile. Vogel invokes familiar icons of American culture—cars and popular music—and familiar American stereotypes—dysfunctional families, seductresses, sexual predators, confused teenagers, troubled middle-aged men—and invites us to see them from a new angle.

Vogel's use of negative empathy, here and elsewhere, invites us to identify with those we might rather disavow. This feeling-with-the-other is neither the traditional empathy of realist drama (where we identify with a protagonist because she is familiar) nor the pathos of tragedy (where we identify with a flawed hero because we too have flaws). By encouraging the audience to identify with Peck, the play transforms what is shameful or threatening into an experience of recognition. Literary critic Andrew Kimbrough cogently argues that *Drive* "testifies to the radical and self-implicating belief that community begins when we recognize that what we find most abhorrent and intolerable in others is really that which we find most fearful and shameful about ourselves."[20] Vogel articulates a similar perspective in her views of a post-9/11 national climate: "The only way Americans can bond right now is against the terror without. That's the only way we can ignore what I call the terror within."[21] Demonizing Peck for his "deviant" desire is a way of defining "normal" (heteronormative) desire. These categories, however, evade the way, as a culture, we fetishize youth and sexualize girls and boys at an increasingly young age. As sexual images fill the cultural landscape, we become ever more vigilant about identifying and policing nonnormative sexualities. Kimbrough reminds us that "the past two decades have witnessed a sharp rise in the awareness of perceived sex crimes against children and the propagation of the unquestioned belief that these crimes are on the rise."[22] Indeed, the naming of the crime itself is a performative gesture, a making of the morally and socially pathological category "pedophile," which then fuels the paranoia surrounding his or her classification and secures the boundaries of the "normal." The escape valve for this paranoia is the voyeuristic consumption of hypersexualized images of young people, which offers some of the same titillations sought by the pedophile, but from a morally sanctioned position.

Drive is not structured with conventional acts and scenes. Instead, scene changes are signaled by gear shifts—first, second, reverse, and neutral—which metaphorically register both time and direction, while reinforcing memory as the play's structuring principle. The trope of the driving lesson is extended through narrated excerpts from a driving manual and the occasional road sign, warning of "dangerous curves," "sharp turns," and "bumpy roads ahead." These devices displace psychological realism and linear action with varying speeds and movements, all of which reorient the audience's sense of time and character. The play's form and its nonrealist staging revise the structure of shame and social stigmatization associated with sexual abuse. That Peck first made sexual contact with L'il Bit when she was eleven years old is revealed late in the play, after the audience has seen their relationship develop through a different lens, not the one that would automatically stigmatize him as a pedophile or pervert. Vogel's dramaturgy works as a kind of pedagogy in the way it uses form to encourage audiences to expand their critical thinking and feeling capacities beyond habituated assumptions or predetermined moral categories. Instead we see their relationship as one formed out of larger cultural attitudes and affective structures.

L'il Bit begins the play by saying to the audience: "Sometimes to tell a secret, you first have to teach a lesson" (7). The invocation of a "secret" at the heart of the play recalls French philosopher Michel Foucault's "repressive hypothesis." Aptly capturing the lure of L'il Bit's opening line, Foucault states, "What is peculiar to modern societies, in fact, is not that they consigned sex to a shadow existence, but that they dedicated themselves to speaking of it *ad infinitum*, while exploiting it as *the* secret."[23] In both Christian confession and psychoanalytic "talk therapy," the aim has been to uncover and expose this sexual secret, which is understood as the hidden secret of an individual's identity. *Drive* draws the audience in with the promise of an exposed secret, "the dirt" buried in this woman's past. However, L'il Bit does not perform a confession, but instead situates her story within the historical landscape of a Maryland littered with the detritus of America's cultural history: "the crumbling concrete of U.S. One . . . one-room revival churches, the porno drive-in, and boarded up motels with For Sale signs tumbling down."[24] She exploits the seductive lure of a (private) secret, subverting it with a (public) lesson. Her lesson teaches us something about the complexity of sexual desire, the alienation of heteronormative gender conventions, and the formative and performative function of memory.

The play connects the concept of memory to the metaphor of the lesson in a manner that suggests the way memories function like an embodied archive, an individual's library of cultural messages and affective traces. From her Uncle Peck's driving lessons to her mother's lesson on how to get drunk like a lady, L'il Bit's memories revolve around the multiple, often conflicting ways she learned how to see and live in her body, how to perform her gender and sexuality, and how to use these as "tools" that, depending on the context, can be mobilized as a strategy either of defense or of seduction. The first

Figure 7: *How I Learned to Drive*. David Morse and Mary-Louise Parker. Vineyard Theatre, New York City, 1997. Photo: ©Carol Rosegg.

scene shows a seventeen-year-old L'il Bit in a car with her Uncle Peck, as he gives her a driving lesson at the same time as he fumbles to unlatch her bra. The Vineyard production provided emotional distance from this and other moments like it through nonnaturalistic acting and an abstracted set design. Facing the audience and sitting in two chairs that signal a Buick Rivera, Peck fondles L'il Bit's breasts, while their bodies remain *"impassive,"* and *"only their facial expressions emote"* (8). The characters' emoting faces and unmoving bodies create affective distance from the action being mimed, while their position facing toward the audience implicates the audience from the outset. Refusing the comfort (or voyeurism) of the fourth wall, and other conventions of realism, the play works as a kind of public staging, an encounter between audience and performers. Further defamiliarizing the action is the voice of the driving instructor, whose disembodied authority guides us through the lessons, telling us what gear is being used, the direction in which we are moving, and the precautions we should take. The driving instructor also signals the shifts in L'il Bit's memories, as they move back and forth between 1962 and the play's present.

Driving lessons are the play's primary conceit, working analogously as lessons in gender formation. Looking back, L'il Bit sees Peck's love of cars as his own heterosexual training, preparing him to love—and assume control over—women. In a scene titled "The Initiation into a Boy's First Love," we see Peck enthusiastically showing L'il Bit all the specialized parts of "the tightest squeeze Chevy ever made," while L'il Bit says knowingly to the audience, "Long after a mother's tits, but before a woman's breasts" (46). Through Peck's driving lessons, L'il Bit learns to take a masculine position, both in the driver's seat and in broader social interactions. In a scene entitled "You and the Reverse Gear," Peck instructs a fifteen-year-old L'il Bit:

> When you are driving, your life is in your own two hands. Understand? . . . You're the nearest thing I have to a son I'll ever have—and I want to give you something. Something that really matters to me. There's something about driving—when you're in control of the car, just you and the machine and the road. . . . A power. I feel more myself in my car than anywhere else. And that's what I want to give to you. There's a lot of assholes out there. . . . And you have to be ready for them. I want to teach you to drive like a man. . . . Men are taught

to drive with confidence—with aggression. . . . Women tend to be polite—to hesitate. And that can be fatal. (50)

This passage is rife with all the contradictions that animate the relationship between Peck and L'il Bit: he wants to protect her, and yet he also violates her; he wants to invest her with a sense of power and authority, and yet he also leaves her powerless to his advances; he wants her to experience the freedom and autonomy of driving, and yet he damages the possibilities she may have had to experience her body in that same way. Peck teaches L'il Bit "to drive like a man," how to assume a masculine position and survive in a world that constructs her as an object, even as he sexualizes her body. L'il Bit learns this conflicted lesson and seeks to find the ontological middle road between active subject and passive object, masculine and feminine, power and powerlessness. The metaphor of the driving lesson reinforces that gender is not something that originates in the body, but something that is taught. Gender emerges in the attitudes and acts we learn and internalize. In his above lesson, Peck describes driving in erotic terms, as an oscillation between domination and submission, surrender and control. When L'il Bit asks Peck why he refers to the car as "she," he responds, saying, "It doesn't have to be a 'she'— but when you close your eyes, think of someone who responds to your touch—someone who performs just for you and gives you what you ask for." Considering Peck's advice, L'il Bit says, "I close my eyes—and decide not to change the gender" (51).

The play also incorporates the device of a Greek chorus, or in this case, three choruses—the Male, Female, and Teenage. This classical convention of the communal choric voice is, in *Drive*, revised as a collection of disparate, conflicting, and often very funny voices. The multiple choruses theatricalize the relationship between individual and collective, private and public, while at the same time dispelling understandings of a singular culture or unified set of memories. The choruses suggest that an individual's voice is, like memory, not actually individual, but a learned, internalized script made up of multiple cultural messages. The gendered and generational specificity of the three choruses further complicates the notion of a unified cultural voice, while also showing the way beliefs and lessons are passed on over time and repeated. The three actors who play the Male, Female, and Teenage choruses enact various parts, such as L'il Bit's family, her classmates, and even L'il Bit herself. The choruses give advice; they criticize; they insult; they sing doo-wop songs in three-part harmony; they witness the relationship between Peck and L'il Bit; they give L'il Bit a voice when she is unable to speak. They provide both comic relief and formal complexity, and they provide distance from the action onstage. Above all, the choruses are the contradictory cultural voices that teach L'il Bit how to live in the world.

When playing the roles of L'il Bit's family, the choruses reveal the way conventional family structures reproduce the norms of a heteronormative culture. The Female Chorus, as L'il Bit's mother, teaches an adolescent L'il Bit how to perform "proper" femininity, which includes drinking politely and tolerating sex. In the tradition of the "Mama Said" advice songs of the 1950s and 1960s, L'il Bit's mother offers "A Mother's Guide to Social Drinking." Here, L'il Bit learns the delicate art of getting drunk like a lady, which means not getting "sloppy," but rather "tipsy and a little gay." If she has had too much to drink, she should dunk her head in water, since "a wet woman is still less conspicuous than a drunk woman" (24, 27). The Male Chorus, as L'il Bit's grandfather Big Papa, acts as the voice of a generation that tended to talk down to women and reduce them to their (reproductive or sexual) bodies. When L'il Bit expresses a desire to go to college, for example, Big Papa asks, "How is Shakespeare going to help her lie on her back in the dark?" Goading further, he continues, "What does she need a college degree for? She's got all the credentials she needs on her chest" (17). Emphasizing the connection between family and sexual development, L'il Bit explains, "In my family, folks tend to get nicknamed for their genitalia" (13). While Peck and Big Papa's names are self-explanatory, her name comes from the "little bit" her family discovered between her chubby newborn legs. This subtle and seemingly whimsical detail disrupts the supposed sexual dimorphism upon which gender is constructed and works in dissonant relation to L'il Bit's well-developed chest.

Complicating a perception of L'il Bit as sexual victim is the Female Chorus, as Peck's wife, Aunt Mary, who sees L'il Bit as the knowing nymphet, the seductress luring Peck away from her, the loyal wife. Aunt Mary's speech constructs a different understanding of L'il Bit as the Lolita-like young woman practicing her wiles on an innocent man. Aunt Mary's speech also cultivates a sense of empathy for Peck, whom we see here through the eyes of a wife who knows more about him than she will admit, to herself, him, or the audience. Directly to the audience, Aunt Mary has her say:

> (*Sharply*) I'm not a fool. I know what's going on. I wish you could feel how strongly Peck fights against it—he's swimming against the tide, and what he needs is to see me on shore. . . . And I want to say this about my niece. She's a sly one, that one is. She knows exactly what she's doing; she's twisted Peck around her little finger and thinks it's all a big secret. Yet another one who's borrowing my husband until it doesn't suit her anymore. (67)

This speech broadens the play's treatment of sexuality well beyond the category of pedophilia, confronting the audience with two female sexual stereotypes—the temptress and the long-suffering wife—that reveal the limited language we have to define female sexuality and agency. As in *Desdemona*, this speech also suggests the way women often see one another as competition for male affection and judge one another through an internalized male gaze. Significantly, sexuality is again invoked here as L'il Bit's "big secret," the truth she is hiding from her family and the world. This monologue also implies that it is within heteronormative marriage that "big secrets," like sexual abuse, are kept hidden. Aunt Mary explains why "we don't talk about it," justifying her role as complicit wife-in-denial, by insisting, "I think domesticity is a balm for men when they're lost" (67). Marriage and the domestic sphere are here depicted as the primary zone of cultural repression. What Aunt Mary seems not to know is that L'il Bit is not the only one to whom Peck is giving lessons.

In a scene that precedes Aunt Mary's, Uncle Peck teaches Cousin Bobby how to fish. Idling in the ambiguous temporal register of "The Neutral Gear," Peck stands alone on stage, performing the lesson to an imagined Bobby in a monologue that is both tender and disturbing. Like the driving lessons he gives to L'il Bit, Peck's lessons to Cousin Bobby are coded as lessons in how to perform gender and sexuality. Peck teaches Bobby how to bait the hook in ways that recall his lesson to L'il Bit on being a defensive driver. "Sand fleas should always keep their back to the wall" (34), he tells Bobby, instilling a slightly homophobic message of masculine self-protection. When Bobby begins to cry after catching a fish, fearing that it is in pain, Peck teaches him a lesson in heteronormative masculinity, which means censoring emotional responses like compassion:

I don't know how much pain a fish feels—you can't think of that. Oh, no, don't cry, come on now, it's just a fish—the other guys are going to see you. —No, no, you're just real sensitive, and I think that's wonderful at your age—look, do you want me to cut it free? You do? (35)

The coded lesson in masculinity in this scene suggests the way boys learn early to be ashamed of their emotions. And yet Peck tells Bobby, "There's nothing you could do that would make me feel ashamed of you," only to disturbingly transform these reassuring words into an act of violation. Peck exploits Bobby's vulnerability by insisting that they are sharing "something special just between you and me," in this "secret place" (35). Peck's highly ironic lesson to Bobby eases the young boy's shame about his sensitivity, while simultaneously taking advantage of the boy's emotional exposure. The audience, in this moment, recognizes the actions Peck mimes and inevitably feels an uncomfortable shame, and even shock. Because Peck performs alone on stage, the audience becomes, in a way, Bobby's surrogate, compelled to inhabit the place of this fictive figure and to imaginatively experience the violation of this encounter. Peck's monologue puts this "secret place" and the act performed there into public view, redirecting traditional circuits of identification and empathy by placing the audience in the position of witness. In a move characteristic of Vogel's dramaturgy, this unsettling theatrical moment is followed by a comic scene performed in the style of a vaudeville sketch.

Directly after the encounter between Peck and Bobby, we see L'il Bit's indoctrination into the vexed and painful world of female sexuality. Three generations of women sit at the kitchen table to offer their advice to L'il Bit on sex and men. Lil Bit's mother tells her, "It's important that he loves you," while her grandmother comically overstates her case for abstinence, proclaiming, "Tell her it hurts! It's agony! You think you're going to die! Especially if you do it before marriage!" (42). Learning, alternatively, how to defend, contain, and suppress her sexuality, a baffled L'il Bit wonders, "Why does everything have to hurt for girls?" (43). Indeed, one of the play's points is that there are few options for representing or talking about female sexuality as a source of pleasure; instead, it is caught up in a discourse that defines it as an experience of pain, shame, and secrets. Moreover, L'il Bit's question echoes her own prescient warning to Peck that "someone is going to get hurt" (32, 33) if they develop an intimate relationship. However,

Peck's driving lessons have also put her "in the driver's seat" of their relationship. After the two celebrate her driver's license with dinner and drinks, it is a sixteen-year-old L'il Bit, having successfully learned Peck's lessons on defensive driving and remaining in control, who decides not to consummate their relationship.

Vogel explains Peck and L'il Bit's relationship through the story of "The Gift of the Magi": "I wanted the play to be that they give each other . . . the wrong gifts, with great love."[25] There is, indeed, a great deal of reciprocity in L'il Bit and Peck's relationship. L'il Bit listens to Peck, keeping him company in his restless loneliness, which enables him to abstain from alcohol. Likewise, Peck treats L'il Bit with a loving respect that few others in her life offer her. In their relationship, there is both love and a mutual recognition of one another's loneliness. As Judith Butler points out, following Hegel, our desire for recognition is necessary for "our very sense of personhood," and it is a desire that, like seduction, "places us outside ourselves, in a realm of social norms that we do not fully choose, but that provides the horizon and the resource for any sense of choice that we have."[26] The hurt that Peck both tries to prepare L'il Bit for and subjects her to is the inevitable result of their relationship, which simultaneously transgresses and reinforces the social norms that define them both.

The play's central scene is entitled "1965. The Photo Shoot." A thirteen-year-old L'il Bit moves swiftly through the performative gestures of feminine embodiment: self-consciousness, shame, and defiance. As David Savran argues, "it is in this scene that L'il Bit most graphically—and theatrically—becomes an object for her Uncle Peck and, more ominously, for herself as well."[27] Looking back to this moment without any visible traces of emotion, L'il Bit sets the scene, which takes place in Peck's basement, a place where, she says knowingly, "he keeps his secrets" (59). In this space of domestic privacy and secrets, L'il Bit learns how to perform as a sexual object, but she also learns to transform shame into seduction. As Peck prepares her for the session, we see his desire for L'il Bit as, in part, a desire for command over her body. As he *"unbuttons her blouse to the midpoint, and runs his hands over the flesh of her exposed sternum, arranging the fabric, just touching her. Deliberately, calmly. Asexually,"* his movements register as calculated, detached, not erotic. Peck's motivation in this scene is not directly sexual at all, but more strategic and, perhaps for that reason, more unsettling. Vogel's stage directions are so remarkably precise that the scene's trajectory is mapped in them through descriptions of L'il Bit's affective transformations. As Peck takes the first pictures, *"L'il Bit turns to him like a plant to the sun"* (61), a gesture of adoring, unguarded compliance that also suggests the symbiotic relationship between sun and plant, with L'il Bit turning toward Peck for sustenance. *"At first a bit self-conscious,"* L'il Bit *"blushes"* under her uncle's gaze. However, this shame is swiftly transfigured into an awareness of her capacity to please him with her body and its postures. A *"faint smile"* replaces her blush. Encouraging her to dance to the background music as if she is "alone on a Friday night," Peck choreographs her movements: "just move for me, L'il Bit" (62). Eagerly, Peck snaps photographs, declaring L'il Bit "beautiful," as she responds to his gaze by looking at him *"a bit defiantly"* (62–63). Peck champions these new postures—"Ooooh, great" (63)—and L'il Bit learns how to see herself through Peck's eyes; she learns to move her body in response to his affirming voice and desiring gaze. Assuring her, "No—I'm not here—just my voice" (62), Peck eerily evokes the disembodied male gaze that women internalize as "their own." In this scene, L'il Bit *becomes* for and because of Peck's gaze.

What L'il Bit thinks is an intimate encounter is yet another lesson. Here, Peck prepares L'il Bit to live in a sexualized marketplace, where her body and sexuality can be a source of profit, rather than shame. When he tells her, "If we keep this up, in five years we'll have a really professional portfolio" (64), L'il Bit feels betrayed, realizing that Peck is taking her picture for *Playboy*. She begs him to keep the photos private, and although he insists, "It's not anything shameful" (65), he agrees. This scene of objectification is characterized by an atmosphere of violation and exposure. After realizing Peck wants to sell her pictures, L'il Bit feels like he can "see right through" her, a vulnerable transparency incited as her exposed body is made into a public commodity. Peck replies with misguided tenderness, telling her, "I love you. I have loved you every day since the day you were born" (65–66). His sentiment is genuine. However, it betrays Peck's own loneliness, thus making his attachment to L'il Bit seem self-serving. Mark Brokaw's production at Signature Theatre further complicated interpretations of this scene by projecting the images of L'il Bit that Peck was taking on a screen above her, interspersing them with images of *Playboy* bunnies, popular celebrities, and even

Alice Liddell, Lewis Carroll's child muse. In this way, the "private secret" unfolding in Peck's basement is contextualized within a long tradition of sexualized images in visual art and media. The audience is invited into the complexity of this coming-of-age scene and divested of the comfort of clear moral responses.

The photo-shoot scene is structurally connected to a poignant trio of scenes that directly precede it entitled "The Anthropology of the Female Body in Ninth Grade—Or A Walk Down Mammary Lane." These scenes are affectively linked to the preceding scene with Peck through L'il Bit's feelings of exposure and self-consciousness and the gestures of shame she performs in both contexts. The unconventional structure and arrangement of these short scenes enable the audience to look closely at the many ways young girls learn to see their bodies as objects, often foreign ones. The three choruses play various roles as L'il Bit's peers, and in these brief interactions, we witness the isolating effects of shame and how swiftly this affect is learned and internalized as both script and performance. In the gym shower, L'il Bit's peers burst into laughter at the sight of her naked, rapidly developing breasts, which have become a target of mockery. The driving instructor's voice booms, "Were You Prepared?" while "(L'il Bit tries to cover up; she is exposed)" (54). L'il Bit's physical and emotional exposure contrasts sharply here with the formal, detached tone of the driving instructor's voice. Suddenly the scene shifts in setting and tone, as "1960s Motown fills the room and we segue into: . . . The Sock Hop" (55). L'il Bit tries to explain her feelings to a group of girls at the Sock Hop:

> But sometimes I feel like these alien life forces have grafted themselves onto my chest, and they're using me until they can "propagate" and take over the world and they'll just keep growing, with a mind of their own until I collapse under their weight and they suck all the nourishment out of my body and I finally just waste away while they get bigger and bigger and—(L'il Bit's classmates are just staring at her in disbelief).(57)

As in *Twins*, this scene invokes the campy terror of 1950s sci-fi films; only here, the alien other is L'il Bit's own body. Both alienated from her body and shackled to what it signifies, L'il Bit becomes, in these scenes, acutely aware that her body is not entirely hers, but the property of a cold and unfriendly culture. Trying to find relief from her shame by commiserating with a female peer, L'il Bit asks her directly, "don't you ever feel . . . self-conscious? Like you're being watched all the time?" "That's not a problem for me" (55), replies the young teenager. Peck hovers in the background in these scenes, and when an awkward young boy asks L'il Bit to dance, *"she tenses, aware of Peck's gaze"* (54), and declines the invitation. The audience sees Peck in the background, *"star[ing] at L'il Bit's body [and] setting up a tripod"* (55), in preparation for the photo shoot he is about to stage and that we are about to see. As a fourteen year-old L'il Bit stands self-conscious and alone at a high school dance, Peck prepares for L'il Bit's next lesson—the photo-shoot scene we have just witnessed, in which she learns to see herself as sexualized object. The temporal arrangement of these scenes suggests the way sexual objectification works as a kind of compensation for bodily shame, a necessary reinforcement of a fractured subjectivity. While her peers mock L'il Bit's body, Peck praises it. Both encounters have indelible effects on the way L'il Bit sees and lives in her body.

L'il Bit is an astute student, transforming Peck's lessons into a form of sexual authority. This authority is demonstrated on a bus trip to upstate New York in 1979, during which she meets and seduces a seventeen-year-old boy. She is twenty-seven and, significantly, a teacher. In this scene, both seduction and teaching are represented as theatrical performances that involve attraction and persuasion. Significantly, L'il Bit is not the driver here, but the director, actor, and playwright. L'il Bit's encounter with the high school boy illustrates that, just as Peck taught her, she is in control, directing how the scene unfolds, even before it begins. She says to audience, "I was only into the second moment of conversation and I could see the whole evening before me." Implicitly addressing Peck, L'il Bit describes her seduction in theatrical terms:

> And dramaturgically speaking, after the faltering and slightly comical "first act," there was the briefest of intermissions, and an extremely forceful and *sustained* second act. And after the second act climax and a gentle denouement—before the post-play discussion—I lay on my back and thought about you, Uncle Peck. Oh. Oh, this is the allure. Being older. Being the first. Being the translator, the teacher, the epicure, the already jaded. This is how the giver gets taken. (41)

This scene is both metatheatrical and metasexual, emphasizing gender, power, and sexual desire as learned roles. Seduction is defined here as a conventional two-act comedy, complete with a climax and resolution, which underscores the way dramatic form shapes our expectations and our desires. L'il Bit plays the leading role in this comedy and acknowledges the man from whom she learned her timing and techniques.

We also witness the more destructive ways in which L'il Bit has transformed desire for Peck into identification with him. A scene titled "During 1970. A Nixon recession" comes early in the play and shows an adult L'il Bit alone and driving recklessly along the back roads of Maryland. While Nixon was justifying the invasion of Cambodia, and Myra and Myrna were in Long Island, L'il Bit was getting kicked out of college because she may or may not have "fooled around with a rich man's daughter." (On this, however, L'il Bit is, "not talking.") Like Peck, L'il Bit has taken to drinking—"a fifth a day"—and driving her 1965 Mustang "fully tanked" down the Beltway. She contemplates the precariousness of this act, realizing that "just one notch of the steering wheel would be all it would take." And yet, she adds, "he taught me well" (21). L'il Bit brings two memories into view here, one of Peck's lessons and the other of their future effects. This dialectical recollection enables L'il Bit to see her likeness with Peck and to look for other roads to travel down. Driving allows L'il Bit imaginatively to transform her feelings of isolation into an experience of mobility and control. Significantly, the car she drives down the Beltway was made the same year that a thirteen-year-old L'il Bit learned that her body was a commodity to be sold to *Playboy* by her uncle. Thus, with the 1965 Mustang working as a surrogate for her objectified past self, L'il Bit quite literally takes her life in her own hands.

In the penultimate scene of *Drive*, Peck visits L'il Bit's college dorm room on the eve of her eighteenth birthday, bearing the symbolic gift of a Cadillac to mark her entry into adulthood. Now, L'il Bit can take the driver's seat in a luxury car and, by metaphorical extension, take full control of her relationship to Peck. Realizing that she cannot form intimate relationships with other people until she severs the one with Peck, L'il Bit refuses to see him again. Vulnerable and desperate, Peck asks L'il Bit to marry him, begging her to stay with him. There is a devastating desperation in Peck's desire in this scene, and he becomes jealous, asking L'il Bit, "Are you seeing other men?" As in other moments of the play, L'il Bit refuses here to divulge sexual secrets, telling Peck, "I—no, that's not the reason—I—well, yes, I am seeing other—listen, it's not really anyone's business!" (80). In a last plea for her affection, Peck asks, "Of your own free will. Just lie down on the bed with me. . . . Because sometimes the body knows things the mind isn't listening to." Yielding in compassion, L'il Bit lies beside him on her dorm room bed. And as Peck and L'il Bit lie together, the Female and Male choruses narrate, along with L'il Bit, fragmented, sensual memories of her love for Peck, just the kind of embodied knowing that he asked her to consult in his final request. In her recollections, Peck becomes the object of L'il Bit's desire: "warm brown eyes," "warm hands," "sweat of cypress and sand," "his heart beating Dixie" (81–83). After this poignant convergence of broken memories and embodied sensations, L'il Bit tells the audience, "I never saw him again. . . . It took my uncle seven years to drink himself to death. First he lost his job, then his wife, and finally his driver's license" (85). Spoken matter-of-factly, this elegiac moment is haunted by Peck's physical presence, as he remains still seated beside L'il Bit on stage. With a present filled to overflowing with memories of Peck, L'il Bit sits, calmly and assuredly, beside him, ready to remember and reperform their first encounter.

In the final scene, the full history of L'il Bit and Peck's relationship comes into focus. The Teenage Chorus speaks all of L'il Bit's lines here, while she sits silently in the passenger seat beside Peck and *"looks at him closely, remembering"* (88). Confronting her past, L'il Bit's disembodied voice is replaced by her direct gaze, the first direct look shared by L'il Bit and Peck during a sexual encounter. The ventriloquism theatricalizes the dislocation of body and voice incited by this experience and also creates a sense of distance between the encounter and its remembrance, between the eleven-year-old L'il Bit and her adult self who remembers. The Teenage Chorus's narration works to distance the audience from the actions being performed. The encounter is further defamiliarized by the age of the adult actress playing L'il Bit, who sits on Peck's lap in a pose that carries connotations of both childhood (sitting on Dad's lap) and sex work (a lap dance). Peck asks L'il Bit, "Do you want to drive?" (88), thus initiating their first driving lesson in 1962, an ironic lesson on how to drive with caution and control. Peck instructs L'il Bit while simultaneously placing *"his hands on her breasts,"* an image of violation that contradicts the words he speaks. L'il Bit sees in retrospect Peck's conflicted desires: he wants both to protect and prepare L'il Bit and also to satisfy his sexual desire and exercise his control. As Peck *"tenses against L'il Bit,"* she sits on his lap, facing the audience, *"trying not to cry,"* comforting herself by insisting, "This isn't happening." The audience watches her words disproved, in a disturbing moment filled with a mixture of uncomfortable eroticism, sadness, and panic. There is an urge to plead with Peck, along with L'il Bit, who begs him, "please don't do this" (90). And yet there is also a moment of shameful recognition, a painful awareness of the inevitability of such an encounter in a culture saturated with images far less sensitively drawn.

L'il Bit concludes the play with a direct address to the audience, a narrative strategy that brings the audience back to the beginning of the play and suggests that the lesson was, itself, the secret, the lure to look at sexuality in a different, more difficult way. Of that encounter as an eleven-year-old girl, an adult L'il Bit tells us, "That was the last day I lived inside my body. I retreated above the neck, and I've lived in the fire in my head ever since" (90). She continues, "The nearest sensation I feel—of flight in the body—I guess I feel when I'm driving" (91). Peck's driving lessons both took something from her and gave her something in return. L'il Bit's alienation from her body emerged not only from her relationship to Peck, but also from the lessons taught to her by her family, her classmates, and the broader culture. Peck's lessons, however, also gave L'il Bit something else: agency. If the photo session staged the objectification of L'il Bit's body under Peck's guiding gaze and directing voice, his driving lessons taught her how to assume a position of power and authority. This final scene stages the importance of L'il Bit's narrative voice as the agency with which she gives shape and meaning to her memories and her story. As L'il Bit (and the audience) remembers Peck, she (and we) gets remade through the process. Now "believing in things . . . like family and forgiveness," L'il Bit gets into her car, where *"a faint light strikes the spirit of Uncle Peck, who is sitting in the back seat of the car. She sees him in the mirror. She smiles at him. He nods at her. They are happy to be going on a trip together"* (92). In this final image of recognition and forgiveness, L'il Bit looks at her own image reflecting back at Peck's, as she sees him as part of her remade, recollected self. She redirects traditional narratives of closure and resolution, along with the safety they promise, opting instead for an uncharted path. With the car in first gear, L'il Bit, together with the ghost of Peck, prepares to drive into an unknown future: "And then—I floor it" (92).

Directed by Mark Brokaw and featuring Mary-Louise Parker and David Morse in the lead roles, *Drive* premiered in February 1997 at the Vineyard Theatre before moving across the street to the Century Theatre in April 1997 for a commercial run, where Jayne Atkinson (and later Molly Ringwald) and Brian Davison took over the lead roles. After 450 performances over a fifteen-month run, *Drive* went on to be produced across the country and around the world. Winning the 1998 Pulitzer Prize for drama confirmed Vogel's reputation as a daring and important American playwright. In an interview shortly after the premiere of *Drive*, Vogel articulated her desire "to *seduce* the audience," to get them to "go along for a ride they wouldn't ordinarily take, or don't even know they're taking," and, on the way, see "highly charged political issues in a new and unexpected way."[28] Ben Brantley of the *New York Times* went along for the ride, writing, "It is hard to say who is the more accomplished seducer . . . Uncle Peck, surely the most engaging pedophile ever to walk across an American stage, or the woman who created him."[29] The reviews of *Drive*'s original New York production were almost unanimous in their praise of the playwright's keen sense of balance and the play's nuanced depiction of a delicate subject.[30] Vogel told the *Observer's* Matt Wolf during *Drive*'s May 1998 London premiere at the Donmar Warehouse (John Crowley directing) that she "hopes the play is seen as a study in shades of grey."[31] Michael Feingold begins his review in the *Village Voice* with a critique of Vogel's "last two productions," which he describes as "weak, overly cute early works."[32] Like Brantley, Feingold praises Vogel's boldness in *Drive*, writing, "She doesn't flinch from any of the awfulness involved . . . but the mixture of gentleness and precision in her touch is so reassuringly authoritative that you accept the picture completely." He concludes, "This is, quite simply, the sweetest and most forgiving play ever written about child abuse."[33] Jill Dolan's pithy review in *Theatre Journal* points out, however, that "*Drive* is only 'about' incest after the scene of Li'l first molestation,"[34] which occurs very near the end of the play. Until then, it is a play about "forgiveness and family, about the instability of sexuality, and the unpredictable ways in which we learn who we are, how we desire, and how our growth is built on loss."[35]

Not all critics responded positively to the play. In his review of the 1997 Vineyard Theater production, *New York* magazine's John Smith was ambivalent about the play's lack of moral judgment, wondering, "A play has every right not to answer the questions it raises—most works of art don't. But just how many unknowns is an equation entitled to?"[36] The *New York Observer's* John Heilpern took issue with Vogel's admission that she wanted to see whether the audience would "allow themselves to find this erotic," writing facetiously, "Ms. Vogel would like us to be turned on by child molesters like Uncle Peck. . . . Come on in, folks! See the safe pedophilia!" Sarcastically reacting to the play based on moral prejudgments and unexamined buzz words, Heilpern argues that Vogel "hasn't written the provocative drama she claims; she has neutralized the issues making them more or less harmless."[37] Heilpern was unable to see the play beyond the level of sensationalized "issues," and the subtlety of the relationship was lost on him; his review registers more than a little disappointment that the blunt categories of victim and pedophile were not maintained. Similarly, in his review of a 2004 production of *Drive*, Michael Toscano of the *Washington Post* argued that, because Uncle Peck was played "with such skill and precision, combined with Vogel's seeming inability to clearly state who or what is right or wrong," the play's "message becomes so muddled as to be nonexistent." Disturbed by a lack of clear moral messaging, Toscano was disappointed that a "courageous feminist, lesbian playwright" like Vogel did not "take a strong position" and make it clear "who is preying on whom" by portraying "the predator" as "clearly . . . evil."[38] Assuming that, since she is a feminist and a lesbian, she should portray the woman as the unequivocal victim is exactly the kind of essentialism that Vogel's plays work to unravel. Also seeking moral clarity, London reviewer Paul Taylor singles out Vogel's play from a cluster of sexual abuse plays that were produced in the 1990s.[39] He argues that *Drive* represents "an ambiguous image of empowerment, sexual temptation and suggested [a] complicity" that leaves the spectator "feeling faintly soiled."[40] And yet this ambiguity and affective aftermath are the play's greatest achievements. Vogel seeks not moral certainty, but moral complexity, situating ethical questions within the flux and interconnections of history and culture and in the unpredictable movements of shame and desire. It is a drama about the culture that created Peck. Ultimately, *Drive* was canonized using highly traditional terms, as a play that manages to transcend—rather than problematize—moral issues. As Robert Brustein writes, "Vogel moves her characters out of the provisional world of morality into the timeless world of art."[41] To praise the play using such sanitizing aesthetic terms simplifies and dehistoricizes the subjects, bodies, and sexualities it complicates. Nonetheless, it is a remarkable work that takes its rightful place among a canon of other remarkable works.

Memory is one of the ways normative embodiment is established, repeated, and also transformed. The disjunctive memories that give shape to *Drive* also shape the temporal structure of the plays examined in the next chapter, *The Baltimore Waltz* and *The Long Christmas Ride Home*. In these three plays, Vogel presents a model of theatrical time understood as both propelling forward and pulling back, a complex temporal movement in which the past is encountered as part of the present, and the body operates as the site and means of that encounter. In *Baltimore Waltz* and *Long Christmas Ride Home*, the focus shifts away from female sexuality and toward more diffuse explorations of family, memory, and sexuality. Vogel continues with her bold formal experimentations, while mobilizing memories animated by fantasy and rooted in her personal history. Like the contrasting tones of *Twins* and *Drive*, *Baltimore Waltz* and *Long Christmas Ride Home* approach similar topics (family, memory, homophobia, AIDS), but from different directions and in different registers. The irreverent comedy of *Baltimore Waltz* becomes, in *Long Christmas Ride Home*, a poetic contemplation, and yet both plays take audiences on journeys and use theater as a forum for remembering and questioning, moving and being moved.

CHAPTER SIX

Stopping Time: *The Baltimore Waltz* and *The Long Christmas Ride Home*

A play plucks human experience from time and brings aesthetic completion to a process we know to be endless. The play imitates the timely in order to remove it from time, to give time a shape.

> —Bert O. States, *Great Reckonings in Little Rooms*[1]

Dear Paula: I thought I would jot down some of my thoughts about the (shall we say) production values of my ceremony. Oh God—I can hear you groaning—everybody wants to direct. Well, I want a good show, even though my role has been reduced involuntarily from player to prop.

> —Letter from Carl Vogel to Paula, outlining his
>   funeral wishes

Since the theatrical event itself stages two different temporal frames—the time of the audience and the time of the playworld—theater offers a unique opportunity for rearranging conventional patterns of past-present-future/beginning-middle-end and for bringing into conversation the enduring, repeatable time of the play—"a process we know to be endless"—and the finite, forward-moving time of the audience. *The Baltimore Waltz* (1992) and *The Long Christmas Ride Home* (2003) commemorate Vogel's brother, Carl, who died of AIDS-related complications on January 9, 1988. Both plays repeat and suspend a personal moment of loss, examining its affective repercussions and expanding it into a public commemoration—a ceremony of celebration and remembrance. Time is paradoxically both suspended and reshaped as a recursive journey in these plays; the European tour in *Waltz* and the family car trip in *Home* bypass linear movements and final destinations in favor of circuitous journeys that return to the point of departure, leaving the travelers changed by what they have seen along the way. While the journeys in both plays spatially map out a recursive movement, the commemorative impulse initiates its own recursivity, as memories of the past fill the present moment. Reconfiguring time in these three ways—the theatrical event, the round-trip journey, and the act of remembering— *Waltz* and *Home* stage a complex temporality that involves stopping time, folding the past into the theatrical present, and bringing the past/passed back to life.

Just as *The Mineola Twins* and *How I Learned to Drive* both trace a social history of postwar female sexuality, *Waltz* and *Home* explore the same subject but in different registers: a post-1980s cultural climate of homophobia. The bawdy physical comedy of *Twins* and *Waltz* generates different meanings than the poetic lyricism of *Drive* and *Home*; the humor and dream/fantasy sequences of the former plays displace the subject matter, while the minimalistic playworlds and lyrical language of the latter two plays condense it. Vogel adjusts the tone as a way to shift perspectives and revise the questions being posed. *Waltz* deploys camp as a dramaturgical strategy, using juxtaposition, irony, and humor to defamiliarize cultural stereotypes and prejudices, especially those surrounding AIDS and homophobia. Theater scholar David Román articulates the capacity of theater to produce counterhegemonic representations of homosexuality and AIDS, emphasizing the equal roles performed by playwrights, actors, directors, and spectators in this process. Román writes,

> Such a project—to intervene in the dominant representations governing AIDS—must involve a serious interrogation of the discourses, imagined or available, by which we fashion our identities to counter AIDS. The goal to fight back and stop AIDS is, moreover, securable to all of us who participate in the collective and localized enterprise we call theatre. No doubt, for some of us, it's the role of a lifetime.[2]

Román's call for a revised language and newly fashioned identities positions theater as a public forum and activism as theatrical performance. The suspended moments in *Waltz* and *Home*, seen in this light, become intensely collective losses that reverberate in every direction. Mobilizing theater in this way is politically important, especially since, as Judith Butler points out, so "few deaths from AIDS were publicly grievable losses."[3] In *Waltz* and *Home*, theater functions as a site of commemoration—an opportunity to stop time, in order to grieve, remember, debate, and celebrate.

Translating Loss: *The Baltimore Waltz*

Vogel has said, "*The Baltimore Waltz* will be for me the greatest play I ever wrote."[4] The play's dedication reads, "To Carl—because I cannot sew," which implies that this is Vogel's version of an AIDS quilt. She asks that all productions of *Waltz* include in their program Carl's letter to her, excerpted in an epigraph to this chapter, as well as below, which he wrote after his first bout of pneumonia at Johns Hopkins Hospital in Baltimore, Maryland. With a flair for the theatrical and a charming wit, Carl offers Vogel five options for "the piece of me I leave behind":

1. Open casket, full drag.
2. Open casket, bum up. (You'll know where to place the calla lilies won't you?)
3. Closed casket, internment with the grandparents.
4. Cremation and burial of my ashes.
5. Cremation and dispersion of my ashes in some sylvan spot.

In his suggestions for the funeral score, Carl reveals his interest in the full spectrum of the aesthetic hierarchy: "I would really like good music. My tastes in these matters run to the highbrow: Fauré's 'Pie Jesu' from his *Requiem*, Gluck's 'Dance of the Blessed Spirits' from *Orfeo*, 'La Vergine degli Angeli' from Verdi's *Forza*. But my favorite song is 'I Dream of Jeannie.'"[5] Prefacing the play with Carl's words imprints every production with his humor, warmth, and presence. Carl is immortalized in *Waltz*, his memory brought back to life every time the play is staged and in that suspended moment from which the action unfolds, where it remains always.

The entire action of *Waltz* occurs in the moment that Anna hears her brother has died. As David Savran points out, Vogel borrows the structure of *Waltz* from the conceit employed by Ambrose Bierce in his story "An Occurrence at Owl Creek Bridge," of a dilated moment that comes when confronted with the shock and finality of death.[6] Crucially, however, the audience does not realize this until the play has ended, and so we watch the action unfold believing in Anna's fantasy. We watch the play believing that Anna has just been diagnosed with Acquired Toilet Disease (ATD), while Carl is the healthy brother who accompanies his sister on a European adventure. Suspending time and endlessly deferring the conclusiveness of death, *Waltz* is a celebration of Carl's life, a theatrical translation of loss into remembrance, and a dramatic condensation and displacement of the emotion that emerges in a moment of grief, when there is an urge to flee from the finality of death, if only through fantasy.

The premise of a European trip in *Waltz* stems from a trip Carl asked Vogel to take with him in 1986, an invitation that she declined, not having the money and not realizing that Carl was HIV-positive. He died just over a year later, and Vogel wrote her play as a way to take that trip with him. Although the play came from a very personal moment of loss, it is not a play of mourning, in the traditional sense. Performance studies scholar Peter Dickinson compellingly characterizes *Waltz* as a "queer ritual of remembrance," pointing to the way it "challenge[s] fundamentally the standard Freudian model of mourning."[7] Indeed, the play parodies psychoanalytic models of mourning, as well as traditional theories of female sexuality (as passive, problematic) and fantasy (as illusion, escape). In *Waltz*, Vogel's personal loss becomes a public commemoration, with stylistic juxtapositions, campy humor, and vibrant theatricality inviting spectators to imagine their own place within the story.

Just as *How I Learned to Drive* is not "about" pedophilia, *Waltz* is not "about" AIDS. AIDS—with its associations with immoral sexual activity among gay men—is defamiliarized in the play through the parodic humor and displacement of the causes, symptoms, and group associated with the disease. In *Waltz*, ATD is an incurable illness contracted primarily by single female schoolteachers and transmitted through contact with the toilets used by their young students. Since ATD is not sexually transmitted, Anna intends to "fight the sickness of the body with the health of the body,"[8] by sleeping with every "Thomas, Deiter, and Heinrich" (42) she encounters in Europe. As Dickinson points out, "one of the things that was so refreshing about Vogel's play when it first appeared was how exuberantly 'unchaste' it was in its AIDS dramaturgy."[9] Indeed, the play eschews sexual moralism and the privatization of sex in favor of an exuberant promiscuity and pointed political statements, which punctuate the otherwise comic play and remind the audience that, over a decade later, the lack of public attention to the still-growing global AIDS pandemic remains.

The classic film noir *The Third Man* (1949) operates as the intertextual backdrop of the play, animating the playworld with the subcultural drama of the genre and riffing on the mysterious double death of *The Third Man*'s central character, Harry Lime. The film depicts a desolate postwar Vienna still occupied by the Allied forces and Russians seeking out defectors, conjuring a social climate of paranoia and suspicion that parallels the social context surrounding AIDS in the late 1980s and early 1990s. As "a cinema of moral anxiety,"[10] film noir offers a productive lens through which to examine the secrecy, paranoia, and moral panic surrounding AIDS and homosexuality in post–Cold War America. *Waltz* revises *The Third Man* as a parody of the moral panic surrounding AIDS, juxtaposing the suspicions surrounding postwar communist activity with the suspicions surrounding homosexuals. Stylistically, the lighting design in *Waltz*—the lush atmosphere of European scenes and the stark white hospital scenes—also references *The Third Man*'s aesthetic fusion of expressionistic cinematography with harsh lighting and Dutch angle shots. Vogel recasts the devoted Anna Schmidt as the licentious Anna and restages Harry Lime and Holly Martins's mysterious encounter in the Weiner Riensenrad Ferris wheel scene as a homoerotic rendezvous between the Third Man and Carl, where a stuffed rabbit— Carl's cherished childhood toy and an oblique symbol of his sexuality—is exchanged for an underground ATD drug.

The play not only defamiliarizes the associations between homosexuality and AIDS but also questions the rhetoric surrounding AIDS discourse. When Carl hears the news that his sister is sick with an incurable illness, he remarks angrily, "If Sandra Day O'Connor sat on just one infected potty, the media would be clamoring to do articles on ATD. If just one grandchild of George Bush caught this thing during toilet training, that would be the last we'd hear about the space program" (12). Implicitly confronting the rhetoric of 1980s AIDS activism, which emphasized the "innocent victims" of the disease— "as if there were those who invited and hence deserved the disease and those who acquired it innocently"[11]—Vogel makes the "innocent victim" a single, female, heterosexual schoolteacher, a move that disables the moralizing impulse underlying debates about the illness. Awake worrying over the effects of ATD on her body, Anna asks Carl whether people will know she is ill. In one of the play's most pointed lines, Carl reminds her, "It's not a crime. It's an illness" (17). The rhetoric of "innocent victim" clearly emerged in reaction to the characterization of homosexuality and AIDS as "criminal deviance." Vogel defamiliarizes right-wing definitions of AIDS, which saw the disease as a form of retribution for the immoral "crime" of homosexual activity, defining it instead as a disease contracted by a teacher who neglects the Department of Health and Human Services' ATD safety precautions: "Do squat. Don't sit" (19). Innocence and deviance are, in *Waltz*, reversed, and the play overturns conservative AIDS rhetoric along with the reactionary rhetoric of AIDS activists. People with AIDS/ATD are neither criminals nor victims in Vogel's playworld. To borrow the words of Orson Welles–as–Harry Lime in *The Third Man*: "Victims? Don't be melodramatic."[12]

Lighting, music, and dramatic structure contribute to the play's exhilarating capriciousness, conjuring a playworld somewhere between dream, fantasy, and stark realism. *Waltz* is structured as a montage of scenes that, like a Viennese waltz, move seamlessly between forward and backward movements. Language lessons, political satire, travelogues, scenes from *The Third Man*, parodies of psychiatric models of grief, and frisky sex scenes make this more vaudeville than O'Neill. It is a play built on juxtapositions, with the sterile realism of the hospital scenes standing out against the fecund chaos of the fantasy scenes they frame. Reality and fantasy in *Waltz* are, as in *Hot 'n' Throbbing*, interconnected registers distinguished visually through lighting. Most of the action in *Waltz* takes place in lighting that is "stylized, lush, dark and imaginative," which sharply contrasts with "the hospital white silence of the last scene" (6). As in all of Vogel's plays, music evokes social context and subtext, and in *Waltz*, the score recycles "every cliché of the European experience as imagined by Hollywood" (6).

Waltz has a triangular structure, with three characters—Anna, Carl, and the Third Man—and three registers—Anna's European fantasy, her Baltimore reality, and her memories of Carl and their childhood together. This tripartite dramaturgical structure undermines

Figure 8: *The Baltimore Waltz*. Left to right: Cherry Jones,
Richard Thompson, and Joe Mantello, Circle Repertory Theater,
New York City, 1992. Photo: Gerry Goodstein

dualistic perceptions of fantasy/reality, protagonist/antagonist, past/
present, homo/hetero, and loss/recollection. In Mark Brokaw's 2004
Signature Theatre production, this structure was visually reinforced
with a backdrop of three large windows, which loomed like portals
opening to three possible worlds beyond that of the stark space in
which Anna begins and ends the play. Similarly, Anne Bogart's 1992
production emphasized the play's triangular structure, using only a
hospital bed, curtains, and a couch as the set. In Bogart's production,
Anna was continually positioned in the center of the play action,
even as all three characters move fluidly among the three registers of
the playworld.

Like characters in a dream or film, the characters in *Waltz* are
part reality and part fragmented figments of Anna's imagination. The
costumes immediately signal this ambiguity, with "Anna . . . dressed

in a full slip/negligee and a trench coat" and "Carl . . . in flannel pajamas and a blazer or jacket" (6). Carl is in many ways the most realistic and stable character, whereas the Third Man morphs most dramatically from one role to the next, narrating the language lessons and childhood memories that Anna recites throughout the play and playing the roles of Harry Lime, Anna's string of sexual partners, and each of the three doctors. As the first doctor, the Third Man diagnoses Anna's ATD using incomprehensible medical jargon that leaves her powerless and vulnerable; in his role as the Strangeloveian urologist, Dr. Todesrocheln, he develops dubious methods that leave Anna fearful and skeptical; and in his role as the doctor in the play's final scene, he compassionately though futilely consoles her after her brother has died. The Third Man acts, paradoxically, as both the ineffectual force of the American medical establishment and the curative partners in Anna's self-prescribed sexual therapy. In his turns as doctor, translator, sexual partner, airport security guard, and noir villain, the Third Man mediates between Anna's fantasy and her reality, while disrupting all attempts to construct the playworld and the characters in it in binary terms.

Waltz, like *Drive*, uses the trope of the lesson as a framework for the play's action, a trope reinforced by Anna's work as a kindergarten schoolteacher and Carl's as a children's librarian at the San Francisco Public Library. In the play's opening scene, Carl, who has been fired from his job because he is gay (the play's first hint that Anna's ATD is Carl's AIDS), gives a lesson to a group of visiting schoolchildren on his last day of work. Showing the children the pink slip he received from the branch manager, Shelley Bizo, Carl instructs the children on how to cut out triangles from pink construction paper to match the one he wears on his lapel. He coordinates the craft exercise with a revised version of the familiar nursery rhyme: "Here We Go Round the Mulberry Bush," adding the irreverent line, "This is the way we pick our nose, pick our nose, pick our nose, so early in the morning," as well as the politicized line, "This is the way we go on strike, go on strike, go on strike" (8). This satiric revision is both a call for action and a reminder that we learn things like homophobia, paranoia, and prejudice at an early age, and so we can also learn (and teach) more inclusive models of community as well.

Anna opens the play with a direct address to the audience, which is both a plea for help and an invitation into the playworld. Feeling lost and disoriented, she asks the audience to help her understand and remember:

> Help me please. (*Recites from memory*) Dutch: "Kunt U mij helpen, alstublieft?" "There's nothing I can do." French: (*Searches in vain*) I have no memory. (*Reads from the* Berlitz) "Il n'y a rien à faire." "Where are the toilets?" "Wo sind die die Toiletten?" I've never been abroad. It's not that I don't want to—but the language terrifies me. (7)

Anna's opening address establishes the play's focus on language, memory, and loss. These lines are Anna's response to the words of the doctor at Johns Hopkins Hospital in Baltimore, Maryland: "I'm sorry . . . There's nothing we can do" (9).These words, spoken in the present tense, signal Carl's death and Anna asks the audience to "help [her] understand." On one level, she is teaching herself foreign languages in preparation for her European adventure with her brother, and on another level, she is trying to translate the meaning of her brother's passing. All of Anna's language lessons in the play relate back to this moment, and it is this moment that *Waltz* stops and expands into fantasy. The ominous line—"There's nothing we can do"—echoes throughout the play, in various tenses, and provides the point of return at the play's end. Anna's fantasy journey works to translate this moment and these words—their meanings and affective reverberations—so that loss and helplessness become remembrance and reconciliation.

Anna's language lessons are a metaphor for the process of grieving, which begins with an experience of isolation and moves toward acceptance. The lessons also translate the impenetrable jargon used by the doctor into the language of Anna's fantasy journey. The Third Man gives "Lesson Number Three: Pronouns and Possessive Case. I, you, he, she, and it. They and we. Yours, mine ours." This lesson is correlated with the primary verb of action: "to do":

> THE VOICE OF ANNA: There's nothing I can do. There's nothing you can do. There's nothing he, she, or it can do. There's nothing we can do. There's nothing they can do.
> ANNA: So what are we going to do?
> CARL: Start packing, dear sister.
> ANNA: Europe? You mean it? (14)

Using the verb "to do," a verb that describes the work of all performatives, Anna mobilizes the performative power of fantasy—its capacity to create and remake—in order to gain a sense of agency. While Anna can *do* nothing to change the reality of Carl's death, she can use her imagination to transform how she lives with it.

At the center of the play is a comic theatricalization of Elisabeth Kübler-Ross's five stages of the terminally ill. In her influential 1969 book, *On Death and Dying*, Kübler-Ross challenged the dehumanized approach to illness, asking: "Is the reason for this increasingly mechanical, depersonalized approach our own defensiveness? Is this approach our own way to cope with and repress the anxieties that a terminally ill patient evokes in us?"[13] As a corrective to this approach, Kübler-Ross posited five emotional stages that the terminally ill travel through while coming to terms with death: denial, anger, bargaining, depression, and acceptance. In *Waltz*, Vogel adds a sixth stage: lust. With the Third Man announcing each stage, Carl and Anna lie together in the bed, shifting positions in conjunction with each stage of grief Anna enacts. In "The First Stage: Denial and Isolation," Anna confesses, "I feel so alone"; in "Second Stage: Anger," Anna asks, "How could this happen to me! I did my lesson plans faithfully for the past ten years. . . . Which one of them did this to me? . . . Susy Higgins? Because I called her out on her nosepicking?" Through each stage, Carl is there to comfort her:

> CARL: Calm down, sweetie. You're angry. It's only natural to be angry.
> Elizabeth Kübler-Ross says that—
> ANNA: What does she know about what it feels like to die?! Elizabeth
> Kübler-Ross can sit on my face!
> *(Carl and Anna change positions on the bed)*
> THE THIRD MAN: The Third Stage: Bargaining.
> ANNA: Do you think if I let Elizabeth Kübler-Ross sit on my face I'll
> get well? (26–27)

Kübler-Ross describes hope as a constant throughout all the other five stages, writing, "The one thing that usually persists through all these stages is hope," adding, "Even the most accepting, most realistic patients left the possibility open for some cure, for the discovery of a new drug."[14] Hope, a necessary ingredient of fantasy, plays an important role in confronting the absoluteness of death, alleviating the weight of its overwhelming finality. Lust, Vogel's contribution to this paradigm, introduces sex as a healing act that does not carry disease, but combats it. By turning lust into a form of therapy, a physical remedy rather than a moral vice, the play translates the associations often attached to nonmonogamous sex—illicit, secretive, dirty, deviant—and replaces them with positive connotations that link it with robust health and restoration. And as Anna and her Parisian Garçon make love in the bed center stage and reach a climax of self-in-relation—shouting in unison "I—I—I—I—/Je—Je! Je!! Je!"—Carl tells the audience, "In art, as in life, some things need no translation" (23). Indeed, sex is the only literal thing in the play—nothing more and nothing less than what is it: a bodily act.

By presenting an active female sexuality unencumbered by shame or social stigmas, the play also reworks conventional stereotypes of female sexuality. Anna is neither innocent victim of a disease nor stigmatized whore, and her virile sexuality is characterized in the play in terms traditionally coded as masculine; it is active, inherent, and spontaneous. In fact, since female sexuality masquerades as male homosexuality in this play, then we could say that the play as a whole, with its broad humor, parody, social satire, erotic subtext, and sketchlike structure, burlesques female heterosexuality *and* male homosexuality. Attitudes surrounding sexuality and AIDS are displaced under the stylized light of *Waltz*, with Carl's low-key demeanor accentuating Anna's amplified libido. And as her sex drive propels them through Europe, it becomes the therapeutic life force that counters the death with which she is actually confronted.

Coinciding with the play's temporal movements, the language lessons also teach Anna about time, specifically verb tenses (past, present, and future perfect), and its role in shaping subjectivity. Both semantically and syntactically, these linguistic exercises link subjectivity, agency, and temporality, reflecting Anna's search for the power to change the course of events, to turn back time, and to translate loss into something she can accept. The repeated refrains, "I don't understand" and "the language terrifies me," suggest a suspension of linguistic meaning in moments of grief, which leave the subject in a state of fearful helplessness. As Judith Butler contends, "grief displays the way in which we are in thrall of our relations with others . . . in ways that challenge the very notions of ourselves as autonomous and in control."[15] Pointing to the way loss is often experienced as a rupturing of the self, Anna's first language lesson deals with "subject position. I. Je. Ich. Ik" (9). Here, Carl is her teacher. It is through learning the first-person singular—in four different languages—that Anna begins the process of translating loss into reconciliation—a reunion through memory and fantasy that will allow her to incorporate Carl into her sense of self. Anna's fantasy trip—indeed the entire play—can be read as the transformative work of mourning, in the sense that "mourning has to do with agreeing to undergo a transformation the full result of which you cannot know in advance."[16] These unpredictable transformations emerge from the work of fantasy and memory. That Anna spends much of the play reconstructing pieces of her memory and learning languages suggests that remembering is itself an act of translation, a transposition of past into present and loss into recollection. Anna learns a new vocabulary in order to assimilate—discursively and emotionally—her grief, and the play's juxtapositions and composite characterizations create the effect of a dreamlike splintering of self, in which all the players seem to refract the emotional upheaval of a single moment.

Alongside the language lessons are, like in *Drive*, memory lessons. *Waltz* develops an understanding of language and memory as social, embodied acts. In particular, the play emphasizes memory as an experience activated by sensations, like smell and touch. And yet memory, the play suggests, is always accompanied by loss, even as the act of remembering also retrieves what has been lost. In scene 8, Anna recalls the moment when her and Carl's parents told the five-year-old sister and seven-year-old brother that it was no longer appropriate for them to share a bed. The Third Man introduces the scene as "first separation—your first sense of loss," then narrates Anna's memory of sneaking back into her older brother's room and snuggling up next to him, "breathing in the scent of [her] own breath and his seven-year-old body" (17). Memory becomes a compensation for the inevitability of loss. As Butler writes:

> Let's face it. We are undone by each other. . . . If this seems so clearly the case with grief, it is only because it was already the case with desire. One does not always stay intact. . . . Despite one's best efforts, one is undone, in the face of another, by the touch, by the scent, by the feel, by the prospect of the touch, by the memory of the feel.[17]

When she enters "the Fifth Stage: Acceptance," Anna says to Carl, "when I hold your hand, and I kiss it . . . I try to memorize what it looks like, your hand. . . . I wonder if there's any memory in the grave?" (28). Remembering here is an act of acceptance and reconciliation. The "undoing" of the self that grief initiates, memory—and theater—gathers back together and performs.

On the subject of memory, Anna is a gifted teacher. During her tryst with the Munich Virgin, who is ambiguously described as *"very young"* (40), Anna assumes a position not unlike that of L'il Bit in relation to the young man on the bus trip in upstate New York. However, Anna's seduction of the Munich Virgin has a tender, almost maternal quality. It is a lesson in compassion and seduction at once. She tells the virgin:

> ANNA: Listen. I'm a schoolteacher. May I tell you something? A little lesson? When you're a much older man, and you've loved many women, you'll be a wonderful lover if you're just a little bit nervous . . . like you are right now. Because it will always be your first time.
>
> MUNCH VIRGIN: You are a very nice woman.
>
> ANNA: The human body is a wonderful thing. Like yours. Like mine. The beauty of the body heals all sickness, all the bad things that happen to it. And I really want you to feel this because if you feel it, you'll remember it. And then maybe you'll remember me. (41)

Here, Anna articulates a mode of remembering that is inextricably bound to sensual experience. Remembrance reanimates moments of past pleasures, and pleasure, here, is a form of healing. The lesson Anna teaches the Munich Virgin, and herself, is how to remember with and through the body—its affects, pleasures, and desires—and how to create memories of pleasure out of experiences of pain. In this way, memory is experienced as a sensation of fullness in one's body. Just as Anna seeks to translate her brother's death from a clinical, discursive abstraction or political issue into a language of remembrance and love, so too does she seek to recreate loss as embodied recollection. The emphasis on memory in the play suggests that bodies can act as a living archive where the memories of those we are connected to are stored and reanimated through sensations.

Anna's final language lesson introduces the three moods of the verb *"verlassen*: to leave, to abandon, to forsake" (40), a signal that she is beginning to confront her loss. In the play's penultimate scene Anna, sitting alone, remembers a game she used to play "in the days before I could read." In this prelinguistic game, Anna would "make up stories about my hands—Mr. Left and Mr. Right." Using her body, not words, the game acts as a microcosm of the play. She explains to the audience:

> Mr. Left would provoke Mr. Right. Mr. Right would ignore it. The trouble would escalate, until my hands were battling each other to the death. *(Beat)* Then one of them would weep. Finally they became friends again, and they'd dance. (52)

This game uses the body to externalize psychic conflict, a struggle between denial and acceptance, between antagonism and reconciliation, between fantasy and reality. Further, the war between her two hands acts as a condensed metaphor for the play itself, as Anna tries to translate her brother's death from language that "terrifies" into memory that consoles. Imaginatively recreating a time before language defined her world, *"Anna's two hands dance together"* (52), while her mind returns to her Baltimore present.

Jarring her into this return is Dr. Todesrocheln (translation: "death rattle"), who enacts a darkly comic performance of Anna's childhood game. Donning a fright wig and *"one sinister black glove"* (52), the Third Man revises the role of Dr. Strangelove, the schizophrenic scientist from Stanley Kubrick's 1964 satire of Cold War panic. This intertextual echo once again connects Cold War and AIDS paranoia, though this time through the figure of the mad scientist, rather than the noir villain. The scene also works as a dark parody of the underground AIDS remedies circulating during the 1980s and 1990s. After collecting Anna's urine sample, Dr. Todesrocheln becomes increasingly preoccupied with consuming the specimen himself, and the scene turns into an eerie reenactment of Anna's childhood game, with Dr. Todesrocheln's right hand trying to stop his left hand from drinking the urine elixir. As his *"left hand seizes the flask,"* his right hand *"trembling, with authority . . . replaces the flask on the table"* (53). After a series of brief struggles, his left hand finally outwits his right, and with his back to the audience, he drinks the urine in one gulp. Revolted by this display, Anna begins to question the veracity of her own fantasy, asking the doctor, "Is that your real hair? . . . I don't believe that's your real hair." Her disbelief signals the return to her Baltimore reality, and Dr. Todesrocheln's alarming question, "WO IST DEIN BRUDER?" jars Anna back toward the moment that begins the play. As she turns to see her brother lying on the hospital bed, the "Emperor Waltz" blares. Anna, still somewhere between fantasy and reality, tries to awaken Carl, whose body "*becomes animated, but with a strange, automatic life of its own*" (56). He and Anna dance an awkward waltz, but Carl's body gradually "winds down," and a shrill alarm clock sounds, abruptly ending Anna's fantasy and returning her to the initial scene of loss.

In the final scene, the Johns Hopkins doctor reappears, and the harsh white light extinguishes the warm glow of the fantasy journey. Now, back in the present tense, Carl's death is understood by Anna in/as the past tense: "I'm sorry. There was nothing we could do" (56). As the doctor gives Anna the odds and ends from Carl's hospital room, including travel brochures for Europe, she says, "I've never been abroad. We're going to go when he gets—*(Stops herself) (With control)* I must learn to use the past tense." And yet, she refuses the finality of the past tense. As a Strauss waltz softly begins to play, "*Carl, perfectly well, waits for Anna. He is dressed in Austrian military regalia. They waltz off as the lights dim*" (57). The play yields to fantasy, using the theater as a public place of commemoration that remains in "a process we know to be endless." In this sense, Vogel's play participates in a reparative project that promotes a particular mode of spectatorship, in which spectators can actively generate meanings from a text or performance and take their own journeys. Sedgwick writes:

> No less acute than a paranoid position, no less realistic, no less attached to a project of survival, and neither less nor more delusional or fantasmatic, the reparative reading position undertakes a different range of affects, ambitions, and risks. What we can best learn from such practices are, perhaps, the many ways selves and communities succeed in extracting sustenance from the objects of a culture—even a culture whose avowed desire has often been not to sustain them.[18]

This reparative approach aptly captures the way *Waltz* rearticulates the cultural discourse surrounding AIDS, translating the homophobic script and moral panic used to stigmatize those with HIV into a celebratory journey.

The Baltimore Waltz was Vogel's breakthrough play, receiving almost unanimous praise from critics. It premiered in 1990 at Alaska's

Perseverance Theatre, under the direction of Molly Smith, moving to New York City's Circle Repertory Company in 1992, under the direction of Anne Bogart. It won an Obie award and, as Carolyn Casey-Craig states, "marked a turning point in Paula's career."[19] In his review of the 1992 Circle Repertory production David Román writes that *Waltz* is not only "one of the funniest plays of the past few years" but also "a beautiful play that celebrates with such honesty, warmth, and conviction the relationships we continue to lose twelve years and counting into this epidemic."[20] *Waltz* not only marks a particular historical moment in American history; it also remains as a living cultural archive and ongoing commemoration.

In contrast to the almost unanimous praise *Waltz* received, Frank Rich's review for the *New York Times* registered an impatience with the tone and structure of Vogel's play. His review begins by quoting the play's dedication—"To the memory of Carl—because I cannot sew"—only to wonder, "Who Carl is we can only imagine." (If he had read Carl's letter printed in the playbill, he would have found out.) Rich describes the play as "a crazy-quilt patchwork of hyperventilating language, erotic jokes, movie kitsch and medical nightmare—that spins before the audience in Viennese waltz time, replete with a dying fall." Barring the barely veiled tone of disdain, this is an apt description of the play. Rich felt that *Waltz* was, by turns, "too clever by half or less funny than it wants to be" and "too flagrantly defies translation, lacking the internal logic that can make some dream plays . . . add up to their own idiosyncratic terms." What kind of "internal logic" the play is failing to follow Rich does not say. Perhaps most curiously, Rich critiques the play for enacting a kind of hubris in its attempt "to rise above and even remake the world in which the disease exists." Whether he deems AIDS a subject deserving of more somber, realistic treatment, he does not make clear. Rich concludes his review favorably, however, stating, "I respect what Vogel is up to and was steadily fascinated by it." He paid particular praise to Anne Bogart's direction, Cherry Jones's "bravura display of seamless acting technique," and Joe Mantello's winning "burlesque turns in cameo roles of several nationalities and sexual dispositions."[21]

Reviewing the 2004 Signature Theatre production, Charles Isherwood argued that the play had lost its resonance. While over a decade earlier, the play had "touched a chord in audiences who recognized in its wild, reckless shifts in tone and style the authentic note of those confusing times," now, he claims, it "serves to illustrate the cruel tricks time can play on a once-potent work of art." Kristen Johnston's Anna, Isherwood rightly points out, ably performed the comic scenes but "doesn't do vulnerability convincingly."[22] Both Rich and Isherwood define *Waltz* as a "play about AIDS" (to quote Rich's headline), basing their evaluations largely on *Waltz*'s approach to a social "issue." The play's continued vitality lies not in the social issue it invokes, however, but in the way it invokes it. *Waltz* defamiliarizes the affective, moral, and social meanings surrounding AIDS; but even more, it demonstrates the way theater can operate as a civic space, in which fantasy and memory can indeed be mobilized, if only provisionally, to remake the world. As Román writes, "Anna remains, as do we, joined for a moment in the fantasy of the theatre where AIDS can be rewritten as ATD and the living can stand in for the suffering of loved ones."[23] *Waltz* stops time, allowing us to remain in that liminal place of commemoration—between memory and celebration—so we can remember together.

Memory's Ghosts: *The Long Christmas Ride Home*[24]

Like *Waltz*, *The Long Christmas Ride Home* commemorates Vogel's brother, Carl, who appears in this play as Stephen. Vogel states that with this play, "I am revisiting one of my primary concerns, which is that it's homophobia, not so much as AIDS, which kills us in this country."[25] *Home* bears all the Vogel trademarks—stylistic juxtapositions, a combination of humor and pathos, the use of circular form, and a focus on a political issue refracted through the lens of the family—but it is also markedly distinct from her previous work. Highly conceptual, poetic, and formally complex, *Home* departs from the embodied historicity and social specificity of Vogel's other plays, invoking notions of time and place that are, at once, more abstracted and more immediate. The play also marks a shift in her oeuvre away from a central female character and toward a more diffuse ensemble of perspectives, striking notes of solemnity and reverence in contrast to the irreverent humor of her previous plays. In its experimentation with Japanese Nō drama and Bunraku puppet theater techniques, *Home* also marks Vogel's first experiment with a nonwestern theatrical tradition.

"For an American dramatist, all roads lead back to Thornton Wilder," writes Vogel in her foreword to Wilder's *The Skin of Our Teeth*.[26] *Home* revises Wilder's one-act plays, *The Happy Journey to Trenton and Camden* and *The Long Christmas Dinner*, which take a family car trip and an endless Christmas dinner, respectively, as their point of departure for contemplating the rituals and repetitions of everyday life. Reminding us of Wilder's "subtle blend of humor and pathos, and his masterful balancing of abstraction and empathy," Vogel contends that, "of all his innovations we are most indebted to the way Wilder transformed the passage of time on stage."[27] Indeed, Wilder used the theater to comment on the passage of time itself, developing an understated dramaturgical style that focuses on abstracted yet affecting impressions of everyday places, events, and characters. Borrowing Wilder's devices of a car trip and a Christmas dinner, *Home* examines one family's Christmas Eve, which is interrupted by a moment of crisis that returns and reverberates ad infinitum in the lives of the children every year thereafter. The family is, in *Home*, radically defamiliarized, with second-person narration, puppet-children, and rapid temporal shifts displacing the realism of more conventional family dramas. And yet invoking the most nostalgia-laden of holidays enables a trenchant examination of the affective structures underlying both Christmas and family.

Home fuses the principles of the one-act play and the techniques of Bunraku puppet theater to dramatize a family car trip to Grandma's for Christmas dinner, along with the emotional repercussions of this trip in the lives of each family member. Vogel says of the play, "I chose Christmas because for us in America, regardless of whether we are Christian, it is the closest thing to myth we have."[28] Vogel suggests that the play be produced not during Christmas, but instead in the "before [or] the aftermath."[29] Displacing the immediate present, the play focuses on the enduring nature of annual rituals and on the halo of memories and emotions that cluster around them. The play begins in an undetermined past, then flashes forward in time and, at a critical moment of crisis, stands still. The action pivots around a fight between the mother and father, referred to generically as Man and Woman, which erupts in the family car, signaled in Mark Brokaw's production simply by a bench. The Man and Woman argue in the front seat, while their two daughters, Claire and Rebecca, and their son, Stephen, sit anxiously in the back seat. As the argument escalates and the Man raises his hand to strike the Woman, the car veers out of control, coming to a stop on the edge of a slippery cliff. Vogel stops this moment, a violent memory that echoes throughout the play as the "before and the aftermath" of the play action.

The violence of this moment, and others throughout the play, is divested of its expected affective impact through the juxtaposition of a Japanese aesthetic with western cultural content. As Vogel puts it, *Home* exemplifies "one westerner's misunderstanding of Bunraku. The misunderstanding is key."[30] Vogel's use of Bunraku techniques defamiliarizes subjects such as family, violence, religion, and sexuality, undermining habituated responses by demanding a constant negotiation between drama and aesthetics, identification and distance, affect and intellect. Emotional values associated with familiar cultural symbols are radically altered, for example, when Good King Wenceslas is played on a samisen at Christmas mass or when Bunraku puppets perform the parts of children. Vogel draws on the nonrepresentational aesthetic of Bunraku as a way to disorient the conventional modes of spectatorship associated with western realist drama; to dramatize time in a nonlinear pattern; and to problematize the notions of individual agency, privacy, and interiority that are central to constructions of the modern western subject and modern western theater.

Deriving its name from eighteenth-century playwright Uemura Bunrakuken, Bunraku developed out of earlier forms of sixteenth-century doll theater. Unlike Nō theater, which emerged in the fourteenth century under the support of the shogunate, Bunraku emerged as a popular form that appealed to the general public. And yet Nō and Bunraku are both highly literary forms. As theater scholar Donald Keene points out, "Bunraku is the one theatre of dolls for which literary masterpieces have been especially composed,"[31] and this literary emphasis both connects it to Nō and differentiates it from Kabuki, a popular form that places primary focus on the actor's body and gestures. The text of Bunraku is sung by chanters who occupy a central role in the performance. As Keene explains, "the chanter was moved from backstage to a place before the audience, as if to deny the illusion that the puppets were speaking for themselves, and to insist on the primacy of the written word."[32] The chanted narrative is embodied and performed by the puppets, which are three to four feet tall and operated by three puppeteers. The senior puppeteer wears elaborate traditional robes and holds the puppet upright, while observing its movements and reacting to them expressively. The two assistants, who dress in black cloaks, move the arms and legs in minute and intricate movements that take a lifetime of training to master. As Keene points out, the senior puppeteer "makes no attempt to conceal the fact that she is manipulating the puppet," since "the illusion that the puppets [are] moving and speaking of their own accord" is not the aim of the spectacle.[33] The aim of Bunraku performance is the unity of elements, from the unified breath of the puppeteers to the coming together of the three components—text, music, and puppets. Keene explains: "If the three operators of a puppet must 'breathe' as a single entity, it is no less essential that the three component parts of Bunraku, the narration, the music, and the puppets, 'breathe' as one."[34] As the three puppeteers breathe together, the puppet comes to life for the audience; the more unified the breath, the more lifelike the puppet appears. Similarly, the more indivisible the dramatic components seem, the more animated the spectacle becomes.

Bunraku splits the conventions of western theater into three separate elements, thus presenting a total, though divided, visual display. In his essay "The Dolls of Bunraku," French cultural theorist Roland Barthes writes:

> Bunraku practices in effect three separate modes of writing, which allow us to read simultaneously three areas of the spectacle: the marionette, the manipulator, the vocalizer: the effected gesture, he who effects the gesture, and the vocal gesture.[35]

Barthes connects the divided elements of Bunraku theater and Brechtian epic theater, which challenged the unity of the "total work of art." Barthes explains that, in Asian acting techniques, Brecht saw a social action being *cited*, rather than an individual gesture being performed. As Barthes puts it, Brecht recognized that "here reigns the *quotation*," the social act that is "freed from the metonymic contagion of voice and gesture, of the spirit and the body, which cements together [the western] actor."[36] This performative "quotation," which takes apart—or deconstructs—voice and gesture, spirit and body, would be called, by Walter Benjamin, "*gestus*." Similar to Barthes, Benjamin defines Brecht's drama as a "theatre of interruption," identifying the interruptive element as *gestus*, "the quotable gesture," which disrupts the flow of action and creates a distance between the actor and the action being performed. "'Making gestures quotable' is one of the essential achievements of epic theatre,"[37] concluded Benjamin. As the crystallization of a social condition, the *gestus* aims to separate actor and consciousness and to suspend the citation of a social action long enough for the spectator to see other possible actions that might be performed in its place. Vogel too mobilizes this suspension of a social action and interruption of linear time, quoting a past moment long enough for the audience and actors to analyze its continued resonance in the present.

The dialectical image, like the *gestus*, is an interruption in historical time that yields social meanings in the present. It is an image in which the past is infused with the immediate present—the nowtime (*Jetztzeit*) of Jewish mysticism. As Benjamin writes:

> The dialectical image is one flashing up momentarily. It is thus, as an image flashing up in the *now* of its recognizability, that the past . . . can be captured. The redemption which can be carried out in this way and in no other is always to be won out of the perception of that which is being lost irretrievably.[38]

Benjamin's Marxism is shaped by Messianic Judaism, and his notion of the dialectical image comes out of this political-religious worldview. Now-time articulates a perspective through which one sees history as a series of quotable moments; it is a convergence of linear and theological history, a moment in which history becomes meaningful, not discursively, but as a collision of fragments, memories, and repetitions. Art, and especially theater, opens itself to encounter with nowtime, as it is already somewhat removed from everyday temporality. In *Home*, the moment that is suspended is, in effect, taken "outside of time," a private memory opened up for public witness. From this perspective, we see the way time—and our methods for organizing time and history—shapes actions, thoughts, and choices.

The subtitle—*A Puppet Play with Actors*—points to the puppets' central role in *Home*. The puppets visually complicate some of the fundamental dualisms structuring western theater and culture: body/voice, interiority/exteriority, active/passive, past self/present self, private/public, individual memory/collective memory, performativity/theatricality. The actors playing the adult children operate the puppets, which stand in as their child-selves, and the movements are

Figure 9: *The Long Christmas Ride Home.* Left to right: Mark Blum, Enid Graham, Will McCormack, Catherine Kellner, and Randy Graff. Vineyard Theatre, New York City, 2003. Photo: ©Carol Rosegg.

orchestrated in response to the dialogue narrated by the Man and Woman. In this way, the puppets become animated representations of the past, while the puppeteers witness a reenactment of this past (their past) from an objective perspective. And as the actor-puppeteers replay their memories in an improvisational performance, they gain an opportunity for critical examination and revision of these memories. Like the Brechtian actor, the puppet-puppeteer relationship enacts a critical distance between actor and action performed, between memory and affect, and between past and present. Like Bunraku puppeteers, the actor-puppeteers in *Home* remain visible when manipulating the puppets. However, unlike Bunraku puppeteers, with their animated facial expressions and precise manipulations, the puppeteers in *Home* operate the puppets somewhat awkwardly, with expressions that remain "neutral and unemotive."[39] The actor-puppeteers appear like a diegetic audience, watching the action that they are making the puppet perform and placing the audience in the same position of detached analysis, rather than emotional (over)involvement. Making the puppets the primary focus also displaces conventional practices of interpretation and identification, discouraging the moralizing tendencies that often accompany representations of gender, sexuality, religion, and family.

Along with the theatrical displacement of body-voice, act-agent, past-present, effected by the puppets, Vogel draws on the narrative technique of Bunraku to problematize western notions of psychological interiority, privacy, and individuality. The first section of the play uses nonrealistic dialogue, with the parents narrating the thoughts of their children and of each other aloud to the audience, in past tense, verse form. This technique disrupts not only naturalistic conventions of character but also notions of individuality and interiority so central to western constructions of selfhood. The Man, for example, narrates his wife's thoughts during Christmas mass: "The mother thought perhaps she should have an affair / To feel the heat and motion of a man's body next to hers" (17). The Man and Woman also narrate the thoughts of their children. As Stephen struggles with anxious thoughts about his burgeoning sexuality, his father speaks these thoughts aloud to the audience: "Was he bad? For watching boys? / Think, Stephen, of something else / Without heat and motion"(17). Similarly, the Woman narrates her daughter Claire's thoughts: "She had asked for cowboy boots and guns / . . . She had not noticed that slight crease in her mother's brow, a concern / A question too soon to be asked" (19). What is experienced initially as private and shameful is here publicly reenacted as a shared experience. Further, the ventriloquism performed by Man and Woman separates performative gestures from the authority that gives them force and meaning. Thus, as the Man and Woman (the authority) narrate the thoughts of their puppet-children, the puppets perform or "cite" these narrated thoughts in the form of gestures. The relationship between thought and act is in this way taken apart and made visible. And although the parents are invested with the authority to speak the thoughts of the children, it is the adult-puppeteers who are the agents of the performative act. Like the *gestus*, this disjunctive narrative technique disrupts the autonomy of the speaker, positioning the social aspects of the voice in dissonant tension with individual bodies, thereby radically disrupting the notion of a private, inner consciousness with a circulation of thoughts and feelings that, although believed to be individually felt, are actually collectively experienced.

This distinctive narrative strategy also suggests that sexuality is neither private nor individual, but part of a shared system of internalized codes, gestures, and affects. As Judith Butler writes, sexuality is relational and resists claims to possession:

> And so when we speak about *my* sexuality or *my* gender, as we do (and as we must) we mean something complicated by it. Neither of these is precisely a possession, but both are *modes of being dispossessed*, ways of being for another or, indeed, by virtue of another.[40]

Gender and sexuality can never be "mine," then, but are always products of the social world from which I speak. This displacement of body and voice in the play stages a unique challenge to understandings of gender and sexuality as the essence or secret truth of one's identity. As the seemingly private thoughts and feelings of the children are made public by the parents' narration and performed by the puppets, the audience sees the subjectivities of the children formed through a kind of dispossession; the children are dispossessed by the authority of their parents and the heteronormative culture of which they are a part, and the puppets become emblems of this dispossession, homeless materialized spirits still seeking refuge.

One of the play's central concerns revolves around questions of belief. Narrated by the Man, Claire repeatedly asks her parents during Christmas mass at the family's Unitarian church, "But What Do We Believe?" (24, 28). In a culture that has lost its faith in universal categories and communal values, the characters in *Home* search for something solid on which to build a belief. Religion, like art, involves constructing a system of belief through which meaning and value are created. Mobilizing theater's capacity to question and produce other kinds of meanings and values, *Home* foregrounds the possibilities of building more diverse and inclusive belief systems. The play works to demystify the systems of belief (religion) and institutions (family) that give value and authority to *certain* bodies and *some* voices. What is at stake in the production of belief systems is the authority to make distinctions between what is real and what is not, to define what is right and what is wrong, and to decide what (and who) matters and what (and who) does not.

Neither theater nor religion is, in Vogel's play, about a belief system based on binary divisions between real and illusion, spirit and flesh, sacred and profane, physical/metaphysical. As the young Unitarian Minister's sermon reinforces, "It is not only Joy To The World! It is Joy In the World" (25). The Minister's didactic function in the play underscores the various ways we learn and internalize cultural beliefs and values. Here, religious authority is used to construct alternative ways of looking at social and spiritual realities that disrupt distinctions between material and spiritual, sacred and profane, public and private. Showing slides of Japan's Edo period as part of his sermon, the Minister inadvertently shows an image of a Japanese prostitute. Transforming his mistake into a teaching moment, he describes the prostitute as "a lady of the . . . um, Theatre district of Edo. A working lady" (26). He elaborates on the image in a neutral tone, describing the position of the prostitute on the bottom, "and on top a very nice gentleman, possibly of the warrior class. In our culture, we revere Mary Magdalene in a similar way. Although Mary Magdalene, um, renounced her line of work" (26). This passage forges connections between the sexualized iconography of women in both western and eastern cultures, past and present. Moreover, his lesson reinforces the working lady's labor *as labor*. Curious, Claire asks her mother, "'Did the Virgin Mary work?'" and her mother answers, "'No. She stayed at home. Like your mother'" (27). Through this cross-cultural comparison, the play constructs a micro-materialist history of female labor and sexuality out of sacred feminine icons. In this way, the sacred is historicized and revealed as part of the larger narrative of the history of sexuality.

The Minister, like Vogel the playwright, looks to Japan to defamiliarize habituated western perspectives. As the Minister points out, "Sometimes using the distance and perspective / Of a Far-off land, of another people / We can return and see our home more clearly" (25). In sharp contrast to the denunciation of bodily desires and pleasures that characterizes much Christian theology, the Minister suggests "putting aside Western notions of guilt and shame about the / body—Why not embrace what will too soon be gone?" (25). Revaluing the body and its pleasures in positive terms, he points to Japanese "artists, courtesans, actors and merchants" as models to follow, since they are "determined to enjoy the flesh because it [is] ephemeral." As the Minister explains, "Artists who wrestle with this relationship of man / And nature called this art 'Ukiyo-e' / The Floating World" (25). *Ukiyo-e*, or the Floating World, is the Japanese term for a type of art that seeks to represent humanity's relationship to nature. Emerging from the urban culture of Edo (modern-day Tokyo) between the seventeenth and twentieth centuries, *Ukiyo-e* is art that is closely connected with the pleasures of theaters and restaurants, of geishas and courtesans. Vogel invokes this notion in her play to reorient the western tendency to view bodily pleasures as morally suspect, presenting pleasure, instead, as something to be honored, celebrated, remembered. In its liminality (to use Victor Turner's term), theater itself is a kind of floating world, an embodied medium that reminds us of the pleasure and impermanence of inhabiting a body. Significantly, the play's epigraph is a poem entitled "Floating World," written by Carl Vogel, whose ghost inhabits the play and whose body is revived in its performance.

As Christmas mass shifts into Christmas dinner at the grandparents' house, the play's focus on religion shifts to a focus on family. And as the Minister narrates the role of grandmother and grandfather, religious and family rituals are implicitly juxtaposed, and the thoughts and tensions simmering beneath the surface during mass and in the family car bubble forth into overt violence. Claire is given a gift that clearly demonstrates that she is her father's favorite child; Stephen is shamed and mocked by the Man for his sexual disposition; and the grandfather rails against the Man for so callously hurting his son, hurling the verbal barb, "'Kike!'" at his son-in-law, to which the Man responds with "'Cocksucker!'" (37). As *"the two men waltzed in a wrestler's embrace,"* they enact a stylized fight performed in the present but narrated as an event of the past, bringing distance to the emotional impact of this moment. And as the Minister narrates the emotion of the moment—"And the women and children keened a collective: 'Aaaahhhh!'" (38)—Claire takes over with the memory of "feeling the shame / . . . And whatever happened from that moment on / Moments linked to moments / It was all her fault" (40). Time reverberates in *Home*, the affective traces of past moments returning as echoes, reminders of what still remains. After the fight at the grandparents' house, the play returns to the family car to stage the fight between the Man and the Woman. As the Woman says bitterly to her husband, "Well. What a lovely Christmas you've given me," the Man responds by *"ritualistically draw[ing] back his hand to strike."* But Claire halts this moment by making a future promise—"I will never have children" (46)—and the play flashes forward to witness the failed relationships of Claire, Rebecca, and Stephen, all of whom are still living out this frozen moment in the family car. Here Vogel references Wilder's *The Long Christmas Dinner* most directly, revising Genevieve Bayard's desire to stop time—"I shall never marry, Mother—I shall sit in this house beside you forever, as though life were one long, happy Christmas dinner"[41]—into Rebecca's promise never to bear children (which, like Genevieve's wish, is a refusal to repeat and reproduce the family unit) and Stephen's promise, "I will never strike a woman like that!" (46). However, while Genevieve wishes to remain in the perpetual present, Rebecca and Stephen promise a future divorced from the present.

In the second half of the play, each adult sibling performs a monologue that reveals intimate details of their respective romantic relationships and suggests that, despite Stephen's and Claire's desire for a different future, their past remains part of their future lives. Spoken in the present-tense prose form and punctuated by Japanese woodblocks, the monologues are directed not to the audience, but to the siblings' partners, who were, in Mark Brokaw's production at New York City's Vineyard Theatre, represented by looming shadow puppets, designed by master puppeteer Basil Twist and positioned behind a screen backstage, without any defining or humanizing characteristics. As the actors stood facing stage left to speak their lines, the shadow puppets performed broad, theatrical gestures, producing an imposing silhouette that suggested both the enormous presence of the past in the siblings' future lives and also their distance from it. Twenty-five years later, Rebecca rails against her lesbian lover, who has been cheating on her and who has locked her out of their apartment; twenty-four years later, Claire shouts at her abusive partner, who also has locked her out; and sixteen years after that fateful Christmas car trip, Stephen laments his partner's infidelity. Each stands outside in the winter cold on Christmas Eve, homeless.

Unlike his sisters, Stephen moves fluidly across temporal and spatial boundaries in this section, as he witnesses his sisters' suffering, reenacts his own, and provides critical distance on the stage action through his direct addresses to the audience. After delivering his dejected monologue to his ex-partner, Joe, which takes place sixteen years in the future, Stephen's scene moves to a gay bar, where he meets a "*hunky version of one of the Village People*" (49) and has an impromptu and unprotected encounter in the backroom, performed by puppets that *"simulate a sexual act that means this play will never be performed in Texas"* (50). As the puppets thrust behind the screen, Stephen, also behind the screen, mimes gestures that suggest at first a state of pain, then relaxation, then pleasure, and finally realization. Stephen's repositioning from upstage to backstage behind a screen metaphorically dramatizes the denial and repression of a homophobic culture. Reaching their own respective moments of hopelessness—Rebecca sitting frozen in a snow bank waiting to die and Claire holding the gun in her mouth—the sisters are suddenly saved by a memory of their brother, a memory that resuscitates their bodies with an infusion of breath. What the audience realizes is that Stephen has since died of AIDS and returns every year on the day after Christmas, St. Stephen's Day, to observe his sisters. Considered to be the first Christian martyr, St. Stephen is invoked as one of the many ways the play works to defamiliarize AIDS and homosexuality, the way it juxtaposes eastern and western religious and cultural traditions, and the way it displaces a habituated moral response with aesthetic distance.

In the latter half of the play, the Ghost of Stephen takes on a central role and acts as a mediator between the theater audience and the playworld. Stephen tells the audience about his love for Joe; his admiration of Zeami, Kabuki, and "all things Japanese" (49); and his yearly return to visit his sisters, adding, "all of our ancestors come back to observe the still breathing" (51). It is the breath—and not the body—that separates the living and the dead in *Home*. This reformulation works to displace the moral significations embedded in bodies, particularly those bodies marked as sexually deviant and contaminated, with an emphasis on the breath as ontological ground zero. Philosopher Mladen Dolar explains, "in many languages there is an etymological link between spirit and breath (breath being the 'voiceless voice,' the zero point of vocal emission); the voice carried by breath points to the soul irreducible to the body."[42] The play's emphasis on the breath positions theater as a sacred space and repositions the social discourse surrounding AIDS as a shared, collective concern, rather than a problem arising from the sexual deviance of a marginalized group.

In its ceremonial solemnity, the middle section of the play borrows more from Nō drama than from Bunraku. And in the tradition of Nō, Stephen assumes the role of *shite*, the first actor and central figure that, Keene explains, is the "only true personage"[43] of a Nō play. Depending on the play, the *shite* performs the role of a demon, a god, a woman, an old man, or a child. Keene points out that the *shite* "has usually died before the play begins"[44] and returns as the incarnation of a powerful emotion left unresolved, such as "enmity, possessive jealousy, or remorse."[45] Not at all the protagonist of western realist drama, "the *shite* belongs to another world, not our own, and the creation of character, in the sense that the term is used in other forms of drama, is meaningless in Nō."[46] Since Nō is nondialectical—that is, it does not rely on the conflict generated between a protagonist and antagonist—the other players, the *waki* (second actor), the *tsure* (companion to the *shite*), and the *jiutai* (the chorus), "are merely observers of the action and not antagonists."[47] This nondialectical, nonrealist dynamic engages the audience in a different kind of theatrical spectatorship, one that demands attention, at once, to affect and aesthetics, dramatic effect and technique, unity and fragmentation. In the tradition of the *shite* figure of Nō drama, Wilder's Stage Manager, and Christianity's first martyr, the character of Stephen assumes a prominent role in the center of the play, not as a moral figure, but as an artistic expression of a social condition.

Reflecting on his contraction of HIV, Stephen describes his illness to the audience in aesthetic terms:

> How my sisters will cry. I could feel the virus entering my body. But I could not undo what had been done. And for the next several years, I could feel the virus multiply with a ferocious beauty—replicating patterns that changed and mutated. I could not see the beauty then, of course. . . . It is a very terrible beauty. But it is a beauty all the same. It takes distance to see the beauty in it. And now I have all the distance in the world. (50–51)

The "terrible beauty" that Stephen describes calls to mind Benjamin's theory of the aura.[48] As a spatial and temporal term, the aura implies both physical and historical distance. As Elin Diamond writes in *Unmaking Mimesis*, "Benjamin links the 'experience of the aura' with a complex temporality." "To destroy the aura," Diamond suggests, "is to *release experiences*—emotions, understandings correspondences—for *exoteric* use in the present."[49] Defining the disease that took over his body from an aesthetic perspective, rather than a pathologizing one, Stephen's above speech uses a different set of correspondences, images, and emotions to define AIDS and to describe the bodies affected—and stigmatized—by it.

Providing the dramatic and aesthetic center of the play is a dance, which is performed by the same actor who plays the Unitarian Minister and the grandparents. Of the dancer, Vogel suggests in her stage directions, *"oh, and let him be beautiful"* (52). The dance is a version of the *mai-goto* of Nō drama, a conceptual dance piece performed to instrumental music. Vogel notes that directors and choreographers should decide for themselves how to interpret this section "for western eyes," admitting that "it is as unknown to me as the backroom of a bar" (52). In a characteristic Vogel note, the stage directions explain the eclectic musical subtext informing this dance section: "I wrote this part to the musical segment of 'Porno 3003' . . . and a very manic version of 'Tomorrow Shall Be My Dancing Day'" (52). That she draws inspiration from the synthetic rhythms of the Japanese pop group Pizzicato Five and a traditional English Christmas carol in order to write a highly abstract, yet erotic dance suggests a great deal about Vogel's use of formal experimentation to disorient cultural stereotypes. The effect is a mesmerizing encounter between two beings hovering somewhere between times and places and yet remaining wholly embodied. As the dancer moves seductively and gracefully around Stephen, the dance becomes an aesthetic revision of Stephen's romantic relationship and of the violent intrusion of AIDS into his life, evoking connections between art and eroticism. The *mise-en-scène* of this section was created by Neil Patel at the Vineyard using a red silk backdrop, which provided the visual and symbolic subtext of the dance. The effect suggested a mode of perception grounded not in dualities, but in immanence, an understanding of spirit *in* the flesh, suffering *in* pleasure, beauty *in* pain. At the end of the dance, with the dancer *"breathing hard . . . he takes Stephen in his arms and pours his breath into Stephen's mouth"* (52). Here, breath is linked to desire, a desire that is both of the spirit and of the flesh, ephemeral and embodied. After the dance, the Ghost of Stephen turns to the audience to say:

> How wonderful it feels to breathe! You cannot know how beautiful it is. When you are alive, you cannot see your breath. But we your ancestors can see the air move when you breathe. Your breathing cre-

ates a spectrum of color; the motion and heat of your life. And often—in a church or a meeting, in a mosque—or like now, in a theatre. . . . Whenever a family or an audience hold your breath together—a moment of silence before you collectively expel the air—Ah, then: Fireworks for the ancestors! (52–53)

Like the unified breath in Bunraku that brings the theatrical spectacle to life, breath is envisioned here as the force that unites metaphysical and physical worlds. And in this moment of a collectively held breath, living and dead are united in the Floating World, and a different kind of temporality is imagined, one in which the past bears witness to the present and those who have passed return to remind the present of what has not yet been remembered. And with the theater audience positioned as both spectator and spectacle, the play returns to the fight in the family car.

Inviting the audience to return with him to that frozen memory on the edge of the slippery cliff, the Ghost of Stephen says, "There is a moment I want you to watch with me. A moment of time stopping. . . . Come back with me now and perhaps you will see it" (53). He breathes life back into the puppets, resumes his place among the living, and the play begins again at the moment when the Man is about to hit the Woman, only now the audience understands the implications of this moment in the future lives of the three children. As *"the man raises his right hand and backhands the woman, slowly, ritualistically"* (53) and the car comes to a halt on the edge of a precipice, a cascade of hopeful "what ifs" erupt from each family member: "If I try harder" wonders the mother, "If I dress a bit younger—If I say softer things" (56). And together, the Man and Woman wonder:

WOMAN and MAN
   If . . .
   (Beat. The Narrators almost turn to each other.)

But it is Rebecca who interrupts their question with:

REBECCA
   And then our father thought of Sheila.
GHOST OF STEPHEN.
   The cream of her breasts

CLAIRE.
   The sliver of her thighs
REBECCA.
   And he wanted to see her.
   He must see her. (56)

Rereading their father's thoughts, his desire to see his mistress, Sheila, the children identify the force—the desire—that eventually propelled the family car back onto stable ground. In the past tense, Rebecca narrates, "As one family and one flesh, / We breathed as one" (57), and with the breath as *gestus*, the past is brought to life in the present. As the siblings assume narrative authority, they look critically at the past and see other possible outcomes of that moment decades ago, revising the thoughts and words of their parents in the theatrical present tense and thus potentially reformulating their future effects. And as the Ghost of Stephen observes *"the currents of color and air"* generated from the breath of the gathered collective, he comments on the spectacular convergence of past and present, living and departed: "Ah! How beautiful!" he says. "Do you see it?" (57). The play concludes, however, with the Man's present-tense imperative—"Children:—let's go home"—followed by Stephen's final line, narrated in the past tense: "And so—we went" (57). The recursive movements of time and memory, in the end, lead back home. In an era in which the nuclear family continues to function as the symbolic center of American culture, Vogel's play sits poised between past and future, unsure of where to go; it registers a nostalgic longing—for home and for hope.

In his *New York Times* review of Long Wharf Theatre's 2003 production of *Home*, directed by Oskar Eustis, David DeWitt described Vogel's approach as "a revelation . . . pure as mathematics in its translation of the prosaic into the abstract."[50] However, "the achievements of this production," according to DeWitt, came "with sacrifices," such as a lack of "gripping momentum" and an overall tone that was "constantly chilly, seldom finding the heat of anything visceral or immediate."[51] The play was lauded as a unique experiment in form, but its lack of conventional conflict and forward movement troubled popular critics and audiences. And although it participates in the recent popularity of puppetry in contemporary theater—from *Avenue Q* to

The Lion King to *War Horse*—*Home* is considerably less spectacular than these more popular shows. Despite its verbal expressions of "heat and motion," the play seemed too detached, its fusion of western subject matter and eastern formal techniques pushing its audiences away, instead of inviting them to "come closer." Literary critic Ann Pellegrini argues, however, that *Home* "reveals the fragility and the hope of human (re) connection," and the characters "yearn for contact with each other, with the past, with lost parts of themselves."[52] The play seems, paradoxically, both alienating and nostalgic, seeking distance from an emphasis on the body but at the same time also yearning for the warmth of embodied connection. This tension resonates productively in our twenty-first century, however, where digital mediation has displaced in-the-flesh sociality.

One way of interpreting the play's two jostling impulses—its nostalgia and its distance—is to consider them in relation to Jill Dolan's theory of the utopian performative, a theatrical experience that "lets audiences imagine utopia not as some idea of future perfection that might never arrive, but as brief enactments of the possibilities of a process that starts now, in this moment at the theater."[53] The utopian performative does not resolve or redeem the past, nor does it promise a better future; rather, it shows us how these temporal arrangements are always (and only) being imagined, constructed, and enacted in the present moment. This theatrical experience does not signal the transcendence of time, history, and difference, but rather a recognition of our participation in "a larger web of culture" and of history that "requires empathy and connection over space and time."[54] Vogel's plays all cultivate such empathic connections, forged out of an engagement with material history and fostered in the present-tenseness of theater. Perhaps no play accomplishes this more resoundingly than her next play, *A Civil War Christmas*.

CHAPTER SEVEN

Haunted History: *A Civil War Christmas: An American Musical Celebration*

> If the past is never over or completed, "remains" might be understood not solely as object or document material, but also as the immaterial labor of bodies engaged in and with that incomplete past: bodies striking poses, making gestures, voicing calls, reading words, singing songs, or standing witness.
>
> —Rebecca Schneider, *Performing Remains: Art and War in Times of Theatrical Reenactment*[1]

> We'll fight for liberty
> Till de Lord shall call us home
> We'll soon be free
> Till de Lord shall call us home.
>
> —Hymn sung by the slaves at Georgetown, South Carolina, when Lincoln was elected[2]

The idea for *A Civil War Christmas: An American Musical Celebration* came to Vogel in 1997 while she was talking to Molly Smith, who had just assumed the position as artistic director at Arena Stage in Washington, DC. Vogel wondered why American theaters staged Dickens's *A Christmas Carol* every year and realized the reason was that no equivalent existed in the American canon. Until now. While *The Long Christmas Ride Home* is meant to be performed in the before- or aftermath of the holiday, this pageant play is situated firmly in Christmas present. Dedicated to her nieces and nephews and her mother-in-law, Dorothy Sterling, who passed away two days before the Long Wharf opening on December 3, 2008, *Christmas* fuses history (the Civil War), ritual (Christmas), poetry (playwriting), and live reenactment (theater) to animate the present with the remains of the past.

The pageant play is a more traditional form than Vogel's previous plays. And yet, written in sixty-two short scenes, *Christmas* is formally complex, moving recursively and disjointedly through the weeks leading up to the last Christmas of the Civil War, while the future—which is our present—hovers everywhere in the playworld. Just as there is no linear history presented here, there is also no static casting. In her production notes, Vogel suggests that, even when not in character and part of the stage action, the actors should remain on stage.[3] The haunted effect of these bodies hovering in the background creates a sense of a history still palpably present and embodied in the shadows. The fourteen actors take on double, triple, and even quadruple roles, crossing lines of gender, class, race, and political allegiance to play the forty-plus characters, which are comprised of actual historical figures (Ulysses S. Grant, Robert E. Lee, Elizabeth Keckley, the Lincolns, John Wilkes Booth), fictional creations (Erasmus "Raz" Franklin, Moses Levy, Chester Manton Saunders), and a combination of the two (Decatur Bronson and Hannah). Although the play's overall scope, purpose, and tone are distinct from Vogel's other plays, many of her trademark questions and impulses are threaded throughout *Christmas*: the centrality of family and community, the persistent hauntings of memory and history, and the importance of theater as a public space.

Visually, the playworld, as designed at Long Wharf Theatre by James Schuette, foregrounded both the pageantry of the spectacle and its haunted quality. Actors performed their scenes in different areas of the wooden thrust stage, often on platforms that were raised to varying heights and built to conjure various uses, such as podiums, bridges, and beds. The nonnaturalistic, minimal stage design conveyed a social landscape still unfinished, full of possibility, populated by characters standing, at once, alone and together, against a backdrop of tall, silhouetted trees that signaled a vast, bleak wilderness. The unifying principle in the play is the Chorus, a communal voice spoken by different actors at different times, as they step out of character, removing themselves from the diegetic narrative to reflect on their character, to comment on another character, or to supplement historical information. The effect of the Chorus is that of the past speaking directly to and in the present. Like Stephen in *Home*, the Chorus in *Christmas* invites the audience to remember the forgotten, to see the invisible, and to feel the presence of the past while gathered together in the liminal space of the theater.

In *God Rest Ye Merry, Soldiers*, historian James McIvor describes the Christmas of 1862 as bleak, with not enough food to even improvise a meal. In contrast to the year before, in 1861, when "war was still a romantic adventure, a chance for dashing feats and excitement," the second Christmas of the Civil War only brought memories of everything that was missing from the present one: family, food, and a festive spirit.[4] However, McIvor recounts a story of this desolate Christmas, in which the Union and Confederate camps, set up within earshot of one another, both began singing patriotic songs to boost morale. When each camp began singing "Home Sweet Home," the two sides were momentarily joined in song. The image that McIvor's story constructs of the Civil War at Christmas is that of a country politically divided by racial and ideological beliefs yet emotionally connected through a shared sense of belonging (to family and nation). It is precisely this dissonant atmosphere that Vogel's play conjures.

Set on the Christmas Eve of 1864, this is a play filled as much with the warmth of community and ritual as it is with conflict and loss. Whereas Vogel's previous work focuses on white, middle- and working-class characters, this story takes its historical moment—the Civil War—and the communities it encompasses as its central concern, examining the promises and outcomes of this important event. Believing that America still lives—socially, affectively, politically—in this ambivalent moment of precarious unity, Vogel uses theater to take a closer look at the moment and its continued implications. Although Vogel began thinking about and researching the play in 1997, she began writing it in 2006. She states, "it was post-Katrina when I wrote this, I was in mourning, thinking we may lose our country and who we are." It was not only Katrina but also "the immigration debate" and "sections of our country still talking about state rights" that reinforced for Vogel that America was still deeply fractionalized. In particular, she believes, "We still have not addressed race."[5] The play premiered in 2008, just as Barack Obama was being voted in as forty-fourth president of the United States, and so the play took on added layers of resonance amid this historic event. In New Haven, Connecticut, to interview Vogel for my doctoral dissertation while the play was in rehearsal, I was invited by the playwright to watch a run-through of *Christmas*. It was fascinating to watch the cast and crew look for ways to fold the exciting present developments in American politics into the play's recollection of the history that made those developments possible. Staging the play during that monumental 2008 election reinforced the ways that theater can participate in a broader cultural dialogue, one that confronts the present and points toward the future by recollecting the past. The commitment of the actors and musicians, together with Tina Landau's masterful direction, underpinned the play's successful performance of community and celebration. Remounted in 2012 at the New York Theatre Workshop, again with Landau directing, *Christmas* tells a story meant to be shared over and over again.

There is a kind of didacticism to the play, which suits its function as a Christmas pageant meant to teach new generations about what came before. If *Christmas* is "about" anything, it might be about the importance of remembering, sharing, and witnessing our stories together. Vogel describes the play as emerging from a promise she made to Carl to "teach the children our family history":

> I wrote this play as a very sentimental aunt and godmother. I wrote this play for every ancestor who celebrates Christmas but also has lit the lights on Hanukkah, I'm writing this for my family who celebrates Kwanza. So, I just wanted to fulfill that promise to my brother Carl. I'm not a historian, but what I'm hoping is that when the kids in my family walk on the streets of Washington, they will think of that place as their legacy. These stories are *our* stories. . . . I'm very lucky to be living at a time when we do have women historians, when we do have African American historians . . . helping us *remember* so we as a country right now . . . can talk to one another and hopefully get in a civic dialogue.[6]

By bringing together public and personal histories, Vogel forges a kind of collective memory that does not oppose individual and community, but makes them indivisible. And as in her "Author's Note" to *Hot 'n' Throbbing*, Vogel attests here to the importance of theater as a civic space for gathering, discussing, and debating how that indivisibility ought best to be negotiated and maintained.

In her research for the play, Vogel sifted through primary archival documents, slave narratives, social histories; she listened to Civil War songs, traditional hymns, and other period music. She toured battle sites all over Virginia, listening to Mosby impersonators and John Brown reenactors relaying the history of each location. Included with the published play-text are many of the sources Vogel drew on while writing the play: excerpts from Lincoln's, Elizabeth Keckley's, and Walt Whitman's diaries; Civil War music; and letters written by Confederate and Union soldiers. Preparing to write her play on the Civil War, Vogel immersed herself in its historical remains and reenactments. In her study of Civil War reenactments, performance studies scholar Rebecca Schneider defines "the syncopated time of reenactment, where *then* and *now* punctuate each other." In this syncopated time, reenactors "romance and/or battle an 'other' time and try to bring that time—the prior moment—to the fingertips of the present."[7] This syncopated time, in which the present touches the past, captures the rhythm of Vogel's play, while the holiday setting and theatrical context give this temporal irregularity an added dimension. The reverberations of recurring rituals, like Christmas, and the "other" time of theater converge with the syncopated "*then and now*" of historical reenactment in Vogel's play. Schneider's study offers an especially productive theoretical lens through which to examine the temporal and affective structure of Vogel's play, which stages a past conflict, revising it as an annual celebration, and which encounters—touches—history through embodied performance.

Schneider poses a question about Civil War reenactments that is also the question animating *Christmas*: "I wonder here not only about the 'as if' but also the 'what if': what if time (re) turns? What does it *drag* along with it?" Especially "interested in the attempt to literally touch time through the residue of the gesture or the cross-temporality of the pose,"[8] Schneider looks for the remains of history in performance. The drag of time invoked here by Schneider suggests that the present is littered with traces of the past. There is something of Benjamin's dialectical image and Brecht's *gestus* here; reenacted gestures, which carry with them a whole social context, both repeat the past and remain as a reminder of that which is being "irretriev-

Figure 10: *A Civil War Christmas*. Left to right: Marc Damon Johnson, Scott Thomas, Rachel Shapiro Alderman, Susannah Flood, Bianca La Verne Jones, Jay Russell, Justin Blanchard, and Ora Jones. Long Wharf Theater, New Haven, CT, 2008. Photo: T. Charles Erickson.

ably lost." Both temporal drag and dialectics envision time and history as a push-pull movement, a forward trajectory accompanied by a recursive dragging back. In Vogel's play, history is what remains, haunting the present with reminders that the past is still unfolding. *Christmas* sets in motion a complex temporality in which the past and present continually remake one another and the affective reverberations of memory generate new cultural meanings.

Christmas is a play with enormous warmth and a reach wide enough to include the diversity of American cultural history, along with its unfinished business. The play encompasses the religious, racial, and ideological diversity of American culture, including both canonical history and the smaller stories—some real, some fabricated—within that narrative. The inclusive embrace of the play is established from the start, as the Chorus says, "Welcome to our story. The season is upon us, and whether it's Christmas, Hanukkah, Kwanza or New Year's—it's a time when we feel our connection to a larger community" (14). Vogel draws a connection between the experience of theater making and of Christmas stating that with both "there is the encroaching deadline. . . . There is gift-wrapping and note-writing and anticipation. And there is melancholy mixed with joy. Friendships lost [and] the knowledge that the present company will disperse."[9] Theater and history also have a close relationship; live performance is one of the ways a culture shares its stories, along with the values and beliefs those stories convey. As a culture's living archive, theater reminds us that history is always in the process of being remade in the present. As Elin Diamond puts it, "the past . . . will always need fresh actors because *it is always under construction.*"[10]

Christmas pivots around the interconnected stories of four characters: Decatur Bronson, a composite character developed from two actual historical figures, both African American Union soldiers who earned a Medal of Honor; Elizabeth Keckley, a former slave who became Mary Todd's modiste and confidante; and Hannah, an escaped slave woman, and her child, Jessa, who together signify as incarnations of Mary and Jesus. Hannah and Jessa's journey from the south to the north side of the Potomac, and from slavery to freedom, is the sacred story at the center of *Christmas.* Abraham and Mary Todd Lincoln play important, yet supporting roles, standing side by side with unknown figures, who often assume a quality best described as dignity. In this juxtaposition of prominent historical figures and unfamiliar characters, there is a kind of democratization of history and a humanizing of both the great men and the forgotten others. Ulysses S. Grant, for example, enjoys the peace of victory while trying hard to abstain from alcohol, and Walt Whitman appears not as a revered poet, but as a compassionate, anonymous hospital visitor, who brings small gifts to injured soldiers. *Christmas* continually brings familiar, canonical history in contact with the forgotten, suggesting that history is simply what we choose to remember. And theater allows us to keep remembering and teaches new ways of encountering a still-present past.

The major historical characters, such as the Lincolns, are finely sketched, not at all caricatures or living statues. As one of America's most symbolically saturated and reenacted presidents, Abraham Lincoln is remembered as a president who brought together a divided cabinet, as well as a divided nation. As historian Doris Kearns Goodwin points out, Lincoln and his memory endure because the integrity of his character enabled him meet the challenges of his time and position. She writes, "His success in dealing with the strong egos of the men in his cabinet suggests that in the hands of a truly great politician, the qualities we generally associate with decency and morality—kindness, sensitivity, compassion, honesty, and empathy—can also be impressive political resources."[11] One of the most striking things about Lincoln's presence in *Christmas* is the unguarded liberty with which he conducts his daily life, walking about the city, riding in his carriage, and talking to citizens in the street. This was a time before the Secret Service, a time when the president worked for the people, and the White House was open to the public. The memory of this kind of democracy is, perhaps, the aspect of *Christmas* that seems *least* like our contemporary moment. The Lincoln we see in Vogel's play is as worried about what to get for his wife for a holiday gift as he is about how to bring together his country, and it is through this balance between the personal and the collective that the play achieves its intricate, affecting texture.

In the character of Mary Todd, we empathize with a loving wife, an ardent shopper, an insecure public figure, and an unpredictable personality. Her mental state was erratic toward the end of her life, and she is depicted in *Christmas* as a woman whose mercurial moods emerge from the pressures placed on her as first lady in a time of national crisis. In scene 29, Vogel captures the volatility of Mary Todd's temperament, as she fusses over the new Christmas tree, while swinging between a hypervigilant zeal and a fretful melancholy. The Chorus registers the state of her mood: "Today we would call it manic" (67). Adding some nuance to Mary Todd's memory, the Chorus elaborates on the difficulties of her public role: "She and her husband had strategized, pillow to pillow, late in the Illinois nights, and now she was barred from all of his meetings. She was told to look to look pretty—" and the second Chorus adds, "—She was criticized for looking pretty while soldiers were dying" (68). The past seems very close here, indeed. Mary Todd was invested in her husband's personal and political well-being, and as Goodwin points out, she "never lost her taste for politics." When things were especially grim late in the war, she tried to lighten her husband's spirits by introducing "a therapeutic 'daily drive,' insisting that the two of them, and sometimes the children, take an hour-long carriage ride at the end of the afternoon."[12] Vogel captures this ritual in her play, and it is yet another moment that gives nuance to these iconic historical figures.

The two Christian Marys, in *Home*, are secularized in *Christmas* as the two Marys in 1860s Washington, DC—Mary Todd and Mary Surratt. Vogel wanted to find a way of bringing these two partisan figures together in a spirit of camaraderie. Her strategy for bringing them together was inspired by a Roz Chast cartoon in the *New Yorker* that depicted the lifelines of Kafka and Daniel Boone running parallel and meeting at a common juncture: they both liked to eat raw dough. And so this became Vogel's guiding idea as she sought to find a point of connection between the two Marys. She needed to find the raw dough, the mutual interest that would unite them.[13] She found it in their shared desire for a Christmas tree. Only vaguely recognized as a Bavarian custom in 1864, trees for Christmas were the height of novelty. Washingtonians in this period used holly to decorate their homes, and yet the two Marys set out on Christmas Eve to search out a new custom. In scene 18, the two Marys, anonymous to one another, have a brief exchange during which Mary Todd describes the difficulty of not being able grieve, publicly, for her southern family members lost in the war. As a fellow southerner, Surratt clasps the first lady's arm, saying, "we must be good to those we have left" (51). Here, the play demonstrates the need and possibility for empathetic connections across ideological divides, with the two Marys enacting a different model of politics and community. Like the two Marys, Elizabeth Keckley, who in addition to being the first lady's seamstress was also the matron of an orphanage, also spends her Christmas Eve searching for a Christmas tree to decorate for her children. The tree becomes the common link among these women as they all seek, in a time of enormous loss, a new symbol around which to celebrate the holiday. In contrast to the female relationships in *Desdemona*, this encounter stages a meaningful connection among women, rather than antagonistic competition.

Christmas accomplishes its complex temporality, in part, by flashing forward and back in time, by staging encounters between characters who are alive and those who have passed, and by placing actual historical figures along side fictional ones. One of the play's most moving encounters is between Moses Levy, a dying Jewish soldier, and Mary Todd. In her desire to bring him comfort in what seem to be his final hours, Mary Todd asks, "What would your mother do? Would she sing?" (88). When he nods yes, she begins to sing "Silent Night," and the Chorus steps forward to recite Kaddish, creating a strangely beautiful elegy for the dying soldier. As he begins to leave his body, Moses prophetically flashes forward to one of the most re-membered moments in American history—the night John Wilkes Booth shot Lincoln during a performance of the farce *American Cousin* at Ford's Theatre. Reciting the line from the play that Lincoln was said to have died while laughing at—"You Sockdologizing Old Man Trap!" (90)—Moses moves across times and subjectivities to stand at the intersection of all the temporal registers—past, present, and future. Moses returns as the Chorus in the penultimate scene, narrating his own passing: "And on Christmas morning, Moses had left his body behind him, cast off like old clothes. And his spirit found itself back in New York, striding down the Lower East Side" (119). This encounter between Mary Todd and Moses has a mystical resonance, taking place simultaneously outside of time and in all times at once. Recalling the women in *Profession*, Moses leaves the material world and returns to his New York City home.

Ghosts pervade the playworld, and the boundaries between past/ passed and present, seen and unseen, are fluid. The play's most haunted characters, Bronson and Keckley, are also the most central. Their centrality is signaled both by their connections to the other characters—alive and deceased, known and unknown—and also by their final address to the audience. They are the hosts of this histori-cal pageant, and their stories exemplify the pain and promise of the history of which they are a part. George, Keckley's only son, was killed in his first Civil War battle. Just five years before, Keckley bought freedom for herself and her son. Bronson's wife, Rose, was killed by Texans on retreat after Gettysburg. Bronson's wife and Ke-ckley's son appear throughout the play, poignant reminders of the enormous losses of this period. The dignified Keckley keeps her mind from dwelling on her son by sewing. "I can't be thinking of you now, George. I've got to put my hands to use" (46), she says, keeping the past at bay. In a flashback later in the play, we realize that sewing was a survival strategy taught to her by her own mother; by learning this valuable skill, she would prove her usefulness and thus not be taken and sold by their slave owner. Keckley's character moves fluidly be-tween boundaries of past and present, living and deceased, and is also centrally connected to the play's sacred center. Throughout the play, she is overcome by "some strange feeling in my bones" (41), a sensation that registers an embodied connection to Jessa and Hannah, who journey through the frigid winter night toward Washington. Late in the play, it is Keckley who finds a frozen Jessa, alone and curled up in a straw-filled crate outside the White House, and calling on George for help, mother and son revive the little girl's lifeless body. Through the act of saving Jessa, Keckley is able finally to accept George's death and to see its broader purpose—the freedom of this little girl.

Like Keckley, Bronson is haunted by loss. After Bronson bought freedom for himself and for his wife, Rose, they purchased a farm near the Potomac. Shortly after that, Rose was stolen off their front porch. Bronson is driven to find her and seek vengeance, and he joined the army motivated by the thought that "every confederate I kill is a bridge to reach her" (24). However, he left his post as sergeant to work as a blacksmith, since the steady labor, like Keckley's sewing, keeps his hands busy and his mind distracted from thoughts of Rose. Echoing Keckley's words to George, Bronson says as he works, "Rose, I can't be thinking of you now" (21). The persistent presence of the past in these characters' lives acts as a microcosm of the hauntings of history in contemporary culture. Moreover, the motif of work highlights a strategy of survival, while also pointing to the physical labor—especially the labor of African Americans—that has built and sustained the country.

Freedom is not sentimentalized in the play, but rather reinforced as an ongoing negotiation, material condition, and incomplete process. In order to fully achieve freedom and practice their citizenship, for example, former slaves had to learn to read, as Rose continually reminded Bronson. Perhaps the most enduring post–Civil War challenges were lingering prejudice among white people and the difficult social adjustments required by African Americans in their role as free citizens of a country whose definition of freedom, historically, did not include them. In her memoir, *Behind the Scenes* (1868), Keckley explains the uneasy transition from slavery to freedom in poetic terms:

> Fresh from the bonds of slavery, fresh from the benighted regions of the plantation, they came to the capital looking for liberty, and many of them not knowing it when they found it. Many good friends reached forth kind hands, but the North is not warm and impulsive.

For one kind word that was spoken, two harsh ones were uttered; there was something repelling in the atmosphere, and the bright joyous dreams of freedom to the slave faded—were sadly altered in the presence of that stern mother, reality. . . . Poor dusky children of slavery, men and women of my own race—the transition from slavery was too sudden for you![14]

This passage tempers any simplistic notions of post–Civil War freedom with reminders of the social, material circumstances that made freedom difficult to achieve. The tendency of the present is often to idealize epoch-marking events like the Civil War, to use them as ideological props for a present political agenda. However, isolating these kinds of events so that they seem discreet from what came before or after obscures their enduring presence and unfinished work.

The complexity of Bronson's character is developed through his relationships with the Quaker boy, Chester Manton Saunders, and the young Confederate, Erasmus "Raz" Franklin. Chester embraces the war with all the ideals and energy of his youth. As a Quaker taught to respect "the Divine spark in every man" (74), Chester does not serve on the battlefield, but as a private with the quartermaster's staff, and his dedication to the war emerges from his abolitionist beliefs. In contrast to Chester's pacifism, Bronson, a recently freed slave who has seen his wife stolen and his fellow troop members shot dead, is a man seeking bloody revenge. And yet, these two find comfort and kinship with one another, building an empathetic connection by sharing their stories. Interspersed throughout their conversations are flashbacks to scenes of Chester and his widowed mother, who together would often sing the hymn:

We'll build us a temple of freedom
And make it capacious within
That all who seek shelter will find it
Whatever the hue of their skin . . . (75)

The play's underlying notes of community and togetherness pervade almost every encounter, even the most antagonistic. Traveling north belatedly to join the Mosby Raiders, Raz Franklin meets Bronson and Chester and is faced with an unexpected battle. Bronson, honoring the vow he made to kill any Confederate soldier who crosses his path, raises his gun to shoot Raz, while Chester says a prayer for "the

Divine spark in every man." Transformed by Chester's belief, Bronson spares Raz's life. Raz and Chester are endearing representations of a deeply polarized nation. They exemplify a new generation that learns and champions the beliefs of their parents and community with energetic optimism.

The Long Wharf production used cross-gender, cross-race casting for the characters of Raz and Chester, complicating the gendered, racial, and political stereotypes associated with their roles. Both characters were played by female actors, Susannah Flood and Bianca LaVerne Jones, respectively. LaVerne Jones, an African American actor, also played Hannah and Rose, and her roles accumulated significations that displaced any fixed class, racial, religious, or political identities. The affective resonance of each role carried over into the next, and in this reduplication there was another kind of ghosting, which theater historian Marvin Carlson calls "the haunted body" of the actor. "The recycled body of the actor," Carlson writes, "already a complex bearer of semiotic messages, will almost inevitably in a new role evoke the ghost or ghosts of previous roles."[15] This ghosting is intensified in plays like *Christmas*, where actors take on multiple roles, which are interlinked and anchored in the same history. The ghosting effect of LaVerne Jones acting the parts of Chester, Rose, and Hannah emerged not only from her shifting roles but also from her embodied presence as an African American woman on stage, which carries its own history. As she played each role—a mother seeking to escape slavery, a wife captured as a fugitive slave, and a young white boy who believes in the divinity of all people—she enacted a multifaceted dialogue with the history she replayed. LaVerne Jones's varied roles encouraged an actively engaged spectatorship and a complex understanding of the history being performed. Complicating the traditional patterns of empathy and identification that we learn watching plays that have static, single-role casting, cross-gender and -racial role-playing asks the audience to read the actor's body not as an individual subject, but as a collective or communal text bearing the codes of history and memory.

Out of the many stories, period songs, and poems threaded throughout *Christmas*, three ideas emerge as *the* galvanizing national forces: country, god, and family. In the soldiers' letters that are included with the published play-text, all of which were written during various Civil War Christmases, every single one registers all three loyalties. While these principles are well-known foundations of America, it is interesting to note the way they also echo back through Vogel's body of work: country, god, and family are both everywhere present and everywhere problematized in Vogel's body of work. Moreover, taken together, country, god, and family cluster around the more intimate ideas of home and belonging. "I want to go home," says a tired and cold Jessa, to which her mother replies, "It's not 'home' since they sold your father. It's not 'home' if you and I can't learn to read. It's not 'home' if we can't go down the road without a paper we couldn't read saying we got permission to go up the road!" (27). Hannah's description of home by negation identifies what erodes the fabric of community: social and racial injustice. There is no freedom for anyone until everyone is free. As the history of slavery and its aftermath brushes up against continuing racial and ethnic divisions in the present, we, the audience, find ourselves in the same moment. By pointing out what destroys the fabric of home and nation, however, Christmas offers an opportunity to stitch up the pieces and rebuild a sense of inclusive belonging.

Hope resonates in Christmas as a powerful yearning and provisional belief. The nostalgic hope that Long Christmas Ride Home leans toward emerges in Christmas as an affective space wherein the promise of peace is suspended indefinitely. As Ely Parker reflects early in the play, "the hope of peace is sweeter than peace itself" (18), which Mary Todd echoes at the play's end (118). Hope preserves the idea of peace in an unspecified future, a future that we are then compelled to strive toward. Recognizing this optimistic hope as their legacy, the audience of Christmas perhaps also realizes that they too remain suspended in this incomplete hope. Interestingly, the play's original ending flashed forward to the future, showing Bronson reunited with his wife, Rose, and seated at a table with their ten children. However, Vogel revised this more familiar and perhaps comforting conclusion so that the play now remains on that Christmas Eve of 1864, where the hope for peace could be collectively preserved, if not the peace itself.

The notes of hope and optimism are further complicated by reminders of the unfulfilled promise of freedom. Separated from her mother and freezing in the unusually cold December night, Jessa—an embodiment of America's future—stands alone on the streets of Washington, DC, saying, "Tonight is my first night of freedom," to which the Chorus adds, "Who knew freedom could be so cold?" (99). The twin poles of hope and freedom circulate complexly in the play-world of *Christmas*. And although the play affirms the necessity and value of both as constituent elements of American culture, it also suggests that they cannot simply exist as abstract ideals. Instead, they must be practiced in civic discourse, public institutions, and social relations.

With the enormous losses of the war felt everywhere in the play, and the conflicts around which the Civil War was waged still deeply embedded in American culture, Lincoln's words remain the hope and the work of the present: "Let us strive to finish the work we are in, to bind up the nation's wounds" (95). This ongoing work of unifying the body politic is achieved, in the play, through the persistent memories of Keckley and Bronson and through the invisible threads of empathy and recognition that foster connections among the characters and between the characters and the audience. Keckley shivers when Jessa shivers; the two Marys meet in a spirit of solidarity and support while buying a Christmas tree; Bronson and Chester share a meal and stories from their pasts; and Lincoln, practicing his second inaugural speech while out for a carriage ride on Seventh Street, feels a "prickling sensation" (95) when he passes a lost Jessa on the street. As he turns around to fetch her, however, she runs away, fearing he is one of the slave catchers that her mother warned her about. This misrecognition, so full of irony, suggests the disparity between grand political rhetoric and the more vexed encounters of everyday social life. This scene, and indeed the whole play, gains an added poignancy, since we know that soon after this first Christmas as a newly united country, Lincoln would be shot. (Booth and his fellow conspirators lurk throughout the play, reminding the audience of the history waiting to happen once the ritual concludes.) In his penultimate line, Bronson, as the Chorus, affirms Lincoln's testament to the labor of nation making, proclaiming, "Our own two hands we shall beat the swords into plowshares" (120). As the physical and ideological work required to rebuild the nation continues and as the labor of African Americans begins to be remembered as history, the play ends with the past, again, speaking directly to the present. Acting as the Chorus, Keckley formally concludes the narrative, stating, "And so our stories end," while Bronson, also as the Chorus, offers a closing gesture befitting the holiday, if not the history: "We share with you the gladness of our hearts, and our wishes for peace. Good night" (120). In its theatrical effect, affective impact, and historical scope, *Christmas* constructs a finely textured yet expansive pageant play that threads the tangible and the intangible and fills the theatrical present with a still-living past.

Describing the 2008 Long Wharf production as "an ambitious, richly detailed, and beautifully mounted new seasonal offering,"[16] the *New York Times*'s Charles Isherwood articulates the play's look, feel, and purpose. Isherwood also reviewed the 2012 production at New York Theatre Workshop, describing the play in similar terms as a "beautifully stitched tapestry of American lives in transition," praising the "embracing expansiveness" of Vogel's writing.[17] The *Boston Globe* credited Vogel's "determination to tell history from the perspective of the disenfranchised."[18] More exactly, however, *Christmas* tells history through a kaleidoscope of complementary and contradictory perspectives, some actual, some fabricated. Far from a museum piece, *Christmas* is a play that manages, quite literally, to touch history.

Where once she sought to complicate, here she seeks to celebrate. And yet *Christmas* is unmistakably Vogel. Generosity, humor, and forgiveness pervade the playworld, animating an embodied history situated in that most haunted of annual rituals: Christmas. There is, fittingly, a recursive movement to this play, a coming-full-circle in Vogel's oeuvre. What, in 1977, began as Meg revising the history of her father becomes, in 2008, Vogel revising the history of her country. And in *Christmas* we can see the ghosts and hear the echoes of her other plays: Sir Thomas More becomes Abraham Lincoln; Desdemona and Emilia become Mary Todd and Elizabeth Keckley; the waltz that concludes *Waltz* becomes the hymn that concludes *Christmas*; and the ghosts of Peck and of Stephen become the ghosts of an entire nation, a country poised between conflict and community, looking with hope toward a future that we, the audience, have inherited as our present. That is Vogel's gift to American theater.

Notes

Introduction

1. Paula Vogel, interview with David Savran, in *The Playwright's Voice: American Dramatists on Memory, Writing, and the Politics of Culture*, ed. David Savran (New York: Theatre Communications Group, 1999), 263.

2. Vogel, interview with Savran, 268–69.

3. Ann Linden, "Seducing the Audience: Politics in the Plays of Paula Vogel," in *The Playwright's Muse*, ed. Joan Herrington (New York: Routledge, 2002), 232.

4. "Marriage Announcement," *New York Times*, Sept. 26 2004.

5. Paula Vogel, foreword, in *Writing: Working in Theatre*, ed. Robert Emmet Long (New York: Ginger/Continuum, 2008), 7–10.

6. Paula Vogel, "Interview with Alexis Greene," in *Women who Write Plays: Interviews with American Dramatists*, ed. Alexis Greene (Hanover, NH: Smith and Kraus, 2001), 430.

7. Vogel, "Interview with Arthur Holmberg," http://www.amrep.org/past/drive1.html, Apr. 3, 2006.

8. David Savran, *A Queer Sort of Materialism: Recontextualizing American Theatre* (Ann Arbor: University of Michigan Press, 2003), 191.

9. Conversation between Paula Vogel and John Guare, Jan. 5, 1998, 92nd Street Y, New York (cassette recording).

10. Pierre Bourdieu. *The Field of Cultural Production*, ed. and intro. Randal Johnson (New York: Columbia University Press, 1993), 84.

11. David Savran, *Highbrow/Lowdown: Theater, Jazz, and the Making of the New Middle Class* (Ann Arbor: University of Michigan Press 2009), 223.

12. Alisa Solomon, *Re-dressing the Canon: Essays on Theatre and Gender* (New York: Routledge, 1997), 9.

13. Paula Vogel, interview with Ann Linden, in Herrington, *Playwright's Muse*, 255, 256.

14. Paula Vogel, email reply to author, July 22, 2011. The following discussion of her teaching practice comes from this email correspondence with the playwright.

15. Victor Shklovsky, "Art as Technique," in *Russian Formalist Criticism: Four Essays*, trans and intro. Lee T. Lemon and Marion J. Reis (Lincoln: University of Nebraska Press, 1965), 12.

16. Vogel, email reply to author, July 22, 2011.

17. Paula Vogel, "An Evening with Paula Vogel," Bruno Walter Auditorium, New York Public Library of the Performing Arts, Nov. 26, 2007, The-

atre on Film and Tape, Billy Rose Theatre Collection, New York Public Library.

18. Quoted in Joan Herrington, "Introduction," in *Playwright's Muse, 9.*

19. Vogel, interview with Savran, 273.

20. Vogel, "Through the Eyes of Lolita: Pulitzer Prize-Winning Playwright Paula Vogel is interviewed by Arthur Holmberg."

21. Judith Butler, "Performative Acts and Gender Constitution: An Essay in Phenomenology and Feminist Theory," in *Performing Feminisms: Feminist Critical Theory and Theatre*, ed. Sue-Ellen Case (Baltimore: Johns Hopkins University Press, 1990), 270.

22. Judith Butler, *Gender Trouble* (New York: Routledge , 1990), 43–44.

23. C. W. E. Bigsby, *Contemporary American Playwrights* (New York: Cambridge University Press, 1999), 295.

24. Quoted in Steven Drukman, "A Playwright on the Edge Turns Toward the Middle," *New York Times*, Mar. 16, 1997.

25. Vogel, interview with Linden, 257.

26. Jill Dolan, *The Feminist Spectator as Critic*, 2nd ed. (Ann Arbor: University of Michigan Press, 2012), 21, 20.

27. Important exceptions to the realism that dominated the stage in the 1980s include David Henry Hwang's *M. Butterfly* (1988); Christopher Durang's farces, such as *The Marriage of Betty and Boo* (1985); Charles Mee's wildly imaginative revisions of Greek plays; and María Irene Fornés's unique take on realism in *Mud* (1983), *Sarita* (1984), and *The Conduct of Life* (1985). In Britain, Caryl Churchill was writing successful Brechtian plays, like *Top Girls* (1982), *Mouthful of Birds* (1986), and *Serious Money* (1987).

28. Vogel, interview with Savran, 283.

29. Elin Diamond, *Unmaking Mimesis: Essays on Feminism and Theatre* (New York: Routledge, 1997), 44.

30. Diamond, *Unmaking Mimesis*, 52.

31. Diamond, *Unmaking Mimesis*, 84.

32. Susan Sontag, "Notes on Camp," in *Against Interpretation and Other Essays* (New York: Picador, 1966), 276–81.

33. Sontag, "Notes on Camp," 281.

34. Drukman, "Playwright on the Edge."

35. Savran, *Queer Sort of Materialism*, 194.

36. Esther Newton, *Mother Camp: Female Impersonators in America* (Chicago: University of Chicago Press, 1972), xvi–xvii.

37. Newton, "Note to the Reader," in *Mother Camp*, n.p.

38. Newton, *Mother Camp*, 105.

39. Eve Kosofky Sedgwick, *Touching Feeling: Affect, Pedagogy, and Performativity* (Durham, NC: Duke University Press, 2003), 149–50.

40. Vogel, interview with Savran, 281.

41. Although this subtitle does not appear in the printed text, Vogel cited

this as her subtitle for the play at a talk she gave at the New York Performing Arts Library. See Vogel, "Evening with Paula Vogel."

42. Savran, *Queer Sort of Materialism*, 191.

43. Savran, *Queer Sort of Materialism*, 190.

44. "Women in Theater: Dialogues with Notable Women in American Theater," Linda Winer, interviewer, CUNY TV, 2002, Billy Rose Theater Collection, New York Public Library.

45. Vogel, "Evening with Paula Vogel."

Chapter One

1. Dolan, *Feminist Spectator as Critic*, 101.

2. Paula Vogel, *Meg* (New York: Samuel French, 1977), 14 (hereafter cited in the text).

3. Raymond Williams, *Marxism and Literature* (New York: Oxford University Press, 1977), 173.

4. Feminist interest in oral histories culminated in 1977–78 in three special issues of the journal *Frontiers: A Journal of Women's Studies.* These issues examined and explained the significance of transmitting, recording, and making public women's forgotten stories in a variety of disciplines, from sociology and ethnography to psychology and literary studies. The essays in these special issues are collected in *Women's Oral History: The "Frontiers" Reader*, eds. Susan H. Armitage with Patricia Hart and Karen Weathermon (Lincoln: University of Nebraska Press, 2002)

5. Vogel, interview with Linden, 256.

6. Vogel, interview with Linden, 256.

7. Vogel, interview with Linden, 255.

8. Vogel, *Meg*, 6.

9. Roland Barthes, *Mythologies* (New York: Hill and Wang, 1977), 143.

10. Amy Green, "Whose Voices Are These? The Arts of Language in the Plays of Suzan-Lori Parks, Paula Vogel, and Diana Son," in *Women Writing Plays: Three Decades of* the Susan Smith Blackburn Prize (Austin: University of Texas Press, 2006), 146.

11. Carolyn-Casey Craig, *Women Pulitzer Playwrights: Biographical Profiles and Analyses of the Plays* (Jefferson, NC: MacFarland, 2004), 217.

12. Bigsby, *Contemporary American Playwrights*, 299–300.

13. Lynda E. Boose, "'Let It Be Hid': The Pornographic Aesthetic of Shakespeare's *Othello*," in *New Casebooks: "Othello,"* ed. Lena Cowen Orlin (Basingstoke, England: Palgrave Macmillan, 2004), 38.

14. Sharon Friedman, "Feminist Revisions of Classic Texts on the American Stage," in *Codifying the National Self: Spectators, Actors, and the American Dramatic Text* (New York: Peter Lang, 2006), 104.

15. David Margolies, "Teaching the Handsaw to Fly: Shakespeare as a Hegemonic Instrument," in *The Shakespeare Myth*, ed. Graham Holderness (New York: St. Martin's Press, 1991), 51.

16. Jill Dolan, "Introduction to *Desdemona: A Play about a Handkerchief*," in *Amazon All-Stars: Thirteen Lesbian Plays*, ed. Rosemary Keefe Curb (New York: Applause, 1996), 438.

17. Anna Jameson, *Shakespeare's Heroines*, 2nd ed. (1833; London: George Bell and Sons, 1908), 181.

18. Margaret Loftus Ranald, "The Indiscretions of Desdemona," *Shakespeare Quarterly* 14.2 (1963): 128.

19. Peter Stallybrass, "Patriarchal Territory: The Body Enclosed," in *Rewriting the Renaissance: The Discourses of Sexual Difference in Early Modern Europe*, ed. Margaret W. Ferguson, Maureen Quilligan, and Nancy J. Vickers (Chicago: Universityz of Chicago Press, 1988), 141.

20. Shakespeare, *Othello*, 5.2.6.

21. Shakespeare, *Othello*, 4.3. 68–79.

22. Boose, "'Let It Be Hid,'" 38.

23. Paula Vogel, *Desdemona: A Play about a Handkerchief*, in *The Baltimore Waltz and Other Plays*, ed. David Savran (New York: TCG, 1996), 193 (hereafter cited in the text).

24. Shakespeare, *Othello*, 4.3.95–104.

25. Vogel, "Note to the Directors," in *Desdemona*, 176 (hereafter cited in the text).

26. Wolfgang Bauer, "Shakespeare the Sadist," *Performing Arts Journal* 3.1 (1978): 105.

27. Marianne Novy, "Saving Desdemona and/or Ourselves: Plays by Ann-Marie MacDonald and Paula Vogel," in *Transforming Shakespeare: Contemporary Women's Re-Visions in Literature and Performance*, ed. Marianne Novy (New York: Palgrave, 2000), 75.

28. Shakespeare, *Othello*, 5.2.7, 23, 79.

29. Shakespeare, *Othello*, 1.3.253.

30. Shakespeare, *Othello*, 5.2.344.

31. Linda Winer, "A New Desdemona Wild and Unbound," *Newsday*, Nov. 12, 1993, 69.

32. Victoria A. Kummer, "Review: 'Desdemona: A Play about a Handerkerchief,'" *Actor's Resource*, Dec. 13, 1993, 20.

33. Ben Brantley, "Iago's Subterfuge Is Made the Truth," *New York Times*, Nov. 12, 1993.

34. Clive Barnes, "In the End, It's Not Half Bard," New York Post, Nov. 12, 1993.

35. John Simon, "Review of *Desdemona*, by Paula Vogel," *New York Magazine*, Nov. 22, 1993, 78.

36. Simon, "Review of *Desdemona*," 79.

37. Kate Taylor, "Played Not Wisely, nor Too Well," *Globe and Mail*, Feb. 2, 2002.

38. Francine Russo, "Review: 'Desdemona,'" *Village Voice*, Nov. 23, 1993, 104.

Chapter Two

1. Samuel Freedman, "Sam Shepard's Mythic Vision of the Family." *New York Times*, Dec. 1, 1985. This passage introduces Freedman's review of Sam Shepard's *A Lie of the Mind*.

2. Vogel, "Through the Eyes of Lolita"

3. Edward Albee, interview with David Savran, in Savran, *Playwright's Voice*, 7–8, 19.

4. Vogel, "Evening with Paula Vogel."

5. Judith Stacey, "The Making and Unmaking of Modern Families," in *Family: Critical Concepts in Sociology*, ed. David Cheal (New York: Routledge, 2003), 94.

6. Michael Warner, *The Trouble with Normal: Sex, Politics, and the Ethics of Queer Life* (Cambridge, MA: Harvard University Press, 2000), 114.

7. Lauren Berlant and Michael Warner, "Sex in Public," *Intimacy*, special issue, *Critical Inquiry* 24.2 (1998), 548, 552.

8. Berlant and Warner, "Sex in Public," 550.

9. Lauren Berlant and Michael Warner, "What Does Queer Theory Teach Us about X?" *PLMA* 110 (1995): 349.

10. Paula Vogel, *And Baby Makes Seven*, in *Balitmore Waltz and Other Plays*, ed. David Savran. (New York: TCG, 1994), 105 (hereafter cited in the text).

11. Peter Brooks, *Reading for the Plot: Design and Intention in Narrative* (New York: Vintage), 1985, 10.

12. Brooks, *Reading for the Plot*, 12.

13. Bilowit, "Bringing Up Baby," 5F.

14. Bilowit, "Bringing Up Baby," 5F.

15. Bigsby, *Contemporary American Playwrights*, 306.

16. Bigsby, *Contemporary American Playwrights*, 305.

17. Ira J. Bilowit, "Bringing Up Baby: Paula Vogel's Newest Born," *Back Stage*, May 7, 1993, 5F.

18. Bigsby, *Contemporary American Playwrights*, 304.

19. Anne Fausto-Sterling, *Sexing the Body: Gender Politics and the Construction of Sexuality* (New York: Basic Books, 2000), 376. Fausto-Sterling is Vogel's wife. They were married in Massachusetts on Sept. 26, 2004.

20. Sue-Ellen Case, "Toward a Butch-Femme Aesthetic," in *Making a Spectacle: Feminist Essays on Contemporary Women's Theatre*, ed. Lynda Hart (Ann Arbor: University of Michigan Press, 1989), 298.

21. Case, "Toward a Butch-Femme Aesthetic," 283, 292.

22. Eve Kosofsky Sedgwick, *Between Men: English Literature and Male Homosocial Desire* (New York: Columbia University Press, 1985), 22.

23. Vogel, *Baby*, 88. The corresponding reference in *Streetcar* occurs on p. 136 in the 1975 Signet edition.

24. Anca Vlasopolos, "Authorizing History: Victimization in *Streetcar Name Desire*," *Theatre Journal* 38.3 (1986): 325.

25. Tennessee Williams, *A Streetcar Named Desire* (New York: Signet, 1975), 99.

26. Vogel, email reply to author, July 22, 2011.

27. Mel Gussow, "Theatre: 'And Baby Makes Seven'" *New York Times*, Jan. 22, 1984.

28. Mel Gussow, "Parents-to-Be Regress to Childhood," *New York Times*, May 7, 1993.

29. Michael Feingold, "Review: *And Baby Makes Seven. Village Voice*, June 8, 1993, 97.

30. Jeanne Cooper, "'Baby': Extended Family Fantasies," *Washington Post*, Jan. 28, 1994.

31. Helen Thomson. "The Web We Weave When We Conceive," *Age*, Aug. 13, 2002, 4.

32. Judith Butler, *Undoing Gender* (New York: Routledge, 1997), 214.

33. Butler, *Undoing Gender*, 29.

Chapter Three

1. Jean Laplance and J. B. Pontalis, "Fantasy and the Origins of Sexuality," in *Unconscious Phantasy*, ed. Riccardo Steiner (London: Karnac Books, 2003), 133–34.

2. Butler, *Undoing Gender*, 217.

3. In the 1997 version, the characters are unnamed, listed only as "Woman," "Man," "Girl," and "Boy." The generic representation positions this as the stereotypical American family, in all its familiar dysfunction. By naming the characters, Vogel particularizes their situation, while at the same time creating a more conventional structure of empathy, especially in relation to Charlene's death.

4. Vogel, *Hot 'n' Throbbing*, 6.

5. This quote is taken from the "Author's Note" (229–31) published with the 1997 TCG version, edited by David Savran. All subsequent quotes will come from the 2000 version of *Hot 'n' Throbbing*, unless otherwise noted (see n. 6).

6. Andrea Dworkin, *Pornography: Men Possessing Women* (New York: E. P. Dutton, 1989), xxvii.

7. "Women in Theatre."

8. Paula Vogel, *Hot 'n' Throbbing* (New York: Dramatists Play Services, 2000), 13 (hereafter cited in the text). Unless otherwise noted, all citations will come from this version of the play.

9. Judith Butler, *Excitable Speech: A Politics of the Performative* (New York: Routledge, 1997), 69.

10. This line was added to the Signature Theatre production; it does not appear in either printed edition of the play.

11. Laplance and Pontalis, "Fantasy and the Origins of Sexuality," 133.

12. Carolyn G. Heilbrun, *Writing a Woman's Life* (New York: Ballantine Books, 1988), 18.

13. Kaja Silverman, *Acoustic Mirror: The Female Voice in Psychoanalysis and Cinema* (Bloomington: Indiana University Press), 1988. 43.

14. Andrew Ross, "Uses of Camp," in *Camp: Queer Aesthetics and the Performing Subject: A Reader*, ed. Fabio Cleto (Ann Arbor: University of Michigan Press, 1999), 320.

15. Frank Krutnik, *In a Lonely Street: Film Noir, Genre, and Masculinity* (New York: Routledge, 1991), 93.

16. Linda Williams, "Film Bodies: Gender, Genre, and Excess." *Film Quarterly* 44.4 (1991): 7.

17. L. Williams, "Film Bodies," 5.

18. L. Williams, "Film Bodies," 4.

19. N. J. Stanley, "Screamingly Funny and Terrifyingly Shocking: Paula Vogel as Domestic Detective," in *Staging a Cultural Paradigm: The Political and the Personal in American Drama*, ed. Barbara Ozieblo and Miriam López-Rodríguez (New York: Peter Lang, 2002), 366.

20. Brian Richardson, "Voice and Narration in Postmodern Drama." *New Literary History* 32.3 (2001): 690.

21. Bigsby, *Contemporary American Playwrights*, 316.

22. Shoshana Felman, *The Scandal of the Speaking Body: Don Juan with J. L. Austin; or, Seduction in Two Languages* (Stanford, CA: Stanford University Press, 2003), 78.

23. Rachel Shteir, *Striptease: The Untold History of the Girlie Show* (New York: Oxford University Press, 2004), 8.

24. Lynne Segal, "Sweet Sorrows, Painful Pleasures: Pornography and the Perils of Heterosexual Desire," in *Sex Exposed: Sexuality and the Pornography Debate*, ed. Lynne Segal and Mary McIntosh (London: Virago, 1992), 66.

25. Kathryn Bond Stockton, *Beautiful Bottom, Beautiful Shame: Where "Black" Meets "Queer"* (Durham, NC: Duke University Press, 2006), 205.

26. Butler, *Gender Trouble*, 171.

27. Lisa Sternlieb, "Molly Bloom: Acting Natural, *ELH* 65.3 (1998): 757.

28. This citation is taken from the 1996 play-text: *Hot 'n' Throbbing*, in *Baltimore Waltz and Other Plays*, 294.

29. Vogel, *Hot 'n' Throbbing*, 1996 edition, in *Baltimore Waltz and Other Plays*, 294.

30. Vogel, *Hot 'n' Throbbing*, 295.

31. Butler, *Undoing Gender*, 201.

32. Vogel, "Author's Note" to *Hot 'n' Throbbing*, in *Baltimore Waltz and Other Plays*, 231.

33. Lloyd Rose, "'Hot 'n' Throbbing': Double Feature," *Washington Post*, Sept. 13, 1999.

34. Jason Zinoman, "Pornography to Prop Up Family Values," *New York Times*, Mar. 29, 2005.

35. Frank Sheck, "Cold and Not So Erotic," *New York Post*, Mar. 31, 2005.

36. Alisa Solomon, "Bump and Grind," *Village Voice*, Mar. 30, 2005, 69.

Chapter Four

1. Gerda Lerner, *Why History Matters: Life and Thought* (New York: Oxford University Press, 1997), 207.

2. Lauren Berlant, *The Queen of America Goes to Washington City: Essays on Sex and Citizenship* (Durham, NC: Duke University Press, 1997), 7.

3. Berlant, *Queen of America Goes to Washington City*, 20.

4. Berlant, *Queen of America Goes to Washington City*, 20.

5. Berlant, *Queen of America Goes to Washington City*, 5.

6. Vogel, quoted in Bigsby, *Contemporary American Playwrights*, 301.

7. Quoted in Bigsby, *Contemporary American Playwrights*, 301.

8. Quoted in Gerald C. Fraser, "Mamet's Plays Shed Masculinity Myth," *New York Times*, July 5, 1976.

9. David Krasner, *American Drama: 1945–2000* (Boston: Blackwell, 2006), 101.

10. This line was added to the Signature Theatre production and does not appear in the published play-text. The published play-text is Paula Vogel, *The Oldest Profession*, in *Baltimore Waltz and Other Plays* (hereafter cited in the text).

11. James E. Combs, *The Reagan Range: The Nostalgia Myth in American Politics* (Madison, WI: Popular Press, 1993), 144.

12. Combs, *Reagan Range*, 144.

13. Svetlana Boym, *The Future of Nostalgia* (New York: Basic Books, 2001), 49.

14. Boym, *Future of Nostalgia*, xii.

15. Walter Benjamin, "Central Park," trans. Lloyd Spencer, *New German Critique* 34 (1985): 40.

16. Benjamin, "Central Park," 53.

17. Deborah Geis, "In Willy Loman's Garden: Contemporary Re-visions of *Death of a Salesman*," in *Arthur Miller's America: Theatre and Culture in a Time of Change*, ed. Enoch Brater (Ann Arbor: University of Michigan Press, 2005), 207.

18. Geis, "In Willy Loman's Garden," 207, 209.

19. C. W. E. Bigsby, *Modern American Drama 1945–2000* (New York: Cambridge University Press, 2000), 83.

20. This line was added to the Signature Theatre production. It is not included in the published play-text.

21. Vogel, email reply to author, July 22, 2011.

22. Ben Brantley, "Portrait of Working Girls Who Are No More," *New York Times*, Sept. 27, 2004.

23. David Rooney, "Review of *Oldest Profession*," *Daily Variety*, Sept. 28, 2004, 8.

24. Susan Sontag, "The Death of Tragedy," in *Against Interpretation and Other Essays*, 135.

25. "Women in Theatre."

26. Vogel, "Interview with Alexis Greene," 430.

27. Hicks, "Playwright Melds Modern Tension and Ancient Convention."

28. Paula Vogel, "Time to Laugh: An Interview with Kathy Sova," *American Theatre* 14.2 (1997): 24.

29. Vogel, interview with Savran, 281.

30. Paula Vogel, *The Mineola Twins*, in *The Mammary Plays* (New York: Theatre Communications Group, 1998), 97, 111 (hereafter cited in the text).

31. "Women in Theatre."

32. Vogel, *Mineola Twins*, 97.

33. Susan J. Douglas, *Where the Girls Are: Growing up Female with the Mass Media* (New York: Random House, 1995), 90.

34. Vogel, "Interview with Arthur Holmberg."

35. Vogel, "Interview with Arthur Holmberg."

36. Vogel, "Interview with Arthur Holmberg."

37. Alex Witchel, "After the Prize is the Pressure: Now What?" *New York Times*, Feb. 7, 1999.

38. *Twins* was workshopped during 1995 at the New York Theatre Workshop and had its world premiere at the Perseverance Theatre in Douglas, AK, in Nov. 1996, with Molly D. Smith as artistic director. It was also produced in Mar. 1997 at Trinity Repertory Theatre in Providence, RI.

39. Mary Ann Doane, *Femme Fatales: Feminism, Film Theory, and Psychoanalysis* (New York: Routledge, 1991), 39.

40. Diamond, *Unmaking Mimesis*, 57.

41. Diamond, *Unmaking Mimesis*, 54.

42. Juliann Sivulka, "The Fabulous Fifties: Selling Mr. and Mrs. Consumer," *Advertising and Society Review* 9.4 (2008): n.p.

43. Peter Biskind, *Seeing Is Believing: How Hollywood Taught Us to Stop Worrying and Love the Fifties* (New York: Pantheon, 1983), 111.

44. Jonathon Green, *Cassell's Dictionary of Slang* (New York, Sterling, 2005), 151.

45. Douglas, *Where the Girls Are*, 5.

46. Sedgwick, *Touching Feeling*, 156.

47. Sivulka, "The Fabulous Fifties," n.p.

48. Sharon Monteith, *American Culture in the 1960s* (New York: Columbia University Press, 2008), 182.

49. Vogel, "Interview with Alexis Greene," 442.

50. Ben Brantley, "Well, at Least She's Not Triplets," *New York Times*, Feb. 19, 1999.

51. Brantley, "Well, at Least She's Not Triplets."

52. Vincent Canby, "A Mad History of Women as Told by Twin Barbies," *New York Times*, Feb. 28, 1999.

53. Michael Feingold, "Double Takes," *Village Voice*, Mar. 2, 1999, 161.

54. John Barry, "Boomer Humor: Charting these Schizophrenic Times Through Two Women," *Baltimore City Paper*, Apr. 4, 2007.

55. "Women in Theater."

56. Vogel, "Interview with Alexis Greene," 441–42.

57. Vogel, "Interview with Alexis Greene," 442.

Chapter Five

1. Marvin Carlson, *Haunted Stage: Theatre as Memory Machine* (Ann Arbor: University of Michigan Press, 2001), 7.

2. Michael Feingold, "All for Love," *Village Voice*, Mar. 25, 1997, 97.

3. Bigsby, *Contemporary American Playwrights*, 319.

4. Vogel, "Interview with Arthur Holmberg."

5. See Bigsby, *Contemporary American Playwrights*, 318; Bigsby, *Modern American Drama*, 233.

6. "Women in Theater."

7. Vogel, "Interview with Arthur Holmberg."

8. Ben Brantley, "Go Along for the Ride with Uncle," *New York Times*, Feb. 13, 2012.

9. Marilyn Stasio, "How I Learned to Drive," *Variety*, Feb. 13, 2012.

10. Vogel, interview with Savran, 276.

11. Alan Shepard and Mary Lamb, "The Memory Palace in Paula Vogel's Plays," in *Southern Women Playwrights: New Essays in Literary History and Criticism*, ed. Robert L. McDonald and Linda Rohrer Paige (Tuscaloosa: University of Alabama Press, 2002), 199.

12. Paula Vogel, *How I Learned to Drive*, in *Mammary Plays*, 21 (hereafter cited in the text).

13. Gilles Deleuze, *Cinema Two: The Time Image*, trans. Hugh Tomlinson and Robert Galeta (Minneapolis: University of Minnesota Press, 1989), 206.

14. Jonathan Boyarin, "Space, Time, and the Politics of Memory," in *Re-*

mapping Memory: the Politics of Timespace (Minneapolis: University of Minnesota Press, 1994), 22.

15. Boyarin, "Space, Time," 23.

16. Boyarin, "Space, Time," 22.

17. Drukman, "Playwright on the Edge."

18. Bigsby, Contemporary American Playwrights, 319.

19. Vogel, interview with Savran, 272.

20. Andrew Kimbrough, "The Pedophile in Me: The Ethics of How I Learned to Drive," Journal of Dramatic Theory and Criticism 16.2 (2002): 49.

21. Robert Hicks, "Playwright Melds Modern Tension and Ancient Convention," St. Petersburg Times, June 3, 2004.

22. Kimbrough, "Pedophile in Me," 49.

23. Michel Foucault, History of Sexuality. Volume 1: An Introduction, trans. Robert Hurley (New York: Vintage, 1990), 35.

24. Vogel, How I Learned to Drive, 7.

25. Craig, Women Pulitzer Playwrights, 230.

26. Butler, Undoing Gender, 33.

27. Savran, Queer Sort of Materialism, 197.

28. Drukman, "Playwright on the Edge."

29. Ben Brantley, "A Pedophile Even a Mother Could Love," New York Times, Mar. 17, 1997.

30. Some of the headlines that suggest praise of the play's balance include: "Play Bypasses Hysteria for Humanity," Globe and Mail (Canada), Oct. 7, 1998; "'Drive' Travels beyond the Issue of Sexual Abuse; Drama Both Compelling and Complex," Washington Times, May 15, 1999; "A Gentle Approach to a Tough Subject," St. Petersburg Times, May 28, 1999; and "A Playwright on the Edge Turns toward the Middle," New York Times, Mar. 16, 1997. Other review headlines seemed to foreground the play's balanced treatment of the subject more sensationally, such as "A Pedophile Even a Mother Could Love," New York Times, Mar. 17, 1997; and "Remarkable Incest Drama Avoids the Standard Clichés," Globe and Mail (Canada), Jan. 9, 1999.

31. Matt Wolf, "The Week in Reviews: Interview: Paula Vogel," Observer, June 21, 1998. For better or worse, since the publication of E.L. James' erotic novel Fifty Shades of Grey in 2011, this metaphor "shades of grey" takes on intertextual meanings, which are at odds with the subtle erotic dynamics in How I Learned to Drive.

32. Presumably, Feingold is referring to And Baby Makes Seven (1993) and Desdemona (1993), both of which were produced by Circle Repertory Theatre in New York City.

33. Feingold, "All for Love," 97.

34. Jill Dolan, "Performance Review: How I Learned to Drive," Theatre Journal 50.1 (1998): 128.

35. Dolan, "Performance Review," 128.

36. John Smith, "When Seduction's All in the Family," *New York*, Mar. 31, 1997, 86.

37. John Heilpern, "Pedophiles, Sock Fetishists . . . Hey, Kids, It's Oprah-Drama," *New York Observer*, Apr. 7, 1997.

38. Michael Toscano, "Ambiguous 'Drive' Takes Audience on Muddled Ride," *Washington Post*, Feb. 5, 2004.

39. In the late 1990s, many British plays revolved around experiences of sexual abuse. Sarah Daniels's *Beside Herself* (1990), David Spencer's *Killing the Cat* (1990), Claire Dowie's *Easy Access* (1997), and Simon Gray's *The Late Middle Classes* (1999) all examine the topic of sexual abuse, tapping into its increasing ubiquity in public discourse. *Drive* taps into this same discourse, as well as the longer feminist tradition of confessional narrative as a means by which women might assume some kind of agency over their bodies and voices.

40. Paul Taylor, "Theatre: The Misuse of Abuse," *Independent*, Apr. 7, 1999.

41. Robert Brustein, "Review: 'How I Learned to Drive,'" *New Republic*, July 7, 1997, 28.

Chapter Six

1. Bert O. States, *Great Reckonings in Little Rooms: On the Phenomenology of Theatre* (Berkeley and London: University of California Press, 1985), 50.

2. David Román, "'It's My Party and I'll Die if I Want To!': Gay Men, AIDS, and the Circulation of Camp in U.S Theater," *Theatre Journal* 44.3 (1992): 327.

3. Judith Butler, *Precarious Lives: The Powers of Mourning and Violence* (New York: Verso, 2004), 35.

4. "Women in Theatre."

5. Paula Vogel, "Playwright's Note" to *Baltimore Waltz*, in *Baltimore Waltz and Other Plays*, 5.

6. David Savran, "Loose Screws: An Introduction," in Vogel, *Baltimore Waltz and Other Plays*, x.

7. Peter Dickinson, *World Stages, Local Audiences: Essays on Performance, Place, and Politics* (Manchester: University of Manchester Press, 2010), 201.

8. Paula Vogel, *The Baltimore Waltz*, in *Baltimore Waltz and Other Plays*, Ed29 (hereafter cited in the text).

9. Dickinson, *World Stages, Local Audiences*, 196.

10. David A. Cook, *A History of Narrative Film*. 2nd ed. (New York: Norton, 1990), 469.

11. Quoted in Bigsby, *Contemporary American Playwrights*, 311.

12. *The Third Man*, dir. Carole Reed, screenplay by Graham Greene, perf. Orson Welles, Joseph Cotton, and Alida Valli (Rialto Pictures, 1949; Criterion Collection), DVD.

13. Elisabeth Kübler-Ross, *On Death and Dying* (New York: Routledge, 1973), 8.

14. Kübler-Ross, *On Death and Dying*, 126.

15. Butler, *Undoing Gender*, 19.

16. Butler, *Undoing Gender*, 18.

17. Butler, *Undoing Gender*, 19.

18. Sedgwick, *Touching Feeling*, 150–51.

19. Craig, *Women Pulitzer Playwrights*, 218.

20. David Román, "Review: *The Baltimore Waltz* by Paula Vogel," *Theatre Journal* 44.4 (1992), 520.

21. Frank Rich, "A Play about AIDS Uses Fantasy to Try to Remake the World," *New York Times*, Feb. 12, 1992.

22. Charles Isherwood, "Death Defying Fantasy Fueled by Love When AIDS was a Nameless Intruder," *New York Times*, Dec. 6, 2004.

23. Román, "Review: *The Baltimore Waltz* by Paula Vogel," 522.

24. An expanded version of the following discussion of *The Long Christmas Ride Home* was published in the Summer 2012 issue of *Comparative Drama*. Sincere thanks to the journal for allowing me to reprint here.

25. Quoted in Gerard Raymond, "Puppets and Politics," *Advocate*, Nov. 25, 2003, 57.

26. Paula Vogel, "Foreword," in *The Skin of Our Teeth: A Play* (New York: Perennial Classics, 2003), viii.

27. Vogel, "Foreword" (*Skin of Our Teeth*), ix, xi.

28. Quoted in Raymond, "Puppets and Politics," 56–57.

29. Paula Vogel, "Author's Note," in *The Long Christmas Ride Home: A Puppet Play with Actors* (New York: Dramatists Play Service, 2004), 7.

30. Vogel, "Author's Note" (*Long Christmas Ride Home*), 5.

31. Donald Keene, *Nō and Bunraku: Two Forms of Japanese Theatre* (New York: Columbia University Press, 1990), 124.

32. Keene, *Nō and Bunraku*, 124.

33. Keene, *Nō and Bunraku* 130.

34. Keene, *Nō and Bunraku* 127.

35. Roland Barthes, "The Dolls of Bunraku," trans. David Savran, *Diacritics* 6 (1976): 44–47 (quotation at 46).

36. Barthes, "Dolls of Bunraku," 47.

37. Walter Benjamin, *Understanding Brecht*, trans. Anna Bostock (London: NLB, 1973), 19.

38. Benjamin, "Central Park," 32–58, quotation at 49.

39. Paula Vogel, *The Long Christmas Ride Home* (New York: Dramatists Play Services, 2004), 6 (hereafter cited in the text).

40. Butler, *Undoing Gender*, 19.

41. Thornton Wilder, *The Long Christmas Dinner: Plays in One Act.* (New York: Penguin, 1959), 15.

42. Mladen Dolar, *A Voice and Nothing More* (Boston: MIT Press, 2006), 71.

43. Keene, *Nō and Bunraku*, 18.

44. Keene, *Nō and Bunraku*, 9.

45. Keene, *Nō and Bunraku*, 18.

46. Keene, *Nō and Bunraku*, 18.

47. Keene, *Nō and Bunraku*, 18.

48. The concept of "aura," which is one of Benjamin's most influential contributions, is best understood as both a temporal and a spatial term, suggesting both physical and historical distance. The aura implies authenticity, although this authenticity is recognized only in its destruction by mechanized reproduction.

49. Diamond, *Unmaking Mimesis*, 145, 147.

50. David DeWitt, "There's Mom and Dad and a Lot of Problems," *New York Times*, Feb. 1, 2004.

51. DeWitt, "There's Mom and Dad."

52. Ann Pellegrini, "Repercussions and Remainders in the Plays of Paula Vogel: An Essay in Five Moments," in *A Companion to Twentieth-Century American Drama* (Malden, MA: Blackwell, 2005), 482–83.

53. Jill Dolan, *Utopia in Performance: Finding Hope at the* Theater (Ann Arbor: University of Michigan Press, 2008), 17.

54. Dolan, *Utopia in Performance*, 162.

Chapter Seven

1. Rebecca Schneider, *Performing Remains: Art and War in Times of Theatrical Reenactment* (New York: Routledge, 2011), 33.

2. This hymn was recorded on Christmas 1864 by Colonel Thomas Wentworth Higginson, a Massachusetts officer who organized freed slaves into the first black regiment. He also recorded that the slaves who sang it were whipped. The hymn is included in the "Further Reading" section of the play-text (155).

3. Paula Vogel, "Author's Note," in *A Civil War Christmas: An American Musical Celebration* (New York: TCG, 2012), 8 (hereafter cited in the text).

4. James McIvor, *God Rest Ye Merry Gentlemen: A True Civil War Christmas Story* (New York: Penguin, 2006), n.p.

5. Vogel, "Afterword," in *Civil War Christmas*, 129.

6. Vogel, "Afterword," in *Civil War Christmas*, 136–37.

7. Schneider, *Performing Remains*, 2.

8. Schneider, *Performing Remains*, 2. Schneider is engaging here with

Elizabeth Freeman's highly productive concept of "temporal drag," which Freeman posits as a way of understanding not individual psychic temporality, but "the movement time of collective political fantasy" (65). Temporal drag conceives of a present littered with detritus of the past, an understanding that disrupts clear demarcations between past and present and complicates linear forward movement. See Elizabeth Freeman, *Time Binds: Queer Temporalities, Queer Histories* (Durham, NC: Duke University Press, 2010), 62–65.

9. Vogel, "Preface," in *Civil War Christmas*, xii.

10. Elin Diamond, "Modern Drama/Modernity's Drama," *Redefining the Field*, special issue, *Modern Drama* 44.1 (2001): 5.

11. Doris Kearns Goodwin, *Team of Rivals: The Political Genius of Abraham Lincoln* (New York: Simon and Schuster, 2005), xvii.

12. Goodwin, *Team of Rivals*, 384.

13. This antidote is told by Vogel in the "Afterward" to *Civil War Christmas*, 127.

14. Elizabeth Keckley, *Behind the Scenes; or, Thirty Years a Slave, and Four Years in the White House* (New York City: New York Printing Co., 1868), 111.

15. Carlson, *Haunted Stage* 8.

16. Charles Isherwood, "A Nation Divided Stands Throughout the Holidays," *New York Times*, Dec. 11, 2008.

17. Charles Isherwood, "Lincoln's Wartime Hope for a Midnight Clear," *New York Times*, Dec. 4, 2012.

18. Don Aucoin, "A Historical Holiday," *Boston Globe*, Nov. 20, 2009, http://boston.com/ae/theater_arts/articles/2009/11/20/.

Bibliography

Albee, Edward. Interview with David Savran. In Savran, *Playwright's Voice: American Dramatists on Memory, Writing and the Politics of Culture.* New York: Theatre Communications Group, 1999. 1-24.

Armitage, Susan H., with Patricia Hart and Karen Weatermon, eds. *Women's Oral History: The "Frontiers" Reader.* Lincoln: University of Nebraska Press, 2002.

The Baltimore Waltz. By Paula Vogel. Dir. Anne Bogart. Perf. Cherry Jones, Richard Thompson, and Joe Mantello. Circle Repertory Company, New York City, February 12, 1992. Recorded. Billy Rose Theatre Collection, New York Public Library.

Barthes, Roland. "The Dolls of Bunraku." Trans. David Savran. *Diacritics* 6.4 (1976): 44–47.

Barthes, Roland. *Mythologies.* Trans. Annette Lavers. New York: Hill and Wang, 1977.

Bauer, Wolfgang. "Shakespeare the Sadist." *Performing Arts Journal* 3.1 (1978): 99–109.

Benjamin, Walter. "Central Park." Trans. Lloyd Spencer. *New German Critique* 34 (1985): 32–58.

Benjamin, Walter. *Illuminations: Essays and Reflections.* Trans. Harry Zohn. Ed. and intro. Hannah Arendt. New York: Schocken Books, 1968.

Benjamin, Walter. *Understanding Brecht.* Trans. Anna Bostock. London: NLB, 1973.

Berkowitz, Gerald M. *American Drama of the Twentieth Century.* New York: Longman, 1992.

Berlant, Lauren. *The Queen of America Goes to Washington City.* Durham, NC: Duke University Press, 1997.

Berlant, Lauren, and Michael Warner. "Sex in Public." *Intimacy*, special issue, *Critical Inquiry* 24.2. (1998): 547–66.

Berlant, Lauren, and Michael Warner. "What Does Queer Theory Teach Us about X?" *PLMA* 110 (1995): 343–49.

Bigsby, C. W. E. *Contemporary American Playwrights.* New York: Cambridge University Press, 1999.

Bigsby, C. W. E. *Modern American Drama 1945–2000.* New York: Cambridge University Press, 2000.

Bilowit, Ira J. "Bringing Up Baby: Paula Vogel's Newest Born." *Back Stage*, May 7, 1993, 5F.

Biskind, Peter. *Seeing Is Believing: How Hollywood Taught Us to Stop Worrying and Love the Fifties.* New York: Pantheon, 1983.

Boose, Lynda. "'Let It Be Hid': The Pornographic Aesthetic of Shakespeare's *Othello*." In *New Casebooks: "Othello,"* ed. Lena Cowen Orlin. Basingstoke, England: Palgrave Macmillan, 2004. 22–48.

Boose, Lynda. "Othello's Handkerchief: The Recognizance and Pledge of Love." *English Literary Renaissance* 5 (1975): 360–74.

Bourdieu, Pierre. *The Field of Cultural Production*. Ed. and intro. Randal Johnson. New York: Columbia University Press, 1993.

Boyarin, Jonathon. "Space, Time, and the Politics of Memory." In *Remapping Memory: the Politics of Timespace*. Minneapolis: University of Minnesota Press, 1994. 1–37.

Boym, Svetlana. *The Future of Nostalgia*. New York: Basic Books, 2001.

Brooks, Peter. *Reading for the Plot: Design and Intention in Narrative*. New York: Vintage, 1985.

Brustein, Robert. "Review: 'How I Learned to Drive.'" *New Republic*, July 7, 1997, 28.

Butler, Judith. *Bodies That Matter: On the Discursive Limits of Sex*. New York: Routledge, 1994.

Butler, Judith. *Excitable Speech: A Politics of the Performative*. New York: Routledge 1997.

Butler, Judith. *Gender Trouble*. New York: Routledge, 1990.

Butler, Judith. "Performative Acts and Gender Constitution: An Essay in Phenomenology and Feminist Theory." In *Performing Feminisms: Feminist Critical Theory and Theatre*, ed. Sue-Ellen Case. Baltimore: Johns Hopkins University Press, 1990. 270–82.

Butler, Judith. *Precarious Lives: The Powers of Mourning and Violence*. New York: Verso, 2004.

Butler, Judith. *Undoing Gender*. New York: Routledge, 2004.

Carlson, Marvin. *Haunted Stage: Theatre as Memory Machine*. Ann Arbor: University of Michigan Press, 2001.

Case, Sue-Ellen. *Feminism and Theatre*. New York: Methuen, 1988.

Case, Sue-Ellen. "Toward a Butch-Femme Aesthetic." In *Making a Spectacle: Feminist Essays on Contemporary Women's Theatre*, ed. Lynda Hart. Ann Arbor: University of Michigan Press, 1989. 282–99.

Claycomb, Ryan. "Staging Psychic Excess: Parodic Narrative and Transgressive Performance. *Journal of Narrative Theory* 37.1 (2007): 104–27.

Coen, Stephanie. "Paula Vogel: No Need for Gravity." *American Theatre* (April 1993): 1–2.

Combs, James E. *The Reagan Range: The Nostalgia Myth in American Politics*. Madison, WI: Popular Press, 1993.

Cook, David A. *A History of Narrative Film*. 2nd ed. New York: Norton, 1990.

Craig, Carolyn-Casey. *Women Pulitzer Playwrights: Biographical Profiles and Analyses of the Plays*. Jefferson, NC: MacFarland, 2004.

Davy, Kate. "Fe/male Impersonation: The Discourse of Camp." In *Critical*

Theory and Performance, rev. and enlarged, ed. Janelle G. Reinelt and Joseph R. Roach. Ann Arbor: University of Michigan Press, 2006. 355–71.

Deleuze, Gilles. *Cinema Two: The Time Image.* Trans. Hugh Tomlinson and Robert Galeta. Minneapolis: University of Minnesota Press, 1989.

Desdemona: A Play about a Handkerchief. By Paula Vogel. Dir. Gloria Muzio. Perf. Fran Brill, J. Smith-Cameron, and Cherry Jones. Circle Repertory, New York City, November 12, 1993. Recorded. Billy Rose Theatre Collection, New York Public Library.

Diamond, Elin. "Modern Drama/Modernity's Drama." *Redefining the Field,* special issue, *Modern Drama* 44.1 (2001): 3–15.

Diamond, Elin. *Unmaking Mimesis: Essays on Feminism and Theatre.* New York: Routledge, 1997.

Dickinson, Peter. *World Stages, Local Audiences: Essays on Performance, Place, and Politics.* Manchester: University of Manchester Press, 2010.

Doane, Mary Ann. *Femme Fatales: Feminism, Film Theory, and Psychoanalysis.* New York: Routledge, 1991.

Doane, Mary Ann. "The Voice and the Cinema: The Articulation of Body and Space." *Yale French Studies* 60 (1980): 33–50.

Dolan, Jill. *Feminist Spectator as Critic.* 2nd ed. Ann Arbor: University of Michigan Press, 2012.

Dolan, Jill. "Introduction to *Desdemona: A Play about a Handkerchief.*" In *Amazon All-Stars: Thirteen Lesbian Plays,* ed. Rosemary Keefe Curb. New York: Applause, 1996. 437–40.

Dolan, Jill. "Performance Review: *How I Learned to Drive.*" *Theatre Journal* 50.1 (1998): 127–28. *Project Muse.* October 5, 2008.

Dolan, Jill. *Utopia in Performance: Finding Hope at the Theater.* Ann Arbor: University of Michigan Press, 2005.

Dolar, Mladen. *A Voice and Nothing More.* Boston: MIT Press, 2006.

Douglas, Susan J. *Where the Girls Are: Growing up Female with the Mass Media.* New York: Random House, 1995.

Doyle, Jennifer. *Sex Objects: Art and the Dialectics of Desire.* Minneapolis: University of Minnesota Press, 2006.

Dworkin, Andrea. *Pornography: Men Possessing Women.* New York: E. P. Dutton, 1989.

Fausto-Sterling, Anne. *Sexing the Body: Gender Politics and the Construction of Sexuality.* New York: Basic Books, 2000.

Feingold, Michael. "All for Love." *Village Voice,* March 25, 1997, 97. Microfilm.

Feingold, Michael. "Double Takes." *Village Voice,* March 2, 1999, 161. Microfilm.

Feingold, Michael. "Review: *And Baby Makes Seven.* " *Village Voice,* June 8, 1993, 97. Microfilm.

Felman, Shoshana. *The Scandal of the Speaking Body: Don Juan with J. L.*

Austin; or, Seduction in Two Languages. Stanford, CA: Stanford University Press, 2003.

Foucault, Michel. *The History of Sexuality. Volume I: An Introduction.* Trans. Robert Hurley. New York: Vintage, 1990.

Freeman, Elizabeth. *Time Binds: Queer Temporalities, Queer Histories.* Durham, NC: Duke University Press, 2010.

Friedman, Sharon. "Feminist Revisions of Classic Texts on the American Stage." In *Codifying the National Self: Spectators, Actors, and the American Dramatic Text.* New York: Peter Lang, 2006. 87–104.

Geis, Deborah R. "In Willy Loman's Garden: Contemporary Re-visions of *Death of a Salesman.*" In *Arthur Miller's America: Theatre and Culture in a Time of Change,* ed. Enoch Brater. Ann Arbor: University of Michigan Press, 2005. 202–18.

Goodwin, Doris Kearns. *Team of Rivals: The Political Genius of Abraham Lincoln.* New York: Simon and Schuster, 2005.

Green, Amy. "Whose Voices Are These? The Arts of Language in the Plays of Suzan-Lori Parks, Paula Vogel, and Diana Son." In *Women Writing Plays: Three Decades of the Susan Smith Blackburn Prize.* Austin: University of Texas Press, 2006. 143–57.

Green, Jonathon. *Cassell's Dictionary of Slang.* New York, Sterling, 2005.

Heilbrun, Carolyn G. *Writing a Woman's Life.* New York: Ballantine Books, 1988.

Herrington, Joan, ed. *Playwright's Muse.* New York: Routledge University Press, 2002.

Hot 'n' Throbbing. By Paula Vogel. Dir. Molly Smith. Perf. Lynnda Ferguson, Colin Lane, Danny Pintauro, Rhea Seahorn, Sue Jin Song, and Craig Wallace. Arena Stage, Washington, DC, September 15, 1999. Recorded. Billy Rose Theatre Collection, New York Public Library.

Hot 'n' Throbbing. By Paula Vogel. Dir. Les Waters. Perf. Lisa Emery, Elias Koteas, Suli Holum, Tom Nelis, Rebecca Wisocky, and Mattew Stadelmann. Signature Theatre, New York City, March 29, 2005. Recorded. Billy Rose Theatre Collection, New York Public Library.

How I Learned to Drive. By Paula Vogel. Dir. Mark Brokaw. Perf. Mary Louise Parker and David Morse. Vineyard Theatre, New York City, April 8, 1997. Recorded. Billy Rose Theatre Collection, New York Public Library.

Jameson, Anna. *Shakespeare's Heroines.* 2nd ed. 1833. London: George Bell and Sons, 1908.

Keckley, Elizabeth. *Behind the Scenes; or, Thirty Years a Slave, and Four Years in the White House.* New York City: New York Printing Co., 1868.

Keene, Donald. *Nō and Bunraku: Two Forms of Japanese Theatre.* New York: Columbia University Press, 1990.

Keyssar, Helene. "Introduction." In *Feminist Theatre and Theory* New York: St. Martin's Press, 1996. 1–18.

Kimbrough, Andrew. "The Pedophile in Me: The Ethics of *How I Learned to Drive.*" *Journal of Dramatic Theory and Criticism* 16.2 (2002): 47–65.

Krasner, David. *American Drama: 1945–2000.* Boston: Blackwell, 2006.

Krutnik, Frank. *In a Lonely Street: Film Noir, Genre, and Masculinity.* New York: Routledge, 1991.

Kübler-Ross, Elisabeth. *On Death and Dying.* New York: Routledge, 1973.

Lanser, Susan. *Fictions of Authority: Women Writers and Narrative Voice.* Ithaca: Cornell University Press: 1992.

Laplance, Jean, and J. B. Pontalis, "Fantasy and the Origins of Sexuality." In *Unconscious Phantasy*, ed. Riccardo Steiner. London: Karnac Books, 2003. 107–43.

Lerner, Gerda. *Why History Matters: Life and Thought.* New York: Oxford University Press, 1997.

Linden, Ann. "Seducing the Audience: Politics in the Plays of Paula Vogel." In Herrington, *Playwright's Muse*, 231–52.

The Long Christmas Ride Home. By Paula Vogel. Dir. Mark Brokaw. Perf. Mark Blum, Randy Graff, Enid Graham, Catherine Kellner, Will McCormack, and Sean Palmer. Vineyard Theatre, New York City, November 25, 2003. Recorded. Billy Rose Theatre Collection, New York Public Library.

MacKinnon, Catharine. *Only Words.* Cambridge, MA: Harvard University Press, 1993.

Margolies, David. "Teaching the Handsaw to Fly: Shakespeare as a Hegemonic Instrument." In *The Shakespeare Myth*, ed. Graham Holderness. New York: St. Martin's Press, 1991. 42–53.

McIvor, James. *God Rest Ye Merry Soldiers: A True Civil War Christmas Story.* New York: Penguin, 2006.

The Mineola Twins. By Paula Vogel. Dir. Joe Mantello. Perf. Swoozie Kurtz, Mo Gaffney, and Amanda Siegfried. Roundabout Theatre Company, Laura Pels Theatre, New York City, February 19, 1999. Recorded. Billy Rose Theatre Collection, New York Public Library.

Monteith, Sharon. *American Culture in the 1960s.* New York: Columbia University Press, 2008.

Newton, Esther. *Mother Camp: Female Impersonators in America.* Chicago: University of Chicago Press, 1972.

Novy, Marianne. "Saving Desdemona and/or Ourselves: Plays by Ann-Marie MacDonald and Paula Vogel." In *Transforming Shakespeare: Contemporary Women's Re-Visions in Literature and Performance*, ed. Marianne Novy. New York: Palgrave, 2000. 67–86.

The Oldest Profession. By Paula Vogel. Dir. David Esbjornson. Perf. Mary Louise Burke, Carlin Glynn, Pricilla Lopez, Joyce Van Patten, and Katherine Helmond. Signature Theatre, New York City, September 25, 2004. Recorded. Billy Rose Theatre Collection, New York Public Library.

"Out Across America, from P.S. 122 to Peoria: A Conversation among Holly

Hughes, Deb Parks-Satterfield, and Paula Vogel, moderated by Cynthia Mayeda." In *Queerest Art: Essays in Lesbian and Gay Theater*, ed. Alisa Solomon and Framji Minwalla. New York: New York University Press, 2002. 168–82.

Pellegrini, Ann. "Repercussions and Remainders in the Plays of Paula Vogel: An Essay in Five Moments." In *A Companion to Twentieth-Century American Drama*. Malden, MA: Blackwell, 2005. 473–85.

Ranald, Margaret Loftus. "The Indiscretions of Desdemona." *Shakespeare Quarterly* 14.2 (1963): 127–39.

Raymond, Gerard. "Puppets and Politics." *Advocate*, November 25, 2003, 56–57.

Richardson, Brian. "Voice and Narration in Postmodern Drama." *New Literary History* 32.3 (2001): 681–94.

Román, David. "'It's My Party and I'll Die if I Want To!': Gay Men, AIDS, and the Circulation of Camp in U.S Theater." *Theatre Journal* 44.3 (1992): 305–27.

Román, David. "Review: *The Baltimore Waltz* by Paula Vogel." *Theatre Journal* 44.4 (1992): 520–22.

Rooney, David. "Review of Oldest Profession." *Daily Variety*, September 28, 2004, 8.

Ross, Andrew. "Uses of Camp." In *Camp: Queer Aesthetics and the Performing Subject: A Reader*, ed. Fabio Cleto. Ann Arbor: University of Michigan Press, 1999. 308–29.

Savran, David. *Highbrow/Lowdown: Theater, Jazz, and the Making of the New Middle Class.* Ann Arbor: University of Michigan Press: 2009.

Savran, David. Introduction to interview with Paula Vogel. In Savran, *Playwright's Voice*, 263–66.

Savran, David. "Loose Screws: An Introduction." In Vogel, *Baltimore Waltz and Other Plays*, ix–xv.

Savran, David, ed. *The Playwright's Voice: American Dramatists on Memory, Writing, and the Politics of Culture.* New York: Theatre Communications Group, 1999.

Savran, David. *A Queer Sort of Materialism: Recontextualizing American Theater.* Ann Arbor: University of Michigan Press, 2003.

Schneider, Rebecca. *Performing Remains: Art and War in Times of Theatrical Reenactment.* New York: Routledge, 2011.

Sedgwick, Eve Kosofsky. *Between Men: English Literature and Male Homosocial Desire.* New York: Columbia University Press, 1985.

Sedgwick, Eve Kosofsky. *Epistemology of the Closet.* Berkley: University of California Press, 1990.

Sedgwick, Eve Kosofsky. *Touching Feeling: Affect, Pedagogy, and Performativity.* Durham, NC: Duke University Press, 2003.

Segal, Lynne. "Sweet Sorrows, Painful Pleasures: Pornography and the Perils of Heterosexual Desire." In *Sex Exposed: Sexuality and the Pornography Debate*, ed. Lynne Segal and Mary McIntosh. London: Virago, 1992. 65–91.

Shakespeare, William. *Othello: The Moor of Venice.* In *Bedford Introduction to Drama*, ed. Lee A Jacobus. Boston: Bedford/St Martin's, 2005. 419–61.

Shepard, Alan, and Mary Lamb. "The Memory Palace in Paula Vogel's Plays." In *Southern Women Playwrights: New Essays in Literary History and Criticism*, ed. Robert L. McDonald and Linda Rohrer Paige. Tuscaloosa: University of Alabama Press, 2002. 198–217.

Shklovsky, Victor. "Art as Technique." In *Russian Formalist Criticism: Four Essays*, trans. and intro. Lee T. Lemon and Marion J. Reis. Lincoln: University of Nebraska Press, 1965. 3–24.

Shteir, Rachel. *Striptease: The Untold History of the Girlie Show.* New York: Oxford University Press, 2004.

Silverman, Kaja. *Acoustic Mirror: The Female Voice in Psychoanalysis and Cinema.* Bloomington: Indiana University Press, 1988.

Simon, John. "Review of *Desdemona*, by Paula Vogel." *New York Magazine*, November 22, 1993, 78–79. Microfilm.

Sivulka, Juliann. "The Fabulous Fifties: Selling Mr. and Mrs. Consumer." *Advertising and Society Review* 9.4 (2008): n.p.

Smith, John. "When Seduction's All in the Family." *New York Magazine*, March 31, 1997, 86.

Solomon, Alisa. *Re-dressing the Canon: Essays on Theatre and Gender.* New York: Routledge, 1997.

Sontag, Susan. "The Death of Tragedy." In *Against Interpretation and Other Essays.* New York: Picador, 1966. 132–40.

Sontag, Susan. "Notes on Camp." In *Against Interpretation and Other Essays.* New York: Picador, 1966. 275–92.

Stacey, Judith. "The Making and Unmaking of Modern Families." In *Family: Critical Concepts in Sociology*, ed. David Cheal. New York: Routledge, 2003. 84–108.

Stallybrass, Peter. "Patriarchal Territory: The Body Enclosed." In *Rewriting the Renaissance: The Discourses of Sexual Difference in Early Modern Europe*, ed. Margaret W. Ferguson, Maureen Quilligan, and Nancy J. Vickers. Chicago: University of Chicago Press, 1988. 123–42.

Stanley, N. J. "Screamingly Funny and Terrifyingly Shocking: Paula Vogel as Domestic Detective." In *Staging a Cultural Paradigm: The Political and the Personal in American Drama*, ed. Barbara Ozieblo and Miriam López-Rodríguez. New York: Peter Lang, 2002. 357–71.

Stasio, Marilyn. "How I Learned to Drive." *Variety*, February 2012. http://www.variety.com/review/VE1117947081/.

States, Bert O. *Great Reckonings in Little Rooms: On the Phenomenology of Theatre.* Berkeley and London: University of California Press, 1985.

Sternlieb, Lisa. "Molly Bloom: Acting Natural. *ELH* 65.3 (1998): 757–78.

Stockton, Kathryn Bond. *Beautiful Bottom, Beautiful Shame: Where "Black" Meets "Queer."* Durham, NC: Duke University Press, 2006.

The Third Man. Dir. Carol Reed. Screenplay by Graham Greene. Perf. Joseph

Cotton, Orson Welles, and Alida Valli. Rialto Pictures, 1949. Criterion Collection. DVD

Thomson, Helen. "The Web We Weave When We Conceive." *Age*, August 13, 2002. 4.

Vlasopolos, Anca. "Authorizing History: Victimization in *Streetcar Name Desire*." *Theatre Journal* 38.3 (1986): 322–38.

Vogel, Paula. *And Baby Makes Seven*. In *Baltimore Waltz and Other Plays*, 59–126.

Vogel, Paula. *The Baltimore Waltz*. In *Baltimore Waltz and Other Plays*, 1–58.

Vogel, Paula. *The Baltimore Waltz and Other Plays*. Ed. David Savran. New York: TCG, 1996.

Vogel, Paula. *A Civil War Christmas: An American Musical Celebration*. New York: TCG, 2012.

Vogel, Paula. *Desdemona: A Play about a Handkerchief*. In *Baltimore Waltz and Other Plays*, 173–224.

Vogel, Paula. Foreword. In *Writing: Working in Theatre*, ed. Robert Emmet Long. New York: Ginger/Continuum, 2008. 7–10.

Vogel, Paula. Foreword. In *The Skin of Our Teeth: A Play*, by Thornton Wilder–. New York: Perennial Classics, 2003. vii–xiii.

Vogel, Paula. *Hot 'n' Throbbing*. In *Baltimore Waltz and Other Plays*, 225–96.

Vogel, Paula. *Hot 'n' Throbbing*. New York: Dramatists Play Services, 2000.

Vogel, Paula. *How I Learned to Drive*. In *Mammary Plays*, 1–92.

Vogel, Paula. Interview with the author. November 7, 2008.

Vogel, Paula. "Interview with Alexis Greene." In *Women who Write Plays: Interviews with American Dramatists*, ed. Alexis Greene. Hanover, NH: Smith and Kraus, 2001. 425–48.

Vogel, Paula. "Through the Eyes of Lolita: Pulitzer Prize-Winning Playwright Paula Vogel is interviewed by Arthur Holmberg." American Repertory Theater. April 3, 2006. http://www.amrep.org/past/drive1.html.

Vogel, Paula. Interview with Ann Linden. In Herrington, *Playwright's Muse*, 253–60.

Vogel, Paula. Interview with David Savran. In Savran, *Playwright's Voice*, 263–88.

Vogel, Paula. *The Long Christmas Ride Home: A Puppet Play with Actors*. New York: Dramatist Play Service, 2004.

Vogel, Paula. *The Mammary Plays*. New York: Theatre Communications Group, 1998.

Vogel, Paula. *Meg*. New York: Samuel French, 1977.

Vogel, Paula. *The Mineola Twins*. In *Mammary Plays*, 93–187.

Vogel, Paula. *The Oldest Profession*. In *Baltimore Waltz and Other Plays*, 127–72.

Vogel, Paula. "Time to Laugh: An Interview with Kathy Sova." *American Theatre* 14.2 (1997): 24.

"Vogel, Paula." *Current Biography Yearbook.* New York: H. W. Wilson, 1998. 587–90.

Warner, Michael. *The Trouble with Normal: Sex, Politics, and the Ethics of Queer Life.* Cambridge, MA: Harvard University Press, 2000.

Wilder, Thornton. *The Long Christmas Dinner: Plays in One Act.* New York: Penguin, 1959.

Williams, Linda. "Film Bodies: Gender, Genre, and Excess" *Film Quarterly,* 44.4 (1991): 2–13.

Williams, Raymond. *Marxism and Literature.* New York: Oxford University Press, 1977.

Williams, Tennessee. *A Streetcar Named Desire.* New York: Signet, 1975.

Wolff, Daniel. "The Strange and Sexless Marriage of Andrea Dworkin and Edwin Meese." *Threepenny Review* 30 (1987): 3–4.

List of Premieres

Meg, A Play in Three Acts. Presented at the Ninth Annual American College Theatre Festival, Washington, DC, 1977.

Desdemona: A Play about a Handkerchief. Staged reading, Cornell University, Ithaca, NY, 1979. Dir. Paula Vogel, Moving Targets Theatre, Brooklyn, 1985. Dir. Gloria Muzio, Sag Harbor Bay Street Theatre Festival, 1993, and Circle Repertory Company, New York City, 1993.

The Oldest Profession. Dir. Gordon Edelstein, Hudson Guild, New York City, 1981. Dir. Tom Bentley-Fisher, Edmonton, Alberta, and Saskatoon, Saskatchewan, Canada, 1988. Dir. Paula Vogel, Brown University, Providence, RI, 1990. Dir. Juanita Rockwell, Company One, Hartford, CT, 1991. Dir. David Esbjornson, Signature Theatre, New York City, 2005.

And Baby Makes Seven. Dir. Paula Vogel, 18th Street Playhouse, New York City, 1984. Dir. Kris Gannon, Theatre Rhinoceros, San Francisco, 1986. Dir. Calvin Skaggs, Lucille Lortel Theatre, New York City, 1993.

Hot 'n' Throbbing. Dir. Anne Bogart, Hasting Pudding Theatre Festival, Cambridge, MA, 1994. Dir. Molly Smith, Arena Stage, Washington, DC, 1999. Dir. Les Waters, Signature Theatre, New York City, 2005.

The Baltimore Waltz. Dir. Annie Stokes-Hutchinson, Perseverance Theatre, Douglas, AK, 1990. Dir. Anne Bogart, Circle Repertory Company, New York City, 1992. Dir. Mark Brokaw, Signature Theatre, New York City, 2004.

The Mineola Twins. Dir. Molly D. Smith, New York Theatre Workshop, New York City, 1996, and Trinity Repertory Company, Providence, RI, 1997. Dir. Joe Mantello, Laura Pels Theatre, New York City, 1999.

How I Learned To Drive. Dir. Mark Brokaw, Vineyard Theatre, New York City, and Century Theatre, New York City, 1997. Dir. Kate Whoriskey, Second Stage Theatre, New York City, 2012.

The Long Christmas Ride Home: A Puppet Play with Actors. Dir. Oskar Eustis, Long Wharf Theatre, New Haven, CT, 2003. Dir. Mark Brokaw, Vineyard Theatre, New York City, 2003.

A Civil War Christmas: An American Musical Celebration. Dir. Tina Landau, Long Wharf Theatre, New Haven, CT, 2008. Dir. Jessica Thebus, Huntington Theatre Company, Boston, MA, 2009. Dir. Tina Landau, New York Theatre Workshop, New York City, 2012.

Printed and bound by CPI Group (UK) Ltd, Croydon, CR0 4YY

10/06/2025

14686729-0001